MY DISCOVERY OF
GOD, ISLAM &
JUDGMENT DAY

Hamza Ali Abbasi

Ghamidi Center of Islamic Learning
www.ghamidi.org AN INITIATIVE OF AL-MAWRID US.

Ghamidi Center
of Islamic Learning
www.ghamidi.org AN INITIATIVE OF AL-MAWRID US.

Publisher: Ghamidi Center of Islamic Learning, Al-Mawrid US
ISBN: 979-8-9886271-6-6

Address: 3620 N Josey Ln, Suite 230 Carrollton, TX 75007
Website: www.ghamidi.org
Email: info@ghamidi.org

CONTENTS

By choosing to read this book and listen to what I have to say, you have given me your precious time. I am truly grateful—thank you! In return, I will strive to be as precise and brief as possible.

After years of grappling with existential questions, science and rationality led me to conclude that it is reasonable to believe an intelligent force might be the creator of everything. This search for the identity of this creator prompted me to explore revealed religions, eventually bringing me to Islam and the Quran. As I revisited Islam in my late 20s—a religion I was born into but had left as a teenager—I found satisfactory answers to most of my existential questions. However, some questions remained unanswered. While popular scholars and interpretations of Islam addressed about 70% of my inquiries satisfactorily, 30% continued to trouble me. Mr. Javed Ahmed Ghamidi, a scholar I accidentally discovered on YouTube around 2015, finally helped me find those answers. Since then, I have continued to learn from him both directly in person and indirectly through his books and online lectures.

This humble endeavor marks my sincere attempt to share with readers all the rationally and morally satisfactory answers to my existential questions. I write as a layperson for laypersons—ordinary people asking similar questions without aspirations to become scholars or academics. In my opinion, the knowledge I acquired during my quest for answers is not advanced or academic; I believe anyone with the time and exposure I had should be aware of these matters.

I am not writing this book as a scholar, nor do I wish to be a writer. I am not even fond of writing, and this is probably my first and last book. It is not meant to be a casual read; it does not promise or aim to entertain readers looking to enjoy it over a cup of coffee on a cozy evening. I share my answers straightforwardly for those seriously interested in existential matters.

Importantly, I write with concern and empathy for my fellow human beings because the answers I found, if true, have crucial implications for everyone. I will endeavor to establish in this book that post-worldly divine accountability is indeed real. This has monumental consequences for each one of us. Hence, I strongly believe that sharing my journey and answers with readers is vitally important.

I don't think I have anything new to say, but I found my answers from many different sources. By writing this book, I aim to compile my answers in one place, hoping it might serve as a helpful resource for anyone seeking answers to similar questions.

Another significant reason for writing this book is that the interpretation of Islam I have come to accept is not widely held, and I wish to play whatever role I can to disseminate this perspective to as many people as possible. Its modern-day flagbearer is Mr. Javed Ahmed Ghamidi. In this interpretation of Islam, contrary to the mainstream view, there is no death penalty for leaving Islam; a woman's testimony is not half that of a man; Muslims cannot fight non-Muslims for their faith; Muslims cannot use violence to impose their interpretation of Islam on other Muslims; women are not obligated to cover their heads; there is no concept of a face veil in Islam; women cannot be captured in wars and enslaved for personal pleasure; Hell is not destined for all non-Muslims; monarchies and dictatorships are against the Islamic political system, which resembles democracy; keeping beards is not a religious commandment for men; gender segregation is not compulsory; and all art forms, including painting, sculpting, and acting, are allowed within certain divinely ordained moral restrictions.

After explaining the reasons behind my beliefs, I want to discuss them with as many people as possible to keep challenging my answers.

There is one more very special reason for writing this book, which I will share at the end. Going through my journey and analyzing my answers will help you understand the sentiment behind that reason, even if you disagree with me ideologically.

Since there are many concepts I have shared in this book that I learned from Mr. Ghamidi, I feel a disclaimer is necessary. I am not a scholarly student of Mr. Javed Ahmed Ghamidi. I am just a layperson who has gained some answers from his teachings. If I make any mistakes in my understanding or in my elaboration of what I learned from Mr. Ghamidi, he bears no responsibility for it.

To ensure the correctness of my understanding of Islam in general and Mr. Ghamidi's teachings in particular, I had this book reviewed by Dr. Shehzad Saleem, a scholarly student of Mr. Ghamidi and an accomplished Quranic scholar with a Ph.D. from the University of Wales, UK. I am extremely grateful to Dr. Saleem for his feedback and for writing a foreword for this book, which I will share in the next section.

Lastly, a very important note for readers: You may find some of the things I write about religion, God, and divine accountability to be quite strange—especially if you do not believe in God or religion. But when you feel that way, remember, we already live in a very strange world. We reside on a round floating rock in an endless sea of other round rocks and gaseous bodies. Atoms—mostly empty space—are arranged into the beautiful and grotesque forms we see around us. Every day, we consume inanimate matter, which transforms into complex life before our eyes, and this mere arrangement of atoms becomes sentient and intelligent.

We live in an age where we have transformed inanimate matter into marvels of modern technology. If we told someone from just 100 years ago about our creations today, they would likely reject our claims as too strange to be possible. Just because strange things happen every day and everywhere, we grow accustomed to their strangeness, and they stop seeming unusual. However, the fact remains that we inhabit a very strange reality. Keep this in mind as we discuss God and divine accountability.

FOREWORD

The quest for truth is one of the loftiest traits a human mind can possess. It is a yearning that may first disturb a person; however, if he continues with this journey undauntedly, it becomes one of the most fascinating experiences of life. More than that, it is an obligation imposed on human beings by their creator.

It gives me great pleasure to introduce and recommend a work produced by one such seeker of truth: Hamza Ali Abbasi. He is known to many as a media celebrity who has won phenomenal acclaim. It seems that the traditional interpretation of religion did not satisfy him, and it became the perfect foil for him to tread into the uncharted territory of atheism. As a true seeker of truth might have it, fate brought Hamza face to face with his future mentor, Javed Ahmed Ghamidi, about 10 years ago. He realized that he had stumbled on the famous Shakespearean tide:

> *There is a tide in the affairs of men Which,*
> *taken at the flood, leads on to fortune;*
> *Omitted, all the voyage of their life*
> *Is bound in shallows and in miseries.*

It was a God-sent chance he capitalized on with great relish and fervor. He set about to unlearn and then learn religion afresh. The basic questions that haunted him began to get answered. The pieces of the jigsaw puzzle of life seemed to fall into place. The mysteries of life and the afterlife began to unravel before him. Like a person possessed with the burning desire for truth, he confronted his atheistic beliefs with his newfound understanding of religion that was based on reason and revelation. He discovered God afresh, and this was perhaps the most cherished moment of his life.

Like any sincere seeker of truth, the process of self-discovery logically led this voyager to the next stage of his enthralling expedition: he decided to share the truth he had discovered with those he could reach. He first used the spoken word to share his incredible odyssey. This led him to meet both young adults and seasoned minds and apprise them of what he had learned. Time then became ripe to dip his pen in the ink of his thoughts and write this book that is now in front of our readers. As a humble student of Javed Ahmed Ghamidi, I can vouch that the author has worked very hard in understanding the views of his mentor and has tried to succinctly and eloquently draft them in the modern idiom. Like any human work, no effort can be fault-free, and neither can any author claim this. The key to understanding religion is critical thinking, which is a lifelong process. I hope that Hamza will not stop at what he has understood and will continue to revisit and improve his findings. After all, real affiliation should be with the truth itself and not with personalities.

My prayers are that the passion for the quest for truth remains ignited in him forever and makes him earn immense reward from his creator both in this world and in the next. May this effort show others the way too and add fuel to the torch of truth personified by these words of Voltaire:

Stand upright, speak thy thoughts declare
The truth thou hast that all may share
Be bold, proclaim it everywhere
They only live who dare

Shehzad Saleem (PhD, University of Wales, UK)
Research Fellow, GCIL

"In the name of God, the Most Gracious,
the Eternally Compassionate."

CHAPTER 1
WHY BOTHER?

My academic interests revolve around domestic and international politics, while my field of work, my business, and my passion is acting in theatre, television drama, and film. Matters of God, the afterlife, and divine accountability don't excite me at all—these subjects are neither on the list of my academic interests nor on the list of my professional passions. However, sheer necessity compels me to engage with these matters. One may ask, though, why the necessity?

Why do I exist? Why does everything exist? Was I deliberately created by someone with a specific purpose, or am I just a product of sheer luck—an accidental outcome of mindless processes? Is there a god or gods? Is there an afterlife, or is my material death my permanent end? Is there a Day of Judgment where I shall stand accountable for the life I lead in this world, or are these just fairy tales?

Why consider these questions to be important at all? For many of us, existential questions and their potential answers do not have any immediate real-world consequences. eem irrelevant in the face of more immediate concerns of daily life that consume most of our time and energy? In short, why bother about such matters when there is a whole life to be lived with all of its pleasures and pains, toils and gains? Why bother at all?

The most straightforward argument often made is that the simple fact that "I" exist—with all my emotional, intellectual, carnal, moral, and aesthetic faculties—set within this bizarre reality filled with its mind-boggling attributes, provides ample reason to seriously contemplate the "Why" aspect of our existence. Moreover, since humans are composed of the same materials as everything else, and only we seem capable of pondering our origins and purpose, we effectively represent all of existence in our inquiry. We are the universe itself wondering about its origin and purpose. Adding irrefutable urgency to this inquiry is the reality that death could occur at any moment, leaving me with an unpredictably limited amount of time to contemplate "Why" do I exist?

But who cares? For me, all such rationale was never compelling enough to consider existential matters as anything more than occasional midnight fleeting thoughts. I was content to let others do this pondering. I believed that deeply exploring existence was something reserved for scholars, thinkers, academics, and philosophers. As someone who does not fit into the above categories, I considered contemplating existence unimportant amid the more engaging aspects of life. After all, life in this day and age has become unprecedentedly engaging in every way.

But gradually, by my late teens, I realized some very compelling reasons to ask such questions and concluded that choosing to be heedless and oblivious toward existential questions and curiosities is by far the worst possible choice one can make. For me, the following reasons make addressing these questions a very serious matter of necessity for everyone—yes, everyone, with whatever time and effort they can invest—and it is in their own ultimate personal benefit no matter what answers one comes to agree with.

Prospects of Unimaginably Severe Consequences

Everyone, everywhere has heard about the idea of some form of divine judgment after death. Billions of people adhere to this belief today, and the notion of post-mortem divine judgment has existed in most - if not all - human societies throughout history, as far as we can tell from written records and orally transmitted stories of ancient peoples. I, too, have encountered this idea, and given the unimaginably profound implications of such a proposition, I felt compelled to seriously investigate this matter at least once in my life to determine if there is any truth to it. The possibilities of permanent bliss, pleasure, contentment, and happiness, or permanent regret, misery, and pain, are too intense to be ignored and not investigated thoroughly.

Two Potential Lives One Can Lead

A reasonably satisfying answer to the question of God and post-mortem divine accountability would define for me the true meaning of what it means to be "ultimately successful" and what it means to be an "ultimate failure." Almost all the choices we make in our lives are, in one way or another, governed by how we define these two concepts. I realized very early in my life that there were two different potential lives I could lead, and I had to decide which one to choose. If the possibility that I will actually be held accountable for the life I lead in this world for a permanent result seems true, then it feels like obvious common sense and the most rational thing to do is to lead one's life in a way that would ensure maximum success in that accountability, or at least ensure safety, to say the least. This kind of lifestyle may have some extremely uncomfortable requirements, like sacrificing some worldly benefits and maintaining an unpleasant level of control over one's desires and instincts. On the other hand, if ideas like God and post-mortem divine accountability seem fictitious, then, for me, the only way to live a worldly life is to relentlessly pursue maximum success, pleasure, and fulfillment, regardless of the cost.

It is valid to point out that many people lead happy and contented lives, seemingly in line with universal human morality, without delving too deeply into existential questions. However, I believe this is an extremely risky approach. I question whether most of us can navigate life without encountering situations where we must choose between aligning with our inner morality, even if it entails some worldly loss, and making choices that benefit us but contradict our inner morality. These are the kinds of dilemmas I frequently faced as I grew older, because life kept presenting choices that, although they felt wrong according to my innate sense of morality, were the most beneficial in terms of immediate worldly outcomes, and vice versa. In such situations, having some understanding of the truth of divine accountability is crucial for making the best possible choices.

Mediocrity Is Not an Option

It might seem like I am taking life too seriously or behaving in an extreme manner, and yes, that is correct. I recommend that you do the same because we—you and I—have only one shot at this worldly life. Soon, death will come, and we will irreversibly and permanently cease to exist in this world. No matter how we live, our loved ones will eventually forget us, perhaps mentioning us only on occasion. If you are famous, you may be mentioned in the news once a year on your birth or death anniversary, but even that recognition will eventually fade away. The world will completely move on and forget about you. Within roughly a hundred years, you, me, our loved ones, and everyone alive today will be gone from this world forever. In the grander scheme of things, the universe as we know it will also ultimately come to an end. Therefore, for me, total and absolute death is inevitable. Given that I have only one shot at this worldly life, mediocrity is not—and should not be—an option.

In summary, the concept of divine accountability after death is a universal idea, marked by its potentially severe consequences. I believe that, for one's ultimate benefit, it is crucial to dedicate time away from everyday duties of life — from the toils of economic survival and maintenance of family, and other emotional/social bonds — to seriously contemplate this matter. It is incumbent upon everyone who is of sound mind to make an earnest effort to reach a reasonable conclusion on this issue as early as possible. Furthermore, it should be a lifelong endeavor to continually reassess the answers one finds and adjust life choices accordingly.

One last reason, which many may not find compelling—and rightly so, as it is more subjective in nature—is, for me, one of the most important factors due to its emotional and ethical value.

Exploring the Identity of My 'True Parent'

I believe that a profound inquiry into the existence of a personal God is a simple endeavor aimed at discovering my true creator—my mother before my earthly mother and my father before my earthly father. I express this with no intention of diminishing the unfathomable emotional value, love, and sacrifice inherent in parental and family relationships. Instead, I am seeking to highlight that if my origin truly stems from a divine being who created me and oversees all aspects of my life—observing and listening to me directly—then my primary relationship is with that being. All other relationships become secondary. Consider this: the family and friends I have, would not be part of my life if I had been born in another time and place. Thus, if a creator does indeed exist, one who fashioned me ex nihilo, then this is my only true relationship. All other relationships are created by the creator who placed me in this world at a specific time and place. Such a revelation carries profound emotional and ethical implications. All primary sentiments such as love, expectation, devotion, and loyalty should be directed foremost to this being, with all other loves, expectations, devotions, and loyalties remaining secondary. Ultimate gratitude for everything good is reserved for this being, while gratitude toward anyone else is secondary.

Likewise, all ultimate expectations and hopes in times of difficulty and distress are directed toward this being, with expectations and hopes from others remaining secondary.

CHAPTER 2

PREPARATION FOR THE JOURNEY

Becoming a Blank Canvas: No Biases Allowed

The environment and surroundings in which we grow up, the education we receive (if any), the social, political, philosophical, religious, and other influences to which we may be exposed, and our positive and negative life experiences contribute significantly to shaping our self-perception and our understanding of reality. As we accumulate ideas and experiences, it is natural to develop biases and inclinations towards accepting or rejecting certain viewpoints. However, if these biases hinder our willingness to listen to opposing views or prevent us from acknowledging what is evidently right or wrong, they transform into detrimental barriers, undermining sincerity and honesty in the quest for truth.

Biases originate from diverse sources, including personal aspects like ego, pride, and self-interests, as well as one's national, racial, political, and religious affiliations. These biases often blind many people to rational and empathetic thinking, forcing us to justify unthinkable absurdities and evils.

Even seemingly harmless biases can cause the most brilliant minds to deny glaring truths. For example, the great theological minds of Galileo's era rejected the obvious truth presented to them by the great scientist. Similarly, Einstein's bias in favor of a static universe initially led him to dismiss the notion of an expanding universe, despite his equations strongly suggesting it. Staying unbiased while analyzing anything is a challenging task, but it is essential because the more we curb our biases, the greater the likelihood of arriving at the correct conclusion. Even if the conclusion turns out to be incorrect, if one reaches that conclusion without any biases through a sincere inquiry, then such an error falls within the realm of genuine mistakes. Genuine mistakes made with sincerity should reasonably merit unconditional forgiveness by both humans and God. Hence, the sincerity and honesty of the inquiry matter more than the conclusion itself.

The human tendency toward bias is more conspicuous in matters of God and religion. This tendency leads individuals to uphold and defend the beliefs they were born into without critically examining them. On the other side of the spectrum, there exists a resistance among many toward organized religion, which makes them refuse to entertain any possibility of evidence supporting the existence of a supernatural creator who has ordained a specific religion or way of life.

During my formative years, I realized the destructive potential of biases. I committed myself to vigilantly monitor this tendency and follow wherever the evidence might lead with all my sincerity and honesty. I resolved not to let my personal attachment to any idea prevent me from rejecting it if the evidence contradicts it. Simultaneously, I pledged not to let my aversion toward any idea obstruct me from accepting it if the evidence supports it.

In Matters of God and Divine Accountability, Simplicity Should Lead to Truth

Exploring ideologies and philosophies that attempt to elucidate the existence of God and divine accountability often leaves seekers feeling overwhelmed amid the multitude of options. The abundance of information about atheism, agnosticism, theism, deism, and the plethora of religions and philosophies—accompanied by a labyrinth of arguments and counterarguments—can lead many to lose interest in the subject entirely. I experienced this firsthand as I delved into a vast array of literature, contemplating different viewpoints, schools of thought, and endless discussions, feeling adrift without a clear path forward.

When I inquired—particularly within religious communities—many clerics told me that to genuinely comprehend my origins and purpose in relation to God and divine accountability, I would need a lifetime of dedication and rigorous study. This is a daunting task for a layperson like myself, who simply seeks answers to fundamental questions without aspiring to become an academic or scholar.

Both proponents and opponents of the existence of God provide an overwhelming amount of information, making the quest for truth about God and divine accountability seem like an insurmountable, exhaustive task. However, an epiphany encouraged me to alter my approach in searching for truth. Consequently, I discovered that the simplest method led to the ultimate truth. I came to realize that if any truth exists regarding the possibility of a God and divine accountability, it must be simple yet capable of addressing basic questions clearly, while also allowing for deeper scholarly exploration. Let me elaborate.God and divine accountability concern all of humanity—everyone's eternal destiny is at stake. Most individuals cannot spare extensive time and energy from the basic struggles and duties of life to immerse themselves in complex literature and discussions. Hence, a simple conclusion can be drawn: if a God will judge all humanity for their actions in this life and has created this present worldly existence with its demanding commitments, then fundamental answers regarding our origins and purpose should be easily accessible and comprehensible to all—both laypeople and scholars alike.

While complexity naturally arises in various fields of human knowledge, if a God exists and holds mankind accountable, the basic essentials should be easily graspable by everyone. It is contradictory to conceive of a God who would create humanity with a purpose yet make understanding the basics so complicated that it becomes an onerous task for most people.

Hence, if a God created me and intends to hold me accountable, then all fundamental knowledge about this matter must be easily and unambiguously discoverable, understandable, and communicable by everyone. After recognizing this, I decided to simplify my inquiry, which led to a pivotal realization.

Humility Is Imperative

There is a disturbing trend among many individuals, especially regarding existential matters. They often assume their worldview, beliefs, opinions, and conclusions are indisputably true, viewing those who differ from them as simply wrong and in need of correction. This leaves no room for discourse aimed at understanding each other's point of view and potentially learning from one another.

Whether within the atheist and agnostic camp or the camp of those who believe in God and religion, it is crucial to recognize the presence of knowledgeable and accomplished people—scholars, academics, and scientists—across the spectrum in all camps, each presenting well-formed arguments and counterarguments. For this reason, it becomes imperative to maintain humility, staying consistently open to the prospect of fallibility and being receptive to learning. We need to move away from the "debate" culture where winning the argument is the sole objective, and instead engage in discussions aimed at exchanging ideas and sharing knowledge. Acknowledging that "I can be wrong" is something that fosters the necessary humility needed to uphold such an attitude.

A Note About Inference

Conclusions are primarily drawn in two ways. The first is through direct observation—such as seeing a tree in front of us and concluding its presence. However, what distinguishes us from many other creatures is our remarkable ability to make highly advanced and intricate inferences, which is the second way we reach conclusions.

For instance, Newton observed an apple falling from a tree and inferred the existence of a force causing the apple to descend toward the ground. This oversimplified example explains what 'inference' entails: it is a conclusion drawn based on available evidence and reasoning. In courts, judges usually render decisions using inference, and in our daily lives, we frequently infer situations—like noticing a friend walk by in school without smiling and inferring that something might be wrong with him. Our inferences can be valid or invalid, resulting in conclusions that are right or wrong based on subsequent direct observation or measurement. Nevertheless, from our routine experiences to the biggest scientific discoveries, our ability to infer remains our most vital faculty in pursuit of any form of truth.

Science's Contribution to Understanding the Existence of a Divine Being

Throughout history, from the remarkable scientific advancements of the Islamic Golden Age to the contributions of Western scientists like Galileo, Newton, Schrödinger, and Francis Collins, it is evident that many religious individuals have excelled in science. Historically, science was not viewed as fundamentally opposed to the divine. The widespread contemporary belief that science has disproved the existence of a personal god and an afterlife is a relatively modern perspective.

Science has undoubtedly helped to dispel dogmatic beliefs originating from both theism and atheism—for instance, it has corrected certain religious groups' misconceptions that the Earth is flat and the universe revolves around it. Conversely, science has also corrected the past belief held by some atheistic and areligious groups that the universe is static, eternal and unchanging.

Often, I hear people state that "science confirms there is no God" or, conversely, that "science asserts the existence of God." Both statements are flawed. Science, as a field of knowledge, does not directly delve into the question of the existence or nonexistence of the Divine. It merely presents facts about how our reality operates. A scientist's role is to provide these facts, but both scientists and laypeople are on equal ground when interpreting whether these facts point towards God or not.

Science: One Tool Among Many

It is crucial to note that in the pursuit of answers to existential questions, science is just one of several faculties one can utilize—but it is not the only tool. One can also employ other equally important tools, such as philosophical inquiry, historical analysis, personal testimony, and arguments derived from ethics and morality.

Understanding "How Something Works" Does Not Negate the Possibility of Its Being Created by God

In the realm of science, the prevalent belief that understanding how and why something works eliminates the need to consider an intelligent origin is misguided. This misconception stems from the belief that if we know how something functions, we don't need "God" to explain it. This falsely suggests that if a divine entity is involved, its actions must be beyond our comprehension—supernatural and unintelligible. However, understanding "how" or "why" something works should not automatically categorize it as a "natural explanation" devoid of intelligent intervention. I disagree with this perception. Perhaps certain religious segments have contributed to this notion by portraying God as primarily a miracle worker whose actions are inherently beyond our comprehension. Nonetheless, the idea that knowing how something works negates the possibility of its creation by an intelligent force is flawed.

The Absence of an Explanation Does Not Invalidate the Explanation

Not having an explanation for the explanation does not render it invalid. To illustrate, if we were to find a wooden chair and table on Mars, we would logically infer that some intelligence is responsible for their creation. We would make this inference despite not knowing who that intelligence is or how they created these items. Not knowing who the intelligence is and where it came from would not be a reason formidable enough to reject the intelligence hypothesis altogether.

BREAKING AWAY FROM AGNOSTICISM & ATHEISM

L et us renew our understanding that humanity has debated atheism and theism since time immemorial. The debate continues
to thrive among accomplished philosophers, thinkers, scientists,
and academics from all sides of the spectrum. Hence, regardless of the
answers we agree with, we must always be open to the possibility of being wrong and be willing to sincerely judge any challenge to our beliefs
based on the reasoning presented. We should strive to decide matters
on their merit as best as we possibly can.

In my late teens, I briefly identified as an agnostic, with a strong
inclination toward atheism. This was largely due to the perceived moral,
rational, and scientific shortcomings of the prevalent religious teachings
around me, combined with the authoritarian attitudes of the religious
clergy I encountered. I refer to myself during that phase as an agnostic
atheist, but it was a very brief period of my life.

14 ● *My Discovery of God, Islam & Judgment Day*

Similarities of Religious Ideas Across Cultures Separated by Time and Geography - A Reason for Serious Investigation

Almost everyone in the world has heard the idea that a God created everything and that this God will hold everyone accountable after death, resulting in a permanent consequence. I heard it too, and initially dismissed it as a narrative humans invented to make sense of the world they didn't understand and to exert control over society. As I discussed earlier, the potentially severe consequences of divine judgment should prompt everyone to continually assess whether there is any truth in these matters. Consequently, I always kept an eye out for information that might challenge my atheism. One peculiar reason, however, persuaded me to seriously investigate these ideas: almost every human culture in recorded history, with very few exceptions like the Amazonian Pirahã people, has held generally similar concepts about God and divine judgment. While the details of these concepts vary widely, they generally include similar themes: a creator God, contact and exchange of information with the divine or otherworldly entities, continuation of consciousness after bodily death, divine judgment following death, and a permanent positive or negative outcome based on that judgment.

At first glance, this might not seem noteworthy, but when you consider it deeply, it becomes quite perplexing. Imagine cultures and societies, separated by time and geography and having never exchanged information, all arriving at generally similar concepts about existence.

> *Religion – the belief in supernatural beings, including gods and ghosts, angels and demons, souls and spirits – can be found throughout history and in every culture. Every known human culture has creation myths, with the possible exception of the Amazonian Pirahã people, who also lack number words, color words, and social hierarchy.[1]*

We will delve into the details of these similarities in a later chapter when I discuss the Quran's explanation of other religions. For now, I want to emphasize what prompted me to consider more seriously the possibility of being created by some intelligence and being held accountable by that intelligence. Why did almost every human culture independently arrive at generally similar ideas about our origins and purpose—about an intelligent creator and some form of accountability by that creator? There are various speculations within expert circles, but for me, this became one of the primary reasons compelling me to investigate the possibility of God and divine accountability.

The question of an intelligent creator kept resurfacing, as it's not just religion that persuades one to consider the idea of intelligence as the source of everything—indeed, the very nature of reality itself compels one to wonder if such a possibility could be true.

The first crack in my atheism appeared around 2004-2005 when the famous and influential atheist philosopher Antony Flew renounced his lifelong atheism at the age of 81. He proclaimed his belief in an intelligence behind everything and detailed his beliefs in his book "There is a God - How the World's Most Notorious Atheist Changed His Mind."--2 Flew rejected religions and the religious concept of God, instead believing in an intelligence that created everything but did not involve itself in the daily affairs of humans. Nonetheless, his conversion made me re-examine my own atheism.

After a serious reassessment, my brief romance with atheism began to wane because the very foundations on which I had based my worldview started to crumble. I used to think I had everything sorted concerning my worldview. I believed that we are a mere speck in an enormous existence, implying that we are nothing more than an accident of probability. The fundamental reality, the uncaused cause of everything, is some primordial mix of energy fields and laws. I believed that random quantum fluctuations caused everything. I considered my brain to encompass all of me, and the termination of my brain meant the end of me. All discussions of a conscious, intelligent entity creating everything and my consciousness continuing after bodily death were deemed by me as mere religious myths, based on subjective human experiences with no evidence or foundation in scientific reality.

However, all of that changed. My belief that science and rationality had completely justified atheism turned out to be false. Here are the main reasons why I could not remain intellectually satisfied with atheism.

Reasons for Doubting My Atheism

1 - Significance of Consciousness and Intelligence

I used to be perplexed by the universe's capacity to allow for the existence of consciousness and intelligence. At the same time, I believed that we humans tend to be narcissistic, attaching undue and undeserved importance to ourselves. This narcissism, I thought, was most pronounced in our religious beliefs—an expression of self-importance driven by the need for a special creator who created us for a distinct purpose. If other animals don't question their existence, why do we? Is it merely because of our higher IQ, or is it also because we cannot bear to feel ordinary, unimportant, and purposeless, doomed to die soon and fade into oblivion? I believed that all notions of humankind's significance, as preached by religion, had been shattered by discoveries demonstrating that we are not the center of the world, and our world is not the center of the universe. We are merely one species among millions, inhabiting a small planet that orbits a medium-sized star in a galaxy containing more than 200 billion stars in a medium-sized galaxy in an ocean of millions, possibly billions, of galaxies. Because we are such a minuscule part of an overwhelmingly large existence, we don't matter in any objective manner and should not feel the need to invoke any special creator to explain our existence.

Size and Value

However, I soon realized that physical size and proportions are by no means adequate criteria for measuring the value of anything. In fact, rarity and scarcity often increase value rather than diminish it. Consider gold and diamonds, for example, or a small oasis of fresh water surrounded by hundreds of miles of barren desert.

Consciousness – The source of All Significance

More importantly, indeed most crucially, consciousness holds fundamental significance because it is the source of all meaning and value, as it requires conscious minds to begin with in order to attach any kind of significance, meaning, or value to anything.

Intelligence: One of the Most Powerful Forces in the Universe

As far as intelligence is concerned, it is significant because it is one of the most powerful phenomena in the known universe. It can overcome supposed natural limits by manipulating the forces of nature at increasingly finer levels, allowing us to utilize these forces and processes to achieve our goals.

Importance of Lifeless Matter Becoming Sentient

Then, of course, there are intangible concepts that some may argue have an independent existence – love, beauty, truth, sacrifice, justice, oppression, pain, and suffering. When lifeless matter becomes alive and acquires the capacity to experience and inflict all the above, to some, that represents the most significant event in the history of an otherwise inanimate pile of matter that constitutes the universe.

To summarize, one pillar of my atheism was the belief that we humans are insignificant, and all stories attributing our significance to God are false. However, my perspective shifted when I realized the true nature of significance and how profoundly significant we are.

2 – An Atheist's Notion of an Uncaused First Cause Is Not Any Simpler Than the God Hypothesis

Our universe exists due to the extraordinarily fine-tuned values of laws and forces that govern matter. Even minor changes to these values would result in a universe drastically different from our own. Consider gravity: an increase in its force, however slight, would cause everything to collapse inward, while a decrease, however slight, would prevent objects from clumping together. This would eliminate the possibility of physics, chemistry, biology, planets, stars, and galaxies emerging. Although there is ongoing debate among scientists, it is generally recognized that there are around 26 such constants, with the possibility of many more. The believer points to the fine-tuning of the cosmos as evidence of an intelligent design behind it—meanwhile, the atheist offers counter-theories, such as the Multiverse theory. This theory suggests the existence of an unimaginably large number of universes, each with varying constants, popping in and out of existence; our universe just happens to have the right constants to support life and intelligence. However, there is a point of consensus between believers and atheists: the necessity of an uncaused cause for everything. This uncaused cause was also the subject of my reflections.

Because everything exists, both the atheist and the theist are compelled to accept the existence of an uncaused cause that gave rise to everything. This is a compulsion because we cannot have an infinite regression of causes, as that would imply that nothing could ever come into existence. Let me share an example: if you were to travel to Paris from any starting point and you eventually reach Paris, it implies that the distance traveled was finite. If the distance between Paris and your starting point were infinite, you would never reach Paris, as you would be traveling endlessly without arriving at your destination. This principle also applies to existence itself. The fact that our reality exists implies that there is a finite number of causes behind it. This logically suggests the existence of a fundamental, ultimate reality that exists by necessity, giving rise to both us and the reality that surrounds us. The only difference between those who believe in God and atheists is that the former assert this ultimate reality is a primordial mind or a consciousness capable of realizing whatever it intends, while the latter believe that the ultimate reality is some kind of primordial mix of matter, energy, and laws that cause everything purely through mindless, undirected processes.

I believed in the atheistic solution because it seemed simpler, and thus more rationally appealing than the ever-so-complex entity known as God. However, as I pondered more about the non-theistic first uncaused cause, it appeared not so simple when compared to the God hypothesis. This "simple something"—the ultimate reality for atheists—needed to encompass all the ingredients and mechanisms required to eventually evolve into intelligent, sentient beings with emotions, ethics, morality, and aesthetics. It also had to support a reality that caters to these attributes, including color, music, beauty, justice, oppression, and everything both wonderful and grotesque. It didn't seem like a very simple assumption that all the above just happened to be contained within that simple something purely by necessity. Matter, even in its most primordial form, has always possessed extraordinary potentialities that require an explanation.

The notion that an ultimate reality, inherently conscious and intelligent, exists by necessity and unfolds through mere chance and coincidence is not, by any means, more plausible on the scale of relative simplicity compared to the idea that such a reality exists intentionally and intelligently, giving rise to everything through deliberate design. This realization put a significant check on my tilt towards atheism, making the hypothesis of a god or divine intelligence seem less complex than the atheistic alternative. It dispelled my false belief that the latter was more rational and scientifically plausible than the former.

But there is more to this—as I delved deeper into our understanding of space and time, I realized that our notion of what is simple and what is complex is too limited. It cannot be used as a basis to consider one hypothesis more plausible than another in the debate between belief in God and atheism. Let me explain this point briefly in the following section.

3 - The Irrelevance of Our Understanding of What Is "Simple" and What Is "Complex"

Emerging theories such as String Theory, Causal Set Theory, and Loop Quantum Gravity propose that space and time are not fundamental. Additionally, proponents of the Big Bang theory argue that time and space themselves emerged from a singularity around 14 billion years ago. Now, purely speculatively speaking, imagine if indeed space and time are not fundamental. This scenario would open the door to the existence of realities beyond space and time—a reality beyond the concepts of "Where" and "When." We, as humans, are limited to experiencing and comprehending reality within the constraints of time and space. If there exists any reality without or outside space and time, we cannot comprehend it at any level. Our definitions of simplicity and complexity would not apply in that reality because all our definitions, perceptions, and experiences exist within the framework of time and space.

Let's conduct a thought experiment—can you imagine anything existing without occupying any space? Or can you imagine anything existing that is not affected by time? Probably not! An overly simplistic parable or analogy of what I am trying to convey might be that in the zero-gravity environment of space, all our definitions and perceptions of weight and how heavy or light something is become irrelevant. Hence, if a reality exists beyond space and time, then our definitions of what is simple and what is complex would become totally irrelevant in such a realm. Rejecting the idea of God because it seems too complex as a first cause, based on our very limited experience within space and time, is a very narrow approach toward reality.

4 - Believing in a Creator Having Similarities With Us: A Justified Belief

Someone once said that if dolphins could wonder where they came from, they would probably imagine a creator who is essentially a great dolphin. I would contemplate such statements and reflect on the folly humankind has committed by seriously entertaining the possibility that a consciousness much like ours could be the creator of everything: a God who is conscious, thinks, intends, talks, feels happy, shows mercy, and gets angry. Attributing such human traits to the uncaused cause of everything is surely no different than the naivety of those dolphins.

However, if a group of dolphins became intelligent enough to contemplate existential questions, while considering all sorts of possibilities regarding who or what created them, they would also be justified in positing the existence of a creator who is at least similar to them in a way that it also possesses intelligence. Moreover, if those dolphins became adept at understanding and manipulating their reality, much like us humans, I would not blame them for thinking that they might share some level of finite similarity with whatever infinite force caused everything, simply because their reality is so intelligible to them. For example, if we discovered an empty alien spaceship on Mars and learned how the spaceship operates, we could reasonably assume that while the owners of the ship could be very different from us in many ways, they are at least mentally similar to us in some ways, because we understand how their spaceship functions. So, if we comprehend reality so well, we can rightfully assume that if the uncaused cause of everything is a someone rather than a something, then that someone is at least similar to us in a way that we can understand many of its actions.

5 - The Idea of an Intelligent Consciousness as the First Cause of Everything - A Realistic Possibility

Consciousness might be a fundamental part of reality

The religious proposition that the first cause of everything is an entity with consciousness seemed entirely fallacious to me. I believed consciousness to be solely a function of the brain—an emergent property of electrochemical reactions. How could a brain function be a part of the first cause of everything? It appeared to be a ludicrous and fictitious religious idea with no grounding in the non-religious realm. However, I discovered theories within non-religious circles—taken very seriously by credible scientists—which suggest that consciousness might not merely be an emergent phenomenon of the brain. It could be something fundamental to reality itself. Of course, I am not implying that this verifies a conscious entity like God created everything. I am simply stating that the non-religious acknowledgment of the possibility that consciousness could be more than just a brain function—and, in fact, a fundamental part of all reality—elevates the idea of a conscious first cause from being merely a religious proposition with no basis in non-religious reality to being a serious possibility rooted in non-religious discourse.

One such theory is Panpsychism, which proposes that consciousness is not an emergent property arising from the complex interaction of matter, but rather a fundamental field that permeates reality. This theory suggests that everything in existence possesses some level of consciousness: humans exhibit a high level of consciousness, dogs possess consciousness on a lower scale, insects on an even lower scale, and even subatomic particles hold an extremely minuscule level of experience and consciousness. A few decades ago, such a theory was considered preposterous. However, there is now growing comfort and acceptance among the scientific community for this idea. Respected and reputable publications in the scientific world, such as "New Scientist" and "Scientific

American," are increasingly exploring and discussing this theory as a very serious scientific possibility.

I read some interesting articles on this matter in the scientific journals "New Scientist" and "Scientific American." When such credible platforms give room to a theory, it signifies that it is gaining serious attention from the scientific community. Michael Brooks writes:

> *The question of how matter gives rise to felt experience is one of the most vexing problems we know of. And sure enough, the first fleshed-out mathematical model of consciousness has generated huge debate about whether it can tell us anything sensible. But as mathematicians work to hone and extend their tools for peering deep inside ourselves, they are confronting some eye-popping conclusions.*

> *Not least, what they are uncovering seems to suggest that if we are to achieve a precise description of consciousness, we may have to ditch our intuitions and accept that all kinds of inanimate matter could be conscious – maybe even the universe as a whole*

> *This could be the beginning of a scientific revolution, says Johannes Kleiner, a mathematician at the Munich Centre for Mathematical Philosophy in Germany.[3]*

The idea that everything possesses some degree of consciousness might have religious or spiritual implications. However, this concept is also gaining popularity among materialist and naturalist circles. Assuming consciousness as a fundamental property of reality offers a very non-supernatural explanation for consciousness.

> *Consciousness, for the panpsychist, is the intrinsic nature of matter. There's just matter, on this view, nothing supernatural or spiritual. But matter can be described from two perspectives. Physical science describes matter "from*

the outside," in terms of its behavior. But matter "from the inside"—i.e., in terms of its intrinsic nature— is constituted of forms of consciousness.

What this offers us is a beautifully simple, elegant way of integrating consciousness into our scientific worldview, of marrying what we know about ourselves from the inside and what science tells us about matter from the outside.⁴

Panpsychism is also gaining acceptance due to the Integrated Information Theory (IIT) developed by neuroscientist Giulio Tononi. As Horgan writes:

Panpsychism strikes me as self-evidently foolish, but non-foolish people - notably Chalmers and neuroscientist Christof Koch - are taking it seriously. How can that be? What's compelling their interest? Have I dismissed panpsychism too hastily? - These questions lured me to a two-day workshop on integrated information theory at New York University last month. Conceived by neuroscientist Giulio Tononi (who trained under the late, great Gerald Edelman), IIT is an extremely ambitious theory of consciousness. It applies to all forms of matter, not just brains, and it implies that panpsychism might be true. Koch and others are taking panpsychism seriously because they take IIT seriously.⁵

I believed that the religious idea of a conscious being creating everything was conclusively negated by science. I thought science had proven beyond doubt that consciousness is merely a product of a material brain. However, when I encountered serious non-religious thinkers exploring the possibility that consciousness might be fundamental to reality rather than just a result of the brain, I began to see the idea of the first cause of everything having consciousness as no longer impossible.

However, consciousness does not equate to intelligence. Do we have similar research and findings that suggest the consciousness, which might potentially be the uncaused cause of everything, also possesses intelligence? Yes, we do. We find hallmarks of intelligence at the very core of the processes that enable life, and signs of intelligence may well be embedded in the very fabric of reality itself.

DNA – Hallmarks of Intelligence

Darwinian evolution is often presented as the ultimate biological proof that God does not exist. However, a significant number of scientists challenge Darwinian evolution—the idea that all species evolved from a single cell—and propose alternative evolutionary mechanisms to explain the origins of biological diversity. 'The Third Way' is an excellent resource for exploring these alternative theories.[6] But my point is, even if Darwinian evolution were true, it wouldn't necessarily negate the existence of a deity; it would merely challenge the concept of a God who does not use evolution through natural selection as a means to generate life's diversity. The proposition that through random mutations and natural selection a single cell evolved into both you and me over a relatively short period, even by our standards of time, is a testament to the efficient nature of DNA. This capacity to produce such diverse life, ultimately culminating in intelligence and all that comes with it, stems from DNA—the cornerstone of all life processes. This has led me to question my atheism rather than reinforce it.

Bill Gates, in his 1996 book "The Road Ahead," aptly stated, "DNA is like a computer program but far, far more advanced than any software ever created."[7] DNA fundamentally comprises instructions on how to create and manage a living organism, written in a four-letter language. These letters represent the nucleotide bases: Adenine, Guanine, Thymine, and Cytosine (in RNA, Uracil replaces Thymine). These instructions are coded and stored within every cell of every living organism and there is a complex mechanism within every cell that reads, deciphers, edits, replicates, and executes the coded instructions. This instructive information—information of the highest order, written in a language—is a hallmark of intelligence. We humans are the only other entities known to produce such information. We achieved the milestone of writing instructions using letters and alphabets relatively recently, around five thousand years ago, with the advent of writing as we became more civilized and sophisticated. The concept of coding information is even more modern, marking the rise of the information age and standing as one of the greatest milestones of human intelligence.

It is quite extraordinary to find something we identify as a distinctive feature of intelligence as a fundamental process of the origin and management of life. However, it is not just at the basis of life that we find coded information; there is also a very strong possibility that coded information might be embedded in the very fabric of reality itself.

Coded Information Embedded in the Fabric of Reality Is a Sign of Intelligence

The notion that some intelligence is responsible for everything is no longer exclusive to religion. The theory that our universe might be a simulation created by an intelligent source is now being discussed among scientists as a serious possibility. Our reality's ability to reveal facts, which lead scientists to consider such a hypothesis seriously, has reinforced my growing suspicion that some intelligence is a cause of everything.

The theoretical discoveries of the renowned physicist Dr. James Gates are the kind of findings that, for me, added plausibility and reasonableness to the idea of some intelligence as the source of everything. I remember watching a discussion entitled "Are We Living in a Simulation?" on YouTube. This discussion, hosted by Neil deGrasse Tyson, was part of the Isaac Asimov Memorial Debate at the American

Museum of Natural History. I was amazed at what Dr. Gates, one of the participants, stated:.

In response to the question, "Where has this pursuit taken you?" Dr. Gates responded:

> **Dr. Gates:** *Well, partly it's taken me to these strange images that are behind your head right now (points to the screen). These are pictures of equations. For the last 15 years, I have been trying to answer the kinds of questions my colleagues have been raising. I have come to understand that there are these incredible pictures that contain all the information of a set of equations that are related to string theory. And it is even more bizarre than that because when you try to understand these pictures, you find out that buried in them are computer codes just like the type that you find in a browser when you go search the web. So, I am left with the puzzle of trying to figure out whether I live in the matrix or not.*

> **Neil:** *Wait! You are blowing my mind at this moment. So, are you saying that your attempt to understand the fundamental operations of nature leads you to a set of equations that are indistinguishable from the equations that drive search engines and browsers on our computers?*

> **Dr. Gates:** *That is correct.*

> **Neil:** *Wait – I have to be silent for a minute here. So, you are saying that as you dig deeper you find computer code written in the fabric of the cosmos.*

> **Dr. Gates:** *Into the equations that we want to use to describe the cosmos – Yes.*[8]

Dr. Gate's theoretical discovery is supported by what we can observe about space itself. If Einstein was right, then there is no such thing as "Empty Space" anywhere. What we perceive as empty space around us is a medium with its own specific properties. This means the fabric of reality, the very space in which everything exists, or what Einstein called "Space-Time," is saturated with information. We understand through gravitational lensing that space can bend and curve. Matter instructs space on how to curve, and space dictates how matter moves. This interaction explains why subatomic particles revolve around the nucleus, planets orbit the Sun, stars orbit within galaxies, and galaxies rotate around their axes, possibly moving in some uniform pattern within the universe.

Empty space is filled with encoded information. This is also the stance of modern string theorists, who propose the "Holographic Principle." According to this principle, space is a hologram generated from information encoded on a lower-dimensional plane. Leonard Susskind, the founding director of the Stanford Institute for Theoretical Physics, supports this view:

> *The three-dimensional world of ordinary experience – the universe filled with galaxies, stars, planets, houses, boulders, and people – is a hologram, an image of reality coded on a distant two-dimensional surface. This new law of physics, known as the Holographic Principle, asserts that everything inside a region of space can be described by bits of information restricted to the boundary.*[9]

The possibility that the very fabric of reality is embedded with coded information, which is crucial for the cosmos to be the way it is and for life and consciousness to exist, is the kind of thing that prompted me to start leaning in favor of the "Intelligence" hypothesis as an explanation of our reality which recognizes instructive information in the form of a code as a distinct hallmark of intelligence.

The only known source of information in the form of coded instructions is us, humans—an intelligence! Considering that a) intelligence is the only known source of coded digital information, b) this type of information is essential for making life possible, and c) there is a possibility that such information is embedded in the fabric of reality, it would be rational and reasonable to infer that there might actually be an intelligence responsible for this. This line of thinking was actually developed by the renowned Charles Darwin himself. Let me explain in the words of Dr. Stephen Meyer:

> *Darwin pioneered a method of historical scientific reasoning where he realized that if you wanted to explain an event in the remote past, you should try to explain it through causes you see now in operation (in the present). He got this principle from the great geologist Charles Lyell. In eastern Washington where I live, there are little patches of white powdery stuff still on the ground from an event that happened in May 1980, and if you don't know what caused that white powdery stuff, you would use a standard historical method of reasoning called the 'method of multiple competing hypothesis' – maybe it was a flood, maybe it was an earthquake or maybe it was a volcanic eruption – which of those explanations is best according to Darwin and Lyell's principle? It's the volcanic eruption, because we have seen volcanos produce white powdery stuff and flood, and earthquakes don't do that. So, if you apply this principle of reasoning and look for a cause now in operation and ask yourself what is the cause now in operation that produces digital information – you come to one and only one type of cause, and that's a mind.[10]*

6 - Non-religious Reasons to Believe in a Soul and an Afterlife

The findings from scientific circles lend credibility to the hypothesis that a conscious, intelligent force could be the uncaused cause of everything;

this sounded like God to me. If God is a plausible reality, might divine accountability also be plausible? For divine accountability to occur, some aspect of this entity known as "Me" must possess a degree of existence independent of my brain and survive beyond bodily death. Is there any reason, from non-religious discourse or our observable and measurable reality, to believe in the plausibility of my existence, independent of my brain and enduring after brain death? Indeed, there is.

Possibility of Consciousness Having an Independent Existence From the Brain - The Binding Problem of Consciousness - No Place in the Brain That Is "For Me"

Consciousness is something we humans know most intimately because we are all conscious—yet it remains completely alien to us because we have no understanding of what makes us conscious. Different sensory inputs are processed in various areas of the brain—for instance, information about the color of an object is stored in one part, while information about its shape is stored in another. Yet, there is no specific location in the brain where this information combines into a unified perception and experience that is "Me!" In neuroscience circles, this is referred to as the "binding problem" of consciousness. But it's more than just not having found the location in the brain that produces this constant, continuous, uniform experience that is "Me"—it's deeper than that. We have evidence suggesting that this "Me," who thinks and decides, might have a separate, independent existence from my material brain.

Penfield Experiment - This "Me" Who Intends to Do Something Might Be Independent of My Brain

Wilder Penfield, an American-Canadian neurosurgeon, applied electrodes to the motor cortex and was able to make patients involuntarily do things such as raise their hands or recall a memory. The cerebral cortex is the part of the brain considered responsible for many higher-level processes including learning, thought, language, emotion, intelligence, personality, and decision-making. This is known because brain activity in this region can be observed when an individual engages in the afore-mentioned activities. In his experiments, although Penfield could make his subjects perform actions involuntarily by applying electrical stimuli, he could not make his subjects "want" to do anything. A causal force was missing from the material brain. In his words:

> There is no place in the cerebral cortex where an electrical stimulation will cause a patient to decide.[11]

> Penfield concluded that this meant that the will (he called it the "mind") was not in the brain, or at least not in any part of the brain that he could stimulate and that the will was not a physical thing. The will was free, in the sense that it could not be evoked by material means.[12]

This implies that even though we can prompt the brain to influence the body through artificial stimuli, we cannot compel a person to make a decision. This "Me" who makes decisions does not appear to be influenced by stimuli to the brain.

I Can Change My Brain With My Intentional Thoughts

Jeffery M. Schwartz, an American psychiatrist and leading researcher in the field of neuroplasticity, demonstrated that conscious thought can literally change the physical brain without any external intervention Schwartz's OCD patients experienced relief from their symptoms as they successfully reorganized and changed their brain patterns by intentionally modifying their thoughts and behaviors. Furthermore, when artificial stimuli were applied to the same areas of the brain that showed improvement in symptoms, it did not yield effective results.

In simple terms, I can intentionally think and modify specific regions of my brain. However, when the same region is artificially stimulated without my conscious input, it does not induce the same change. Swartz describes this process in the following way:

When stimuli identical to those that induce plastic changes in an attending brain are instead delivered to a non-attending brain, there is no induction of cortical plasticity. Attention, in other words, must be paid.[13]

This implies that it's not solely about the signal or stimuli. The involvement of this "I" that I am, or this "Me" who thinks, intends, and acts, is necessary to alter the physical brain. This "Me," which appears to be separate from the brain, can actively influence my material self in a very pronounced way.

It is becoming a serious idea within science that the material brain might not fully explain the mind. This raises the question: could what we are missing in our understanding of the brain also be missing from our understanding of existence as a whole? It appears that the brain and the mind are not entirely separate, yet they are not identical. This opens up the possibility that consciousness might have some kind of independent existence. If consciousness is not solely produced by the material brain, could it be explained by something more fundamental? Or is consciousness itself one of the fundamentals of reality?

This "Me" That I Am Might Continue After Brain Death

I would often make tea for myself around 5 a.m. and marvel at how incredible it is that this "I"—which cannot be pinpointed in my brain—can change my material brain merely through consistent, intentional thoughts. Mind over matter indeed appears to be true. However, this separation of mind and brain could just be some trickery of the quantum world and does not convincingly imply that this "I," seemingly separate from the brain and possibly continuing after bodily death, had to be believed on faith alone with no grounding in observable reality. It seemed unlikely that any serious voice from the scientific community would come forth and bring forth authentic research to directly support the continuation of my consciousness after bodily death—until

I encountered the research of Dr. Sam Parnia. Previously, I discussed that it is a very serious scientific possibility that some part of me might possess an existence independent of my material brain. Dr. Parnia's research advances the matter further by suggesting that this "Me" can survive intact even when the brain ceases to function.

Dr. Sam Parnia, MD, PhD, is the director of Critical Care and Resuscitation Research at NYU Grossman School of Medicine. He led a team of doctors and scientists in a project studying individuals who had suffered cardiac arrests and, in medical terms, passed the threshold of death before being resuscitated back to life. This study, which concluded in 2012, involved 33 investigators across 15 medical centers in the UK, Austria, and the USA. The results of the study were published in October 2014.

> *The researchers on the study represent many medical disciplines, including the neurosciences, critical care, psychiatry, psychology, social sciences, and humanities, and represent many of the world's most respected academic institutions including Harvard University, Baylor University, University of California Riverside, University of Virginia, Virginia Commonwealth University, Medical College of Wisconsin, and the Universities of Southampton and London*

> *Among their conclusions:*

> *Due to advances in resuscitation and critical care medicine, many people have survived encounters with death or being near-death. These people -- who are estimated to comprise hundreds of millions of people around the world based on previous population studies -- have consistently described recalled experiences surrounding death, which involve a unique set of mental recollections with universal themes.*

The recalled experiences surrounding death are not consistent with hallucinations, illusions, or psychedelic drug-induced experiences, according to several previously published studies. Instead, they follow a specific narrative arc involving a perception of - (a) separation from the body with a heightened, vast sense of consciousness and recognition of death - (b) travel to a destination - (c) a meaningful and purposeful review of life, involving a critical analysis of all actions, intentions, and thoughts towards others - (d) a perception of being in a place that feels like "home" - (e) a return back to life.

The experience of death culminates into previously unidentified, separate subthemes and is associated with positive long-term psychological transformation and growth.

Frightening or distressing experiences in relation to death often neither share the same themes, nor the same narrative, transcendent qualities, ineffability, and positive transformative effects.[14]

One major conclusion of this extensive study is:

Cardiac arrest survivors commonly experience a broad range of cognitive themes, with 2% exhibiting full awareness. This supports other recent studies that have indicated consciousness may be present despite clinically undetectable consciousness.[15]

To make it easier, I will quote Dr. Parnia's words from his interview with Robert Lawrence Kuhn in the famous video series "Closer to Truth," titled "Is Life After Death Possible – Sam Parnia":

Robert: Sam, your work in studying the nature of consciousness during cardiac arrests — what some people call Near Death Experiences – some would say casts doubt on scientific assumption that life after death is impossible. Do you think that is right?

Sam: Going through science of it, we don't have all the answers today, but I think we have made enormous strides to answer the question of what happens when we die. We have to remember that death is a process. And just because a person has died and they have been given a time of death and essentially called a corpse, the cells inside the person's body have not become so damaged that we can't bring them back. As science has progressed, we are now able to manipulate those processes for hours after death and bring back a whole person and study their consciousness during that time – which was impossible until very recently. And so, the incredible discovery through this one we can bring back people and send them home, we can really have the miracle of science take someone who is dead and make them alive again – which is amazing! But the other amazing part of it is that we can study what people experience when they have gone beyond death and the evidence so far suggests that – that entity we call the human mind, the consciousness, what the Greeks called 'The Psyche' that was later translated into 'The soul', the Me, Sam – does not become annihilated just after a person has died even if we write him a death note and certify him as being dead. That entity continues and it continues even when the brain does not seem to be functioning raising a question that consciousness maybe a separate entity from the brain, it's not magical, it's just not discovered yet, but it doesn't die. Now I can't tell you what happens 3 hours, 4 hours, 10 hours after a person has died – I can't tell you whether consciousness gradually fades away and disappears into thin air as some people might believe or does it continue

forever longer periods of time – certainly the bodily func-
tions, bodily cells, will die with time there is no doubt about
that - what happens to our real self, consciousness, is as I
explained it continues for a period of time! Now you have to
make your own conclusions - I don't have evidence beyond
that – which is one of two ways: One is that you may say
that Ok, I am going to accept that consciousness may continue
for a few hours after death in some format and gradually
wither away OR you may also argue that if consciousness
was able to continue if the brain wasn't functioning, why
would it suddenly disappear away few hours later because
don't forget even 10 minutes after you have died or even 30
seconds after you have died – your brain does not function
anymore! Even when we do CPR and try to resuscitate
someone there is not enough blood that gets into the brain to
enable the brain to function even during resuscitation – the
brain remains flatlined. And so – certainly there is "Life
After Death" for a period of time but does it continue forever
I don't know but certainly for a period of time afterwards
consciousness remains.[16]

The observation and conclusion by scientists and medical experts that my consciousness—the essence that defines my identity and experiences—can persist in some form despite clinical bodily death, with no observable brain activity, shattered my previous notion that life after death was merely a religious fiction devoid of scientific or medical backing

For me, the concept of an intelligent consciousness as the first cause of everything, the idea that I have an existence independent of my brain, and the notion that my consciousness can continue after my brain has flatlined are not merely religious propositions to be accepted solely on faith without any foundation in non-religious academic and scientific discourse. There are very credible reasons from non-religious discourse that make these ideas a very serious possibility. This realization led me to reconsider God and divine accountability after bodily death as serious possibilities that needed further investigation.

7 - The Fallacy of the Statement: "We Exist Because Given Very Long Periods of Time, Anything and Everything Can Happen"

If one wishes to advocate for atheism, it is comforting to believe that seemingly miraculous events can occur purely by chance, given the factor of unimaginably long periods of time.

Firstly, it is incorrect to say that the universe and we had to come into existence because anything and everything will happen given extremely long periods of time. The accurate statement is that given enough time, anything and everything can happen, but only within the realm of possibilities. Something must have the potential to transform into something else for it to undergo changes over time. For instance, we understand that water can become ice or steam. However, no matter how much time is allotted, water on its own cannot become jet fuel. It would be impractical to assert that, given enough time, water could transform into jet fuel. For water to turn into jet fuel, it must contain specific ingredients — in essence, water must have the potential to become jet fuel in order to transform into it over time.

So, the universe and humanity did not come into existence simply because anything and everything can happen, given enough time. We exist because whatever fundamental reality exists—the base reality that must exist by necessity, from which all other realities emerge—had to have the ingredients necessary to eventually unfold into us over long periods of time. If it lacked the ingredients needed to produce us and our universe, then no amount of time would have resulted in our existence.

As I drifted away from atheism, I could no longer find comfort in the belief that my existence was simply the result of a series of mindless, undirected events over an extensive period. The notion that, given enough time, anything and everything can happen seemed implausible. Instead, I was compelled to focus on the core question: Did the fundamental, underlying reality of the universe contain all the necessary elements to produce me and everything around me by sheer coincidence, or is this fundamental reality an intelligent consciousness that intentionally crafted everything as it is? As previously mentioned, I found the latter idea more compelling.

Secondly, I came to a rather embarrassing realization about time, one that is embarrassing because it is so obvious, yet many of us choose not to think of it this way. Today, we know from everyday science that time is not a uniform entity. Different objects at different speeds experience time very differently. We know that as you approach the speed of light, time significantly slows down. Nowadays, it is understood that a photon does not experience time at all. For a photon, billions and trillions of years mean nothing. If I were to travel near the speed of light, what feels like just one generation in my time could equate to billions of years on Earth. When we refer to "Long or Short Time" and "Billions of Years," we are imposing our very specific and limited perception of time on the entire universe to make sense of it. Our perception of time depends on Earth's rotation on its axis, forming our 24-hour day, and it takes 365 of these rotations for Earth to revolve around our star, marking what we call a year.

For a thought experiment, imagine if it took 1 billion years for our planet to orbit the sun, and our planet's rotation and our perception of time adjusted accordingly—then we might currently be saying that the universe came into existence only 13.8 years ago, which would not seem very long! Similarly, if we were beings the size of the Milky Way galaxy, we might think of the universe as having come into existence just a few months ago, and if we were beings composed of photons, the very question of "When" would become irrelevant.

Realizing that time is such a fluid entity, it seemed like a childish mistake to impose my own specific and limited perception of time on the entire universe to justify its existence as per my worldview.

Again, a reminder—science has not proven the existence or non-existence of God. There are counterarguments and explanations for all of the research and findings I mentioned above. The point of mentioning them was to establish the fact that there are scientific theories, research, and findings that provide a realistic basis for the idea of a conscious intelligence as the uncaused cause of everything. This idea is by no means any less plausible than the alternatives provided by the "No God" camp.

CHAPTER 4
BEGINNING OF MY RE-DISCOVERY OF ISLAM & ROLE OF JAVED AHMED GHAMIDI

I experienced a certain level of comfort as an atheist, believing that there was no life after death and no divine accountability. This conviction allowed me to live my life exactly as I pleased, focusing solely on immediate worldly benefits. During my mid to late twenties, while enjoying my newfound fame as an actor amidst all the glitz and glamor that comes with it, I was, deep down, in a state of severe turmoil. I found myself losing my atheism, and the possibility of a God and post-mortem divine accountability became increasingly realistic.

At this point in my life, I began to consider ideas such as 'an intelligence as the creator of everything' and 'my consciousness continuing after my bodily death' as two very realistic possibilities. As discussed in the previous chapter, I delved into relatively complex ideas to reach this point. Now, I wanted to explore further to find out if there was any ideology that could provide me with the identity of this supposed intelligence and what it expects from me. I expected that the answers would satisfy me intellectually, rationally, and morally.

I reminded myself once again that concerning the idea of God and divine accountability, if there is any truth to this matter, then the basic essentials related to this truth must be easily approachable and understandable by an average layperson. Hence, I decided to keep my inquiry as simple as possible from this point onwards.

Philosophy, Spiritual Religions and Revealed Religions

In comparison to the field of "Philosophy," with its great works from thinkers such as Aristotle, Plato, Kant, Nietzsche, and Locke, or the teachings of wise figures like Osho and Sadhguru, "Revealed Religions" became my initial choice for inquiry. This preference was mainly due to their claims that the creator of the universe has contacted humans and revealed truths about our origins, purpose, and life after death. Thus, I decided to first explore revealed religions, determining that if I didn't find my answers within the framework of these religions, I would certainly explore philosophy and other ideologies.Islam: My first choice of inquiry within revealed religions

Islam: My First Choice of Inquiry Within Revealed Religions

Our recorded history began roughly 5 to 6 thousand years ago, and whatever transpired before that is a matter of wild speculation based on some bones and artifacts. I find it extraordinary that throughout the civilized ancient world, people claimed to make contact with the spirit realm and divine entities. Although shamanism has degenerated in many cultures to mean a host of different things, in ancient Europe, Siberia, China, and the Americas, shamans were regarded as messengers of the divine. In ancient India, sages were known to receive the Vedas are considered revelations from the divine. In ancient Persia, Zoroaster emerged as a messenger of God. The most prevalent tradition of divine contact is found within Judaism, Christianity, and Islam. However, within the framework of revealed knowledge across many religions, which one should I explore, and why?

Ironically, from the available options, Islam — the religion I had initially dismissed — began to seem like the most suitable choice for the first ideology in my investigation. This conclusion emerged for reasons that are purely technical.

The Historical Verifiability of Muhammad (PBUH) and the Quran

The events involving Muhammad (PBUH) and his immediate companions are well-documented, owing to their relatively recent occurrence and significant global impact. It is relatively easy to verify that the Quran, the principal scripture of Islam, remains the same today as the literal word of God originally given by Muhammad (PBUH) to his followers.

Preservation of The Quran in Its Original Language

The Quran claims to be the word of God, preserved word by word in the exact language in which it was given by Muhammad (PBUH).

In contrast, the scriptural texts of other religions did not meet this criterion. The Old Testament and the Vedas date back so far in history that it is nearly impossible to ascertain their true authors, the circumstances surrounding their creation, and whether there have been any alterations to the original texts.

The New Testament is widely recognized not as a document directly handed down by Jesus (PBUH) to his followers, but rather, it comprises accounts of Jesus's (PBUH) words and actions as witnessed by the Apostles. Jesus (PBUH) had a relatively small group of followers through whom this information was transmitted by a few individuals over a few decades, lacking the mass transmission of information seen in the case of Muhammad (PBUH) and the Quran. Unlike the Quran, which was taught by thousands of followers from Muhammad (PBUH) and then mass-transmitted to their descendants, the New Testament's method of information transmission raises questions about possible alterations.

Another essential point is that although Jesus (PBUH) spoke Aramaic, the earliest written manuscripts of the New Testament are in Greek, not Aramaic. These texts represent Greek translations of what Jesus (PBUH) might have taught in Aramaic, and we all know how much can be lost in translation. Hence, the Quran holds a decisive advantage, as it has been preserved in the exact language spoken by Muhammad (PBUH).

Islam Made Sense, But Not Complete Sense

Around 2008, I began exploring Islam as a source of answers to questions about my origin and purpose. I approached the Quran as a compilation of speeches, monologues, stories, and sermons, purportedly from God, delivered by Muhammad (PBUH) to his followers. With a basic understanding of Muhammad's (PBUH) life, I read a straightforward translation of the Quran.

I liked what I was discovering. I understood many things that hadn't made sense to me in the past when I was a teenager rejecting Islam. I suppose it was because I had a broader understanding of reality compared to my teenage years. Also, the behavior of religious clergy in the society around me had become much more accepting of questions and inquiry. As I found more and more satisfactory answers to my existential questions from the Quran, the life story of Muhammad (PBUH), and from my inquiries into written and online video content from learned scholars, both contemporary and historical, I found myself increasingly identifying as a Muslim. I must give credit here to the mainstream scholarship of Islam— both past and present— which has done extremely brilliant work to simplify things for laypeople like me seeking existential answers.

But all was not well. Even though approximately 70% of Islam made sense to me thanks to mainstream scholarly avenues, 30% did not, as it appeared either self-contradictory or problematic on rational, moral, or scientific grounds. However, I remained hopeful, believing that if 70% could be so convincing, the rest would eventually fall into place. Yet, three to four years passed, and I still couldn't find satisfying answers. I began to doubt again, wondering if I had made a mistake by choosing Islam. Perhaps my reasons for exploring it were subjective, possibly because Islam was a familiar ideology since I was born into it, and that influenced my decision. I often thought to myself that, for someone who initially rejected Islam as a teenager, perhaps too hastily, I had proclaimed myself Muslim again. I knew I had to make a decision soon: either I would find reasonable answers in the near future or face the possibility that there might not be satisfying answers to the 30% of Islam that didn't make sense to me—which could mean that Islam might not be divine after all. Given that such a large portion of this religious tradition seemed unclear, considering it divine felt like a substantial error. How could I accept something as divine truth when a significant portion of it appeared either morally, rationally or scientifically flawed?

I will detail all the aspects I found extremely problematic about Islam in the Question-and-Answer section.

It was around 2015, and I was growing tired of my search, teetering on the edge of giving up on Islam again. I wasn't praying very regularly, but on that day, I sat down for the morning prayer (Fajr). Afterward, I sent a request into the universe—I remember my exact words:

> *If there is anyone listening—whomever or whatever you are—you know that I have been searching for answers with all my sincerity. Please let me know if you exist and please*

reveal who or what you are. I promise to devote my life to you. Please! If my doubts aren't resolved to a reasonable extent soon — I will assume there is nothing out there. Please forgive me if I come to the wrong conclusion.

I reminded myself that I must remain sincere, for even if I erroneously conclude that there is no God when there is one, my mistake should be forgiven as long as my efforts are sincere and serious.

For a moment, I believed someone heard me – I felt like something miraculous was about to happen…but nothing happened.

I initially dismissed my prayer as a childish act, feeling that I'd soon need to renounce Islam again and seek answers elsewhere. However, I now believe that someone heard me that day. Shortly thereafter, I stumbled upon a man who not only elucidated the 30% of Islam that perplexed me but also clarified the 70% that already made sense. Additionally, I was introduced to a seldom-discussed aspect of Islam, which now stands as one of the most compelling reasons for everyone to thoroughly explore Islam before forming a definitive opinion on its divine origin.

Javed Ahmed Ghamidi

One point within the 30% of Islam that did not make sense to me is the idea that only those can enter Paradise—who identify as Muslims. This concept troubled me as it seemed inherently unfair. Individuals born into Muslim families have a significantly higher likelihood of dying as Muslims compared to those who are not. This suggests that one's eternal destiny is heavily influenced by their birthplace. On the Day of Judgment, any non-Muslim could justifiably argue that being born into a Muslim family would have made it much easier for them to die as a Muslim and, thereby, qualify for Paradise. Furthermore, I have known many virtuous non-Muslims who devoutly practice the religion of their birth with sincerity. These are hardworking individuals who spend their days earning just enough to support their families and lack the luxury of time to delve into existential questions. These non-Muslims would have easily been very devout Muslims had they only been born into a Muslim family. It just seemed so unjust that some god would condemn them to eternal hell simply because they didn't belong to a specific religious community.

And then, one fine day, I stumbled upon a YouTube video by Javed Ahmed Ghamidi titled "Heaven Only for Muslims and Hell for All Non-Muslims?" I will delve deeper into the issue of non-Muslims and Heaven later in the Question and Answer section. I mention this event here to indicate that this was my introduction to Javed Ahmed Ghamidi. His explanations in the video made sense, and I wanted to learn more about him.

As I discovered, many religious clergy in my surroundings were not very fond of Mr. Ghamidi, even though his research methodology aligns well with traditional religious frameworks. He supports his reasoning with traditional scholarly references. Despite this, he is often labeled as a heretic by many within traditional religious circles. I found such allegations to be fictitious—for example, he is accused of rejecting Hadiths, which is not the case. I will discuss this particular point in detail in the next section titled "Sources of Islam." I learned that much of the slander against him is driven by the fact that Mr. Ghamidi challenges many ideas that popular clergy consider unchallengeable or sacred. I will elaborate on this in the Question and Answer section. On the aspects of Islam that were not making satisfactory sense to me, I found Mr. Ghamidi's answers and reasoning completely satisfactory, and I have yet to find any opposing argument strong enough to convincingly challenge Mr. Ghamidi's reasoning.

How Mr. Ghamidi Fundamentally Changed My Understanding of Islam

There are three extremely important things I learned from Mr. Ghamidi that fundamentally changed my understanding of Islam. They not only helped me understand Islam profoundly but also gave me a significant reason why Muhammad (PBUH) might be speaking the truth. I believe that any layperson can understand these three things with a little effort, and they too can become equipped to understand the basics of Islam themselves. These three things are:

1. Sources of Islam
2. What a Rasool of God Truly is - the most compelling reason to explore Islam.
3. What is the Quran and how to understand it.

The next section of the chapter discusses these points briefly.

4A – Sources of Islam

If I want to understand the message and religion that God delivered through Muhammad (PBUH), where should I look? I received a multitude of answers. The religious clergy around me informed me that much of God's religion is contained in the Quran, but that alone is not sufficient—the Quran is incomplete. There are many commands of God present in the Hadith literature that are independent of the Quran and are not included within it. I was astounded to learn that the Hadith is not just an explanation of the Quran, but it also contains independent commands of Islam that are absent from the Quran. To give a mundane example, the Quran does not directly or in principle prohibit making a picture of a living being, yet this is prohibited in Hadith literature. Specifically, the act of creating a picture of a living thing is said to be severely punishable on Judgment Day (Sunan Nisai, No: 5361). According to this Hadith, if I make a picture of my mother to display in the house, I will be punished on the Day of Judgment.

This realization troubled me deeply. I was disturbed by the fact that the Hadith contains independent commands of God, not found in the Quran itself. This implies that the Quran is incomplete! Imagine—the final book that God sent for humankind is incomplete, leaving portions of His religion within the pages of the Hadith literature, comprising a vast collection of books written and compiled over many decades and centuries following Prophet Muhammad (PBUH), did not resonate well with me. How could God ordain a final book for humankind but leave its guidance incomplete?

However, with Javed Ahmed Ghamidi, I found a clear introduction to the sources of Islam and learned how to analyze them. I discovered the right method to understand what the Quran and Hadith represent, and how to analyze them in relation to each other.

Let me summarize my understanding of this matter as explained by Mr. Ghamidi. Later, I'll describe how Mr. Ghamidi's approach differs from the popular interpretation and why I believe he is correct. I think any layperson who grasps the sources of Islam will find understanding the religion to be significantly more accessible.

Muhammad (PBUH) - The Sole Source of Religion

Muhammad (PBUH) is the final Messenger of God and, therefore, the sole source of the religion. For any element to be added to or removed from Islam, it must have a clear sanction from Muhammad (PBUH). The religion that Muhammad (PBUH) delivered on behalf of God is encompassed within three primary sources of knowledge: the Quran, the Sunnah, and the Hadith. Let's explore what each of these entails..

What is the Quran

The Quran - which literally means "recitation," is the document that Muhammad (PBUH) presented to his followers as the literal speech of God and God's final book to guide humankind. I will discuss in detail in Chapter 4D how Muhammad (PBUH) and his immediate companions made significant efforts to ensure that the Quran was compiled, preserved, and broadly disseminated to hundreds of thousands of followers during Muhammad's (PBUH) lifetime.

The Quran describes itself as:
1) The "Supreme Authority" over other scriptures (Quran 5:48)
2) "The Scale" to judge by (Quran 42:17)
3) "The Ultimate Standard & Criteria" with "Clear Messages of Guidance" on matters of God & religion (Quran 25:1; 2:185)
4) "The Clear Book" (Quran 26:2) which "...explains everything clearly..." (Quran 16:89).
5) A book which is "made easy to remember and understand". (Quran 54:40)
6) A "Straightforward Book" (Quran 18:2).
7) A book "with verses that are well perfected & fully explained" (Quran 11:1)

Quran 2:213 states that the purpose of sending scriptures and books is that, whenever there is a dispute about religion, the divine book can serve as a judge in that dispute. This means that in all matters of religion, the Quran is to be taken as the ultimate criterion to determine what is right and what is wrong.

Hence, according to the Quran's introduction of itself, the book is the ultimate standard for divine guidance. All other literature about Islam, and religion in general, must be analyzed through the lens of the Quran, not the other way around..

What is Sunnah?

Sunnah means "The Way" to do something. It concerns itself with the action aspect of the religion. Ritual prayer, rituals of cleanliness, fasting, Hajj, and marriage (Nikah) are all components of the Sunnah. This practical part of the religion was also mass-transmitted to all followers of Muhammad during his lifetime—everyone knew how to pray, how to cleanse themselves before prayers, how to fast, perform Hajj, and conduct Islamic rituals of marriage (Nikah), etc.

The Nature of Sunnah

The word "Sunnah" means "The Way" and implies action or something practical—it essentially denotes the method of execution. In the Quran, "Sunnah" is used to describe actions undertaken on behalf of God. For instance, in Quran 33:60-62, God issues a warning to the hypocrites and slanderers of Medina, stating that if they continue their misdeeds, they will be seized and killed. This directive of God is referred to as the Sunnah (The Way) of God. Thus, the term Sunnah encompasses both the meaning of how to undertake an action and signifies the practical aspect of Islam.

The Sunnah Predates Muhammad (PBUH)

The Sunnah is not a concept unique to Muhammad (PBUH). The Quran describes it as a tradition inherent to all Messengers of God. It states that Muhammad (PBUH) was bestowed with the same religion given to Noah, Abraham, Moses, and Jesus (PBUT), and he is instructed to follow this very religion (Quran 42:13). This Sunnah of the Messengers predates Muhammad (PBUH); for instance, the ritual worship, or "Salah," existed prior to his time, and historical evidence supports this assertion. It is documented that the Jews of Medina performed Salah, as Muhammad (PBUH) advised his followers to wear attire distinct from the Jews during their prayers (Sunan of Abu Dawood, No: 235). Moreover, prayer is referenced in numerous passages within the Old and New Testaments. Genesis 22:5 recounts Abraham (PBUH) going to pray, Exodus 4:31 depicts the Children of Israel bowing their heads in prayer, and Psalm 95:6 notes David urging people to kneel and bow their heads in worship. Additionally, it is noted in the Sahih of Muslim (No: 6359) that the

Arabs performed 'Salah' to Allah prior to Muhammad's (PBUH) prophethood, as recounted by a companion who said that he offered nightly and morning ritual prayers in worship of Allah three years before he met Muhammad (PBUH).

Fasting existed before the advent of Muhammad, as the Quran states, "Fasting has been prescribed for you as it was prescribed for those before you..." (Quran 2:183). The same applies to charity and Hajj—all these rituals were part of the Abrahamic tradition, already familiar to the Arabs. Muhammad (PBUH) modified the Sunnah according to new divine instructions and corrected errors that had crept into it..

Sunnah Is Specific to Religion

Many Muslims believe that all aspects of Muhammad's (PBUH) life are Sunnah. Verse 3 of Surah 53 of the Quran is widely cited as justification for the belief that everything Muhammad (PBUH) said or did—regarding both worldly and religious matters—is from God. The verse states::

> *He (Muhammad) does not speak of his own desire, it is indeed a revelation sent down to him. He has been taught by a mighty power.*

According to this belief, the style of dress and turban he wore, the type of facial hair he maintained, the foods he preferred, the medications he used and recommended, the posture in which he slept, and even the wooden stick he used for brushing his teeth are all said to be divinely instructed and branded as Sunnah. However, this is incorrect.

The Quranic verse 53:3 states that in matters of God and religion, Muhammad (PBUH) does not speak of his own desire; rather, it is a revelation from God. The Sunnah comprises what Muhammad (PBUH) ordained as part of the religion. However, not everything he did or said constitutes the Sunnah. This distinction is crucial because, firstly, Muhammad's sole mission as God's Messenger is clearly stated to be someone who is designated to deliver God's message. Additionally, Muhammad (PBUH) himself clarified in a saying attributed to him that:

> *I am human. When I command you on anything about religion from God, take it from me, and when I tell you anything from my own opinion (about worldly matters), then remember that I am only a human being...and in many worldly affairs you have better knowledge. (Sahih of Muslim, No: 6126, 6127, 6128).*

Hence, it is justified and very noble if someone desires to follow and mimic Muhammad (PBUH) in all matters of life out of love and admiration for him; however, the Sunnah only encompasses what Muhammad (PBUH) sanctioned in matters of God and religion.

What is Hadith?

Hadith means narration, tradition, or saying. This body of knowledge was formed after the passing of Muhammad (PBUH), as people began to remember, discuss, and articulate his life, words, and actions. On one hand, there is the Quran and Sunnah which an entire generation received directly from Muhammad (PBUH) and his immediate companions, and which has been passed down to successive generations up to the present day. On the other hand, there is the Hadith literature which is based on individuals narrating their personal experiences of seeing Muhammad (PBUH) act or hearing him speak. These individual reports circulated as hearsay until efforts were made to scrutinize and record them decades after Muhammad's (PBUH) death. An entire science was developed by early Hadith researchers and compilers to verify, and then accept or reject, these narrations and their attributions to Muhammad (PBUH). This marked the beginning of the discipline of Hadith sciences—a vast and significant field of knowledge that

Muslims can justifiably take pride in as it has helped preserve a significant amount of historical knowledge about Muhammad (PBUH).

Hadith, in its content, contains life history of Muhammad (PBUH) along with explanations and applications of the religion Muhammad (PBUH) gave through the Quran and Sunnah.

A note of caution here: When quoting from Hadith literature, it is crucial to verify the authenticity of the narration and only quote those traditions that are widely regarded as authentic by most renowned scholars and experts of Hadith. I emphasize this because the practice of quoting weak or inauthentic Hadith is prevalent in some parts of the Muslim world. Weak Hadiths are sayings attributed to Prophet Muhammad (PBUH) whose authenticity has not been satisfactorily confirmed by Hadith experts for various reasons.

Different Methods of Preservation and Transmission of the Quran, Sunnah and Hadith

There are two kinds of histories. The first is established history, which is based on the mass observation, preservation, and transmission of an event. For example, the Indian constitution was adopted by the Constituent Assembly of India on November 26, 1949. This is established history because the event was witnessed and preserved by millions of people. Apart from some fringe conspiracy theories, established history is usually beyond doubt and dispute due to its continuous mass preservation and transmission. The second type of history concerns information that has reached us through individual reporting. For instance, during the 1949 session of the Constituent Assembly, the discussions that took place, and who said what to whom, represent history based on individual reports—meaning it relies on individuals reporting what they saw or heard. Its content is not established beyond all doubt and is always open to scrutiny by experts. Hadith falls into this second category of history.

The terms Sunnah and Hadith are often used interchangeably by many Muslims, but it is crucial to distinguish between the two. Sunnah refers to the actions sanctioned as part of the religion by Prophet Muhammad (PBUH). He ensured that everyone was familiar with the practical aspects of Islam before he passed away. On the other hand, Hadiths are recollections about Muhammad's (PBUH) life by individuals who either knew him directly or belonged to one or two subsequent generations whose predecessors had known him. We will discuss what Hadith literature entails shortly.

All of Islam is contained within the Quran and Sunnah. More than a hundred thousand of Muhammad's (PBUH) immediate followers received the Quran and Sunnah directly from him and transferred them en masse from one generation to the next up to the present. Hadith literature consists of reports about the actions and sayings of Muhammad (PBUH), transferred not through mass transmission like the Quran and Sunnah, but through individual reports from people. This serves as a historical record of Muhammad's (PBUH) life and must be interpreted through the lens of the Quran and Sunnah. This historical record provides an explanation and application of the religion contained within the Quran and Sunnah, but does not introduce any new religious commandments that are not directly contained, or principled in, the Quran and Sunnah.

I want to briefly mention here Mr. Javed Ahmed Ghamidi's principles of understanding Sunnah and Hadith as laid out in his book, "Meezan." These principles are intended for more advanced students of Islam. However, since there is considerable confusion about the difference between Sunnah and Hadith among many ordinary Muslims, I feel it is necessary to mention these principles briefly here, as they have significantly helped me in understanding Islam.

Seven Principles of Understanding Sunnah

1) The Sunnah pertains solely to matters of religion. Aspects such as the type of clothing worn by Muhammad (PBUH), the animal he used for travel, or the food he preferred are not considered part of the Sunnah.

2) The Sunnah pertains to the practical aspect or application of religion.

3) Something cannot be labeled as Sunnah if it does not originate from the practices of God's Prophets. A Qur'anic injunction cannot be considered a Sunnah. For instance, it is known that Muhammad (PBUH) punished fornicators with lashes; however, this cannot be deemed Sunnah because its origin is in the Quran, not in the practices of all Prophets of God. But what about ritual prayer, fasting, charity, and the Hajj? Are they considered Sunnah or commanded by the Quran? These practices are Sunnah because the Quran itself indicates that they were rituals practiced by all prophets, including Abraham (PBUH). Muhammad (PBUH) sanctioned these rituals as following the way of Abraham (PBUH) or the Sunnah of Abraham (PBUH), after making corrections to it. Thus, we observe how the Quran and earlier scriptures detail how people from previous nations engaged in prayers, fasting, giving charity, and performing pilgrimage even before the revelation of the Quran as the tradition of Abraham (PBUH) (Deen-e-Hanif). Therefore, the origin of these rituals is the practice of Abraham (PBUH), which was sanctioned by the Quran. Hence, if there is anything whose origin is a command of God in the Quran, and the Prophet has acted on it or explained it - that is not Sunnah. Only those things are Sunnah whose origin is the practice of the Prophets which are sanctioned by the Quran.

4) If Prophet Muhammad (PBUH) did something voluntarily but did not mandate it as part of the religion, it is not considered

Sunnah. For instance, we know that the obligatory ritual prayer of Fajr consists of two rak'ahs—we also, know that Muhammad (PBUH) voluntarily offered two extra rak'ahs for more blessings but did not ordain them as compulsory—hence, they are not Sunnah but a voluntary part of the religion, or Nafl.

5) According to the Quran, basic guidance is embedded in human nature, although it can deviate from this guidance, it remains ingrained nonetheless. Thus, it is human nature to find some things repulsive and others not. Anything that is an explanation of human nature cannot be regarded as Sunnah. For example, Muhammad (PBUH) prohibited the eating of domesticated donkey meat (Bukhari, No: 436), stating it as an explanation of what human nature should find repulsive and impure. He did not ordain it as Sunnah.

6) Those practices should not be considered Sunnah which Muhammad (PBUH) conveyed to others as guidance, but the very nature of that guidance makes it evident that he did not designate them as Sunnah. For example, Muhammad (PBUH) would recommend certain optional prayers (zikr and duas) to his companions, but it was clear that he did not intend to make them obligatory aspects of the religion.

7) The final principle of understanding the Sunnah is that, just like the Quran is transmitted through mass transmission by Muhammad's (PBUH) followers and not individual reports, so is the Sunnah. Anything that is transmitted through mass transmission is considered Sunnah, while anything that reaches us through individual reports can be taken as a potential explanation of the Quran and Sunnah, but it cannot be taken as Sunnah itself.

Seven Principles of Understanding Hadith

1) The chain of narrators (or Sanad) of a Hadith is of crucial importance. Only those Hadiths should be quoted whose chain of narrators has been declared reasonably reliable by Hadith experts.

2) The content of the Hadith should not contradict the Quran, Sunnah, and fundamental principles of knowledge and reason. In the words of the renowned Hadith expert Khateeb Baghdadi:

   A hadith received through an individual's report is not accepted if it goes against established principles of reason, or if it goes against a clear commandment of the Quran, or if goes against a well-known Sunnah… or if the flaw in that hadith is made clear by a very conclusive argument.[18]

3) Those who ponder on Hadith must possess full expertise in the 6th-century Arabic of the Quraish tribe, the Arabic spoken by Muhammad (PBUH).

4) Hadith has to be understood in light of the Quran.

5) The correct meaning of a Hadith can only be established after understanding the complete context of the Hadith. "What" is being said, "when" it is being said, "why" it is being said, and "to whom" it is being said—all of these factors need to be correctly established to determine the accurate meaning of a Hadith; otherwise, many misunderstandings can occur. For example, one Hadith states that the leaders of the Muslims should only be from the Quraysh tribe.[19] When viewed without context, it appears that Muhammad (PBUH) is proclaiming that all Muslims at all times must only have a leader from the Quraish tribe. However, when the statement is considered in its complete context, it becomes clear that Muhammad (PBUH) was suggesting a remedy for potential circumstances arising immediately after his death, and this was not a permanent directive for

Muslims for all time. Muhammad (PBUH) was applying the Quranic principle, as mentioned in Quran 42:38, that Muslims must determine their collective matters through consultation and the agreement of the majority. He was stating that since the Quraish tribe was supported by the majority of Muslims at that time, they should select their leader from this particular tribe after Muhammad's (PBUH) departure. Hence, when seen in context, it becomes clear that Muhammad (PBUH) was applying a Quranic principle in his own time, and it was not a religious decree or a permanent policy for all Muslims of all times.

6) When analyzing Hadith on a specific subject, it's crucial to consider all relevant Hadith reports to achieve a correct understanding. For instance, examining individual Hadith reports about the prohibition of making pictures of living things might initially suggest that Muhammad (PBUH) declared a comprehensive ban on creating any images of living creatures. However, a thorough analysis of all pertinent Hadith reports reveals that Muhammad (PBUH) specifically targeted the prohibition of images used for idol worship.

7) The entire foundation of God's religion is based on axioms of knowledge and reason. The understanding of these universal truths is something that God Himself has bestowed upon humankind. If a Hadith conveys something that seems to contradict these axioms, then it should neither be accepted with this contradictory meaning nor should it be immediately rejected. Instead, efforts should be made to find a meaning that aligns with the axioms of knowledge and reason. If such a meaning can be derived, it should be considered the true meaning of the Hadith.

A brief Note on the History of the Companions of Muhammad (PBUH)

The history of the immediate companions of Muhammad (PBUH) is also an invaluable resource for understanding Islam. It allows us to examine how they understood and conveyed Islam. After all, who could grasp Islam better than the immediate companions of Muhammad (PBUH)? However, this historical record has also reached us through various individual reports, and therefore, needs to be scrutinized and understood through the framework of the Quran and Sunnah.

A brief Note on Ijma or Consensus of Scholars

Another belief prevalent among Muslims is that if a majority of scholars agree on an idea or interpretation of Islam, then it becomes sacred for all Muslims and cannot be subject to any challenge or review. This assumption elevates a "majority of scholars" to a level of authority on Islam and a source of Islamic injunctions, comparable to the Vatican in Catholic Christianity. On this issue, I find Mr. Ghamidi's approach very apt: for Muslims, only Muhammad (PBUH) is the source of all religious authority and the final arbiter on matters of faith. According to the Quran, only the Messengers of God are to be considered authorities in religion since they receive direct communication from God. After Muhammad (PBUH), no individual or body of scholars can be considered infallible or immune to criticism.

The belief that the consensus of the majority of scholars can never be wrong is primarily justified by the following Hadith:

> God will not allow my nation to gather on an outrageous travesty...(Sunan al-Tirmidhi, No: 2167).

Firstly, the aforementioned Hadith has been graded as weak by Hadith experts and should not be used to substantiate an argument. However, for the sake of discussion, even if we accept it, the Hadith does not imply that the majority of scholars are incapable of making a sincere mistake. Instead, it merely states that owing to the clarity of the fundamentals of Islam in the Quran and Sunnah, it is improbable for all Muslims to concur on a blatant error. For instance, the majority of Muslims will never agree with the notion that there are two or three Gods—or that there are not five but two compulsory prayers, etc. This narration by no means states that the majority of scholars cannot make a sincere mistake while interpreting the religion.

Firstly, the aforementioned Hadith has been graded as weak by Hadith experts and should not be used to substantiate an argument. However, for the sake of discussion, even if we accept it, the Hadith does not imply that the majority of scholars are incapable of making a sincere mistake. Instead, it merely states that owing to the clarity of the fundamentals of Islam in the Quran and Sunnah, it is improbable for all Muslims to concur on a blatant error. For instance, the majority of Muslims will never agree with the notion that there are two or three Gods—or that there are not five but two compulsory prayers, etc. This narration by no means states that the majority of scholars cannot make a sincere mistake while interpreting the religion.

Moreover, some Quranic verses are presented in support of this assumption. However, they appear to be forced justifications. For example, one of the most popular verses used to justify Ijma as a source of religious guidance is as follows:

> And whoever opposes the Messenger after truth has become clear to them and follows a path other than that of believers – then I (God) will let them pursue what they have chosen and then punish them in Hell for it – what an evil end it is indeed (Quran 4:115).

This verse seems to state that if someone realizes the truth of Muhammad's (PBUH) message and acknowledges him as the Messenger of God, then choosing to oppose him for any reason will result in punishment by God on the Day of Judgment. It appears to be a stretch of logic to imply that the 'believers' referred to in this verse are the majority of Islamic scholars—thereby suggesting that deviating from the consensus of these scholars is a travesty. In other words, it seems overly forced to interpret this verse as issuing a permanent decree that a main body of scholars cannot make a sincere mistake. Thus, if the majority of scholars agree on an interpretation of Islam, challenging this consensus-based solely on reasoning might be deemed punishable by God.

Three flawed practices in Understanding Islam

Now that I have hopefully conveyed with some clarity what the Quran, Hadith, and Sunnah entail, I shall discuss the three main reasons that underpin all the concepts within Islam that I found morally or rationally problematic. These reasons are the main points of difference between Mr. Ghamidi and popular interpreters of Islam. The following represent the three flawed practices in understanding Islam.

1) Understanding the Quranic verses or Hadith in isolation without checking their context.
2) Understanding the Quran through the lens of Hadith, rather than vice versa.
3) Considering Hadith as an independent source of Islam rather than merely an explanation of the Quran and Sunnah.

Let's discuss each point one by one.

1 - The Flawed Practice of Understanding Quranic Verses in Isolation Without Understanding the Context

While reading a book or piece of information, it is essential to understand who is saying it, what is being said, why it is being said, and to whom it is being addressed. However, there is a disturbing tendency among many Islamic segments to interpret Quranic verses in isolation without considering these contextual factors. Let us take one example to briefly elaborate on what I am referring to.

Those who view the Quran as merely a collection of God's sayings that can be understood individually and out of context often cite Quran 5:51 as proof that God has issued an eternal command to Muslims, stating that Jews and Christians will never wish them well and that forming alliances or friendships with them is prohibited. The text of the verse, when seen in isolation, appears to suggest this:

> O believers! Take neither Jews nor Christians as allies – they are allies only of each other. Whoever does so will be counted as one of them. Surely God does not guide the wrongdoing people (Quran 5:51).

But when we examine the context from verses 51 to 59, it becomes clear that the Quran specifically addresses those Jews and Christians who were persecuting Muslims based on their faith.

Similarly, when verses are not considered in isolation but in totality, two verses from other sections of the Quran further clarify that the statement in Quran 5:51 pertains to a very specific group of Jews and Christians, not all of them.

> God does not forbid you from dealing kindly and fairly with those who have neither fought nor driven you out of your homes. Surely God loves those who do justice. God only forbids you from being allies of those who have fought you for 'your' faith, driven you out of your homes, or supported 'others' in doing so. And whoever takes them as friends or allies, then it is they who are the 'true' wrongdoers (Quran 60:8-9).

2 - The flawed practice of understanding the Quran through the lens of Hadith instead of vice versa

One opinion prevalent among certain Islamic circles is that guidance through the Quran can only be fully realized when it is studied in conjunction with Hadith literature and the works of great Islamic theologians. However, this approach contradicts the Quran's own assertions about itself. The Book declares itself as:

1) The "Supreme Authority" over other scriptures (Quran 5:48).
2) "The Scale" to judge by (Quran 42:17).
3) "The Ultimate Standard & Criteria" with "Clear Messages of Guidance" on matters of God & religion (Quran 25:1; 2:185).
4) "The Clear Book" (Quran 26:2) which "...explains everything clearly..." (Quran 16:89).
5) A book which is "made easy to remember and understand" (Quran 54:40).
6) A "Straightforward Book" (Quran 18:2).
7) A book "with verses that are well perfected & fully explained" (Quran 11:1).

Quran 2:213 states that the purpose of sending scriptures and books is to ensure that when a dispute arises about religion, the divine book can serve as a judge in that dispute. This means that in all matters of religion, the Quran is to be taken as the ultimate criterion for discerning what is right and what is wrong.

In light of what the Quran says about itself, it is a more precise approach for both Muslims and non-Muslims seeking an understanding of Islam to study all other literature through the lens of the Quran, rather than the other way around. The accuracy of this approach is further reinforced by the fact that the content of Hadith literature is more comprehensible when examined from this perspective. When viewed through the lens of the Quran, Hadith literature fully aligns with rational and moral reasoning and fits within the Quranic framework. I will elaborate on this in the next section below, using the example of the prohibition against making pictures.

3 - The flawed Practice of Considering Hadith an Independent Source of Islam Rather Than an Explanation of Quran and Sunnah

There is a common belief in the Muslim world that Hadith literature not only contains explanations and applications of the religion found in the Quran and Sunnah but also introduces new religious commands that are independent of the Quran and Sunnah. Essentially, this suggests that the Hadith is also an independent source of religious guidance. In simpler terms, it implies that the Hadith includes new directives from God which have no basis in the Quran and Sunnah. However, this perspective raises a question: why would Muhammad (PBUH) make such an effort during his lifetime to preserve and widely transmit the Quran and Sunnah, and yet purportedly dispense some parts of God's religion to only a few individuals on random occasions without making similar efforts to preserve and transmit these teachings? Moreover, why leave the preservation and transmission of these teachings to hearsay, to be scrutinized and recorded decades after Muhammad's (PBUH) death?

There are two problems with this approach. Firstly, it implies a disturbing notion that Muhammad (PBUH) was unable to fulfill what the Quran describes as his sole mission: to "...deliver the message efficiently" (Quran 5:92) and "...deliver the message clearly" (Quran 16:82).

Secondly, numerous contradictions arise within Islam when Hadith is viewed as an independent source—contradictions that require forced explanations. The content of Hadith literature becomes more coherent and free of contradictions when it is regarded as an explanation and application of the religion that Muhammad (PBUH) conveyed through the Quran and Sunnah, rather than as an independent source of Islam.

I will provide detailed examples in a later chapter, but for now, I want to offer a brief one here to illustrate how problematic concepts can arise when the Quran is interpreted through Hadith literature rather than vice versa, and when Hadith is regarded as an independent source of religion. There are multiple Hadiths stating that painting a picture of a living thing is forbidden by God to such an extent that anyone who does so will be punished on the Day of Judgment. Consider the following Hadith narrative:

> Prophet Muhammad (PBUH) is reported to have said: "Those who paint pictures will be punished on the Day of Judgment, and it would be said to them: Breathe soul into what you have created" (Sahih of Muslim, No: 2108)

There are various other Hadiths in which Muhammad (PBUH) appears to show repulsion towards images of animate things. Those who consider Hadith as an independent source of religious guidance assert that the act of painting any picture of a living thing is a sin, punishable by God on Judgment Day. This implies that even if I create a harmless painting of my father, who has passed away, so that I can see his face, remember him, and be comforted - God will punish me for it and ask me to breathe a soul into it. This seems strange because the Quran does not suggest, either directly or in principle, that one can be punished merely for the act of painting a living thing. Why then would God not mention this in the Quran if such actions carried severe consequences? Additionally, there is no rational basis for God to punish me for something as innocuous as painting a picture of my father for the reasons mentioned above—it appears completely unfair and unjust. Similarly, it is nonsensical for God to demand that I breathe a soul into the picture. Since I did not create the picture with the intention to rival God or to worship it as a living entity, why would I be subjected to such a demand?

Those who view Hadith as an explanation of God's religion in the Quran and Sunnah, and understand Hadith literature in light of the

Quran, say that in this Hadith, Muhammad (PBUH) is not prohibiting painting or art altogether but rather prohibiting the creation of images for the purpose of idol worship, as idol worship is strictly prohibited in the Quran. This perspective is logical. If someone creates an image and regards it as a living god worthy of worship, an act God has expressly and emphatically forbidden, then it seems reasonable that God would hold that person accountable and demand that they breathe life into it. I find this approach more appropriate, technically sound, and coherent because the content of Hadith makes complete sense and aligns perfectly with the Quran and Sunnah when viewed from this perspective.

This paradigm of understanding Hadith in light of the Quran and Sunnah is often misunderstood as a rejection of Hadith altogether. However, this is not the case. It's not about dismissing something that Muhammad (PBUH) said or did simply because it does not appear in the Quran. Rather, if a Hadith is technically sound, then anything it contains on behalf of Muhammad (PBUH) is considered sacred and binding for Muslims. The point I am making is that when deriving the correct meaning of Hadith, the more technically apt approach is to understand it, in light of the Quran and Sunnah, rather than the other way around.

4B – Understanding the Role of a Rasool (Messenger) of God – A Compelling Reason to Explore Islam

What I am about to discuss is the most pivotal reason why exploring Islam as a message from God is of paramount importance.

Muhammad (PBUH) did not merely assert himself as a Prophet, or "Nabi," of God; he also claimed the position of "Rasool," a Messenger of God. According to the Quran, through a Rasool, God orchestrates a real-world demonstration of His Judgment for the immediate audience of the Rasool. This demonstration aims to establish conclusive evidence of divine accountability, which all humankind is destined to face after departing from this world. But before diving into the specifics of this topic, allow me to present a contemporary analogy of the events that unfolded in 7th-century Arabia. Understanding these events serves as a potential reason why a serious and sincere investigation into Muhammad's (PBUH) message deserves consideration from everyone.

Human beings often possess a tendency to normalize the extraordinary. Consider, for example, the commonplace video call feature on your phones—a technological marvel that would have astonished someone from a century ago. Explaining that you can visually communicate with someone thousands of miles away through a handheld device would have seemed unbelievable, magical, and miraculous. Yet, because it has become routine in our lives, we no longer find it awe-inspiring; it is now taken for granted.

Because of our extensive familiarity with Islam and its historical context, combined with a lack of discourse and realization within the Muslim world regarding the true essence of a "Rasool of God," it is plausible to say that whether one is Muslim or not, many people fail to fully grasp the profoundly exceptional nature of the events that transpired in 7th-century Arabia, these events demand, at the very least, a sincere and thorough inquiry into the claims and message of Muhammad (PBUH). Subsequently, each individual is free to discern whether these events had any divine connection or significance. Before delving into what precisely constitutes a Rasool of God and the unfolding of events with Muhammad (PBUH) as a Messenger, let us first employ a contemporary analogy to gain a foundational comprehension of the pivotal events in 7th-century Arabia.

Let us envision a Nepalese man named Manav, an illiterate small-time trader living in present-day Kathmandu, Nepal. Manav has no background in military affairs, politics, poetry, or religious learning or activism. At the age of 40, something peculiar occurs: Manav makes an extraordinary claim to his friends and family. He asserts that God has communicated with him through an angel, appointing him as a Prophet of God. His task, as ordained by God, is to guide people on behalf of the divine and to forewarn them about the divine accountability that awaits humanity after death.

This declaration, in itself, is not entirely unprecedented. Many shamans, sages, and holy individuals have preached their beliefs while making similar claims. However, Manav's assertion does not end there. He further claims that God has designated him as a Messenger—the embodiment of God's judgment on Earth for his immediate audience. Manav contends that for all those who do not acknowledge the existence of God or divine accountability based on reasoning, God will implement His Judgment in this world through Manav. The worldly demonstration aims to conclusively establish the reality of Divine Accountability after death—akin to a scientist conducting a laboratory experiment to validate a hypothesis.

The scenario takes an even more peculiar turn. Manav's God tells him exactly how events will unfold beforehand. According to Manav's God, the earthly demonstrations of Divine Judgment have occurred multiple times in human history. Similarly, this earthly judgment through Manav will unfold exactly as it has in the past. God has declared that truth will be revealed through His Messenger to his immediate audience until God informs His Messenger that those who continue to reject the truth are doing so without justification. As a result, they will face God's worldly punishment. Meanwhile, those who accept the truth will receive God's worldly reward. The punishment may manifest in one of two ways: If Manav lacks substantial support, a natural disaster such as a storm, flood, fire, or earthquake will decimate the targeted population. Alternatively, if Manav has substantial support or if total destruction is not warranted, the punishment will be administered through humans, potentially by Manav and his supporters, as agents of God's judgment. For those who embrace the truth and support the Messenger of God, the reward is a mighty kingdom on Earth. Manav is specifically told that he will witness some of these divine judgments during his lifetime, with the remainder unfolding after his death.

Remember - Manav has no background in poetry; however, the divine communication that Manav receives and conveys to the people is not in ordinary Nepalese. Instead, it is one of the finest poetic masterpieces of the Nepalese language.

Remember - Manav has absolutely no background in religious activism, yet through him, God engages in in-depth religious discussions and debates with Christians, Hindus, Buddhists, and Jews. He draws upon their scriptures, offering compelling religious and philosophical arguments.

Remember - Manav does not have any military or political background. Yet, Manav's God continually makes military and political decisions that result in immaculate and complete success on both fronts.

Throughout this unfolding saga, Manav claims no credit, firmly asserting that he merely follows the communications and commands received from God.

But wait, it gets even more bizarre! Manav extends his message beyond Nepal and invites rulers of neighboring countries through letters to accept God's message, even reaching out to superpowers like Russia and China. He warns them that disregarding God's message, sent by a living Messenger of God, will subject them to God's earthly court of judgment, and they will face defeat by Manav and his supporters.

Over the next 35 years following Manav's initial claim, events unfold precisely as prophesied by Manav's God. Those who support Manav are rewarded on earth, while those who oppose God's message suffer resounding defeat, collapsing before Manav and his immediate supporters. The sweeping victory encompasses not only Nepal but also neighboring countries, including superpowers like China and Russia.

Manav and his immediate followers, initially humble farmers and traders from Kathmandu with no notable military expertise, now reign as absolute rulers over Nepal, Bhutan, Myanmar, Laos, Cambodia, Thailand, Russia, and China. They portray this 35-year saga as a divine miracle, asserting it as evidence of Manav's authenticity and the culmination of God's communication through him. This showcases an earthly demonstration of Divine Judgment, serving as proof of the impending ultimate judgment day for all mankind after death.

Now, faced with witnessing these extraordinary events, what would I do? Despite Manav making an almost impossible claim on behalf of God, which was globally fulfilled exactly as claimed, my skeptical nature would prevent an immediate conversion to Manav's ideology. I would consider the possibility that these events might be an unprecedented anomaly in human history, potentially devoid of any divine connection. Nevertheless, due to this 35-year sequence, I would feel a moral and rational compulsion to seriously explore Manav's message. Lingering in my thoughts would be the notion—what if Manav was indeed speaking the truth? If I discover that Manav's message does not morally and rationally satisfy me, particularly concerning fundamental existential questions, then it would be reasonable to assume that the events surrounding Manav were an extraordinary quirk of history, disconnected from any divine involvement.

However, if Manav's message does reasonably address my fundamental questions, combined with the extraordinary 35-year saga of God's earthly judgment, leads me to concede and believe that Manav's message truly originated from God—even if it contradicts my personal desires and interests. To me, this is the sincerest approach to take. I will continue to hold on to that belief until I encounter compelling arguments that challenge it.

In essence, this thought experiment about Manav serves as an exact parallel to the real life events in Muhammad's life (PBUH), making an improbable claim about God and divine accountability while meticulously detailing the plan of its unfolding. The claim unfolded globally exactly as predicted. This serves as the most compelling reason why everyone should, at least once in their lifetime, seriously and sincerely examine Muhammad's (PBUH) message regarding God and Divine Accountability.

Quran's Concept of "Rasool" Elucidates Earlier Scriptures

While I will delve into this in detail in Chapter 5, I would like to briefly touch on this point here. Stories from the Old and New Testaments make more sense when viewed through the Quran's explanation of what truly constitutes a Rasool of God.

Previously, before familiarizing myself with the concept of the Rasool of God, I found Biblical stories such as those of Noah or Lot perplexing. If the nations of Noah and Lot received divine punishment in this world solely due to their sins, why don't we see divine punishments more frequently in today's world, given the ongoing presence of moral and ethical transgressions?

The Quran clarifies that divine punishment on earth is not solely imposed due to corruption and sins prevalent in a society – it is authorized specifically when God communicates directly through chosen individuals, sending them as His messengers to the people - in short, earthly punishments to nations are ordained for rejecting a living Rasool of God and not merely for sinning. Although other sins might provoke God's anger, the rejection of a Messenger of God becomes the reason for infliction of divine punishment on earth.

According to the Quran, a Rasool of God embodies divine judgment on Earth for their direct addressees. They elucidate the truth, and those who believe are saved, while those who reject the Rasool face retribution here on Earth.

Now, revisiting the Biblical stories, they seamlessly align with the Quran's concept of a Rasool. Noah, after being contacted by God, conveyed His message for years. Ultimately, those who supported him were saved, while those who opposed him perished in the flood. A similar pattern applies to other prophetic figures, such as Lot for his nation, Abraham (PBUH) to his people, Moses confronting Pharaoh, and Jesus addressing the Israelites, preceding the arrival of the final Rasool, Muhammad (PBUH).

Thus, the biblical tales of God unleashing divine judgments on earth perfectly coalesce when viewed through the prism of Rasools or Messengers of God.

4C - What is the Quran and how to understand it

To understand this, let's draw a simple parable.

Imagine a Roman king who dispatches his emissary with a mission to the Roman province of Gaul. The king regularly communicates with the emissary through letters which encompass guidance for the emissary and the citizens on personal and collective matters, teachings about history and Roman ideology, and instructions on conducting matters on the king's behalf to fulfill the mission. Once the mission concludes, the king orders compilation and arrangement of all the letters into a book. This compilation aims to offer guidance from the king's wisdom for future generations. Moreover, it allows anyone to understand the king's mission in Gaul and how the king conducted matters through his emissary to fulfill that mission.

That is precisely what the Quran is—a collection of God's sermons and speeches revealed to Muhammad (PBUH), later compiled into book form by God Himself. It encompasses God's messages to Muhammad (PBUH) about immediate situations, God's discourses with Muslims, Jews, Christians, and polytheists of that time, and God's accounts of historical events and how Prophets executed God's judgment on Earth.

Additionally, it includes God's issuance of prayers and other commandments related to moral obligations. The Quran contains both situational content relevant only to Muhammad's (PBUH) immediate addressees and eternal commandments applicable to all people across all times.

As previously discussed, a common trend among certain groups is to interpret Quranic verses in isolation and out of context. I maintain that this approach is incorrect. We have already established that Quranic verses should not be understood in isolation—instead, all verses relating to a particular topic must be considered to derive the correct interpretation.

Language of the Quran

The God of the Quran communicated in the language of His immediate audience - the Arabs of the 7th century AD. The Quran insists it was revealed in clear Arabic so that people could understand God's message (Q 26:195). To comprehend the Quran, one must understand the nature of language itself. The Quran, as a spoken word in Arabic, requires understanding and translation based on the comprehension of its immediate audience or prevailing linguistic norms. Analyzing word usage, sentence structure, and context is essential to determine the meaning of the verses.

Let me stress again—the Quran should be understood just like any other written text, which means::
1) Words should be interpreted based on the meanings most commonly understood by their intended audience.
2) Consider how the word is positioned in the sentence and how that affects its meaning.
3) Take into account the context of the discussion.

For example, if someone were to say, "John said, 'Let's raincheck the lavish dinner today because I want to save some dough to pay the bills,'" it is essential to interpret these phrases within their common understanding rather than derive alternative meanings. The choice of words and their placement in the sentence, along with the context, make it very clear that John wants to postpone the dinner so he can save money to pay for his utilities.

It will be a flawed approach to deviate from the common rules of understanding a written language and assert that because "rain check" can also mean checking for rain outside hence John is saying everyone should check outside for rain during the dinner -- or because "dough" also means a malleable mixture of flour and water hence John wants to save some of that during dinner.

Let us consider an example from the Quran where the word "Torah" has been mentioned 18 times. Historically, the Torah is recognized as the book of guidance and law revealed to, and taught by, Moses and his successor prophets to the Children of Israel. The Jews, and the immediate audience of the Quran, understood the term precisely within that context. To assert that the literal meaning of the Hebrew word "Torah" ("Guidance and Law") implies any book guiding people with legal ordinances is an incorrect way to interpret the Quran or any form of linguistic communication.

The Quran's Relationship to Other Scriptures

There is a popular misconception that the Bible is the direct word of God from cover to cover, but that is not the case. The Bible - both the Old and New Testaments - is a multifaceted collection. It encompasses divine commandments, accounts of Jewish history, and reports about Jesus's life and teachings as recorded by His disciples, such as John and Matthew, which are found within the Bible, which includes the Torah, the Gospels, and the Psalms.

The Quran maintains a unique relationship with the Old and New Testaments. It does not entirely reject them; rather, it acknowledges the divinity of the Torah, the Gospel, and the Psalms (Quran 3:3-4,

5:44-46, 17:55, 4:163, among other passages). However, it insists on interpreting them through the lens of the Quran (Quran 5:48), considering the Quran as the ultimate authority. Essentially, the Quran suggests that while truths exist in the present-day Bible, their validation should align with the Quran.

The correct way to study the Bible in relation to the Quran is to consider that if the Quran revises a Biblical concept, then according to the Quran, this revised idea is the truth, and the original Biblical idea is mistaken. For instance, the Quran clarifies that Jesus was not crucified (Quran 4:157) and claims that Satan belongs to the race of jinns, not fallen angels (Quran 18:50). However, if the Quran briefly touches on a specific topic without going into detail, and the Bible contains more extensive information on that topic, then the Quran is directing the reader to consult the Bible for further detail. For example, while the Quran briefly mentions Gog and Magog (Quran 21:96) without further elaboration, the Bible extensively describes Gog and Magog as descendants of Japheth, Noah's (PBUH) third son in Genesis 10:1-5.

The Best Way to Analyze the Quran for a Layperson

For me, as a layman, the best method to analyze the Quran was to understand its correct introduction, which I mentioned above, and then read a simple translation from cover to cover. If I didn't understand something, I would mark it and seek scholarly opinions on the internet or from books. If something still didn't make sense, then I would endeavor to contact scholars and experts myself and discuss the matter with them. Also, while reading the translation, I made sure to distinguish between the translation and whatever is written in brackets and parentheses, as that is usually the translator's own opinion or addition to the text.

The Issue of the Compilation of the Quran and Its Variant Readings

(For detailed discussion and references please watch the video series entitled "Response to 23 Questions - Qiraat ka Ikhtilaf - Javed Ahmed Ghamidi" - Uploaded on the Youtube Channel of Ghamidi Center of Islamic Learning)

Before we dive into the Quran, it is essential for me to share my learnings about its compilation and variant readings. There is a popular misconception that the Quran was arranged and compiled as a complete manuscript only after the passing of Prophet Muhammad (PBUH). This is not true. Additionally, there are a few manuscripts of the Quran in which some words are written differently from the version of the Quran that is prevalent among Muslims. Why do these manuscripts exist?To understand the issue of the Quranic compilation and its variant readings, we have to briefly discuss how the Quran was revealed to Muhammad (PBUH), how he passed it on to his immediate followers, and what steps they took to preserve and mass transmit it.

Muhammad (PBUH) Presented the Complete Quran in its Current Order To His Followers Before He Passed Away

To comprehend that Muhammad (PBUH) provided his followers with the complete Quran during his lifetime, it is essential to understand the three stages of its revelation.

First Stage

During the first stage, the Quran was revealed in bits and pieces. Verses were often revealed to Muhammad (PBUH) in response to questions and critiques from his addressees or as directives and guidance to Muhammad (PBUH) and his followers on various social and political situations. During this phase, Muhammad (PBUH) would recite the verses revealed to him piecemeal to his followers. While some of the

Companions would memorize them, others would write them down. During this initial phase, it was permissible to recite the Quran in one's own words if one forgot the exact wording (Musnad of Ahmed, No: 16366). In one instance, Muhammad (PBUH) himself forgot some verses of the Quran:

> Narrated by Aisha (R.A): Allah's Messenger (PBUH) heard a man reciting the Qur'an at night, and said, "May Allah bestow His Mercy on him, as he has reminded me of such-and-such verses of such-and-such Surah, which I had forgotten (Sahih of Bukhari. No: 5038).

In another authentic narration, Muhammad (PBUH) informed his followers that they are permitted to recite the Quran in seven different styles, each with its own words and pronunciations. He allowed his followers to choose whichever form they found most convenient (Sahih of Bukhari, Nos. 513 & 514).

Why was this leniency allowed in the initial phase? Firstly, Muhammad (PBUH) himself stated that people should focus on the message rather than the exact words (Musnad of Ahmed, No: 16366). Secondly, a very early Meccan chapter assured Muhammad (PBUH) that a time would come when he would be made to revise the entire Quran under divine supervision, and from that point on, no mistakes would be allowed to persist.

> I (God) will make you recite it (Quran) and then you will not forget any of it (Quran 87:6).

In another verse, Muhammad (PBUH) is advised not to worry about memorizing the exact words immediately at the time of the revelation. He is reassured that, when the right time comes, God will enable him to memorize and recite the entirety of the Quran.

> Do not rush your tongue (O Prophet) trying to memorize the Quran. It is certainly upon Me (God) to make you memorize

and recite it. Then once I make you recite it – follow that recitation (Quran 75:16–18).

Second Stage

In this second stage, Gabriel visited Muhammad (PBUH) twice during his final year, reciting the Quran back and forth twice. This event would later be known as the Recitation of Arza e Akheerah - The Final Recitation. (Sahih of Bukhari: Nos. 4997, 4998, 6285, and 6286).

Several companions of Muhammad (PBUH), such as Zaid bin Thabit (RA), were present at the time. They transcribed the Quran as Muhammad recited it in its final form.[20]

This final recitation was the Quran that Muhammad (PBUH) delivered to his followers in his last year. The followers, en masse, wrote down and memorized the same Quran that is present today in almost every Muslim household.

> *Abeeda Salmani narrates, "The recitation that was presented to him (Muhammad PBUH) the year he died - that is the recitation that everyone is reading" (Musannaf of Ibn Abi Shaiba, No: 30922).*

> *Ibn Sireen states, "Gabriel and Muhammad read the Quran every Ramzan. In his final year this happened twice. That is exactly what we are all reading now (as Quran)" (Sunan of Saeed bin Mansoor, No:57).*

Zarkashi quotes Abu Abdur Rahman al-Sulami, born during the lifetime of Muhammad (PBUH) and one of the earliest scholars of the Quran, saying:

> *Abu Bakr, Uthman, Umar, Zaid Ibn e Thabit, all of Ansar (People from Medina), and Muhajireen (People from Mecca) (may Allah be pleased with them) would read the*

same recitation (Qira'ah) that was the recitation being read back and forth by Muhammad (PBUH) and Gabriel - twice in Muhammad's (PBUH) final year. This was called Arza e Akheerah. I mentioned Zaid ibn e Thabit because he was present at the time Muhammad recited it.[21]

Hence Muhammad (PBUH) in his last year made sure that the Quran we have in present order and form is memorized and written by his followers en masse.

So, if Muhammad (PBUH) delivered the Quran in its current form to his followers during his lifetime, then what is the reality behind the notion that Uthman (RA) was the compiler of the Quran?

The Misconception About Uthman Being the Compiler of the Quran

To understand this misconception, it's essential to grasp the third stage in the history of the Quran.

3rd Stage

This phase consists of efforts made by immediate followers of Muhammad (PBUH) to preserve, and mass transmit the Quran they received from Muhammad (PBUH). In this regard 2 events are very important:

1) By the time Muhammad (PBUH) passed away, the entire Arabian Peninsula had embraced Islam. Estimates suggest he had approximately 150,000 to 200,000 followers. As discussed earlier, all of them were familiar with the Quran, which Muhammad (PBUH) had arranged as Arza e Akhirah (Final Recitation) in his final year. Some companions of Muhammad (PBUH) had written it down, and many others had memorized it. Then came the Battle of Yamama, which resulted in heavy casualties for Muslims. Omar bin Khattab (RA) approached

Abu Bakr (RA), the Caliph, and requested him to create an official written copy of the Quran since many of the casualties at Yamama were memorizers of the Quran. It was deemed prudent to have an official copy of the Quran in case more memorizers were lost. Even though there were existing copies written by individuals, the need was felt for a unanimously agreed-upon official copy of the Quran to avoid any conflicts about its content. Abu Bakr (RA) agreed, and Zaid ibn Thābit (RA), the man who transcribed the final recitation when Muhammad (PBUH) received it from Gabriel in his final year, was appointed to write down the first unanimously agreed-upon official state copy of the Quran on behalf of the vast Muslim empire. This monumental effort was completed, and this official copy of the Quran remained with Abu Bakr (RA) until his death. Subsequently, it was in the possession of the next Caliph, Umar (RA), until his passing. By the time Umar (RA) passed away, the Muslim empire had expanded significantly, and the number of Muslims had increased to the extent that there was no longer a risk of losing memorizers of the Quran. Consequently, this first official copy of the Quran was entrusted to Muhammad's wife, Hafsa (RA), during the time of Uthmān (RA), the third Caliph (See: Sahih of Bukhārī, Book 6, Vol 61, No: 509). Hence, all Abu Bakr (RA) did was create the first official copy of the Quran—the same Quran that Muhammad (PBUH) gave to his followers, the same Quran that hundreds memorized and wrote down.

2) By the time of Caliph Uthman (RA), the new Muslim empire had expanded well beyond the Arabian Peninsula and its neighboring areas. It had become a vast entity, spreading from North Africa to Persia and encompassing modern-day Turkey, Azerbaijan, and Armenia.

A companion of the Prophet (PBUH), Huzaifa bin Yaman (RA), approached Caliph Uthman (RA) and informed him of disagreements about the contents of the Quran that were surfacing in the far-off areas of the empire. Some Syrian and Iraqi soldiers, who were not native to the Arabian Peninsula, had differing interpretations of certain words in the Quran.

Huzaifa (RA) suggested that an official copy of the Quran be delivered to all corners of the vast empire to settle such disagreements. Uthman formed a committee and appointed Zaid bin Thabit, Abdullah bin Zubair, Saeed bin Al-Aas, and Abdur Rahman bin Harith (RA) to collect the official copy of the Quran from the Prophet's (PBUH) wife, Hafsa (RA)—the same official written copy that was made by unanimous consensus during Abu Bakr's (RA) time to create more copies of the Quran for distribution throughout the vast empire.

Their task also included eliminating any other written pieces that might exist in these far-off areas. This duplication and distribution of the official written copy of the Quran throughout the vast Muslim empire is often confused with Uthman (RA) compiling and arranging the Quran. (See Sahih of Bukhārī, Book 6, Vol 61, No: 510) In short, Muhammad (PBUH) received the Quran in its complete present arrangement from Gabriel in the final year of his life. His immediate followers, numbering hundreds of thousands, wrote it down and memorized it.

Within 20 years after Muhammad's (PBUH) passing, efforts by his immediate followers led to the creation of a state-level, official written copy of the Quran with its content unanimously agreed upon. It was standardized and distributed throughout the vast Muslim empire during the time of Uthmān (RA). This standardization and distribution of the official copy of the Quran by Uthman across the vast Muslim empire are often misunderstood as Uthmān (RA) being the compiler of the Quran.

Issue of Variant Readings of the Quran

Various manuscripts of the Quran exist with certain words pronounced differently. Although these differences do not significantly impact the content and message of the Quran, the mere existence of these manuscripts is perceived by many as a negation of the Quran's preservation. However, this perception is not accurate.

As previously discussed, there was unanimous agreement on the Quran. Everyone concurred on the final recitation (Arza e Akheerah) as the Quran that Muhammad (PBUH) presented to his followers as the divinely sanctioned final book of God. Then, why do these manuscripts exist with some differences from the prevalent Quran?

As discussed earlier, during the first stage of the revelation of the Quran, mistakes in recitation were tolerated, and the use of one's own words was permitted instead of reciting the exact words. After Muhammad (PBUH) delivered the complete Quran to his followers and passed away, these early recitations from the Quran's revelation survived in both written and oral forms and reached the companions of Muhammad (PBUH). Two ideological camps emerged among Muhammad's (PBUH) immediate followers regarding how to handle these various readings.

One camp, led by Umar (RA), believed that after Muhammad (PBUH) delivered the final recitation to his followers, they should adhere strictly to that version. The other camp, led by Ubayee bin Kaab (RA), maintained that even though they all possessed the unanimously agreed-upon Quran that Muhammad (PBUH) had delivered to them before his passing, they should still preserve any other recitation or version of the Quran whose attribution to Muhammad (PBUH) was satisfactorily established. This difference of opinion persisted across generations, and hence some manuscripts survived with minor differences from the mainstream Quran, though these small variances make no difference to the message and meaning of the Quran.

In summary, Muhammad (PBUH) presented the Quran to his followers in its current form. The varying interpretations that exist today stem from the early stages of revelation when personal phrasing and errors were permissible. These interpretations have persisted because some of Muhammad's (PBUH) companions chose to preserve them as well.

Now, let us delve into the Quran to explore in detail its comprehensive framework regarding the Rasools (messengers) of God, specifically focusing on how things unfolded with Muhammad (PBUH), the final Rasool of God. I will also explain why I believe the Quran's perspective on this matter aligns rationally and is supported by science, history, and other observable aspects of our reality.

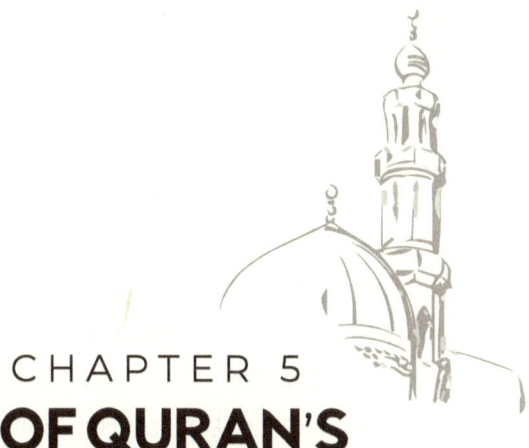

CHAPTER 5

DETAILS OF QURAN'S SCHEME OF THINGS ABOUT RASOOLS

I find it quite perplexing that what I am about to discuss is arguably the most compelling reason for everyone to explore Islam, yet it remains the least understood and discussed aspect of the religion— even among Muslims. If you are a Muslim reading this, there's a 95% chance that you are unaware that, according to the Quran, a Rasool is someone through whom God punishes and rewards people right here on Earth

The Quran elaborately describes every step of how this judgment will be executed through Prophet Muhammad (PBUH) for his immediate addressees. History demonstrates that events unfolded exactly as described in the Quran, down to the minutest details, on a global scale.

Another very intriguing aspect of the Quran's scheme involving Rasools is that it recognizes all the major personalities of the Abrahamic tradition — namely Abraham, Lot, Moses, Jesus, and Muhammad — as well as pre-Abrahamic figures like Noah, not just as Prophets or Nabis of God to guide humankind, but also as Messengers or Rasools to execute His judgment on Earth. From the Quran's perspective, the events surrounding Noah, Lot, Abraham, Moses, Jesus, and Muhammad (peace be upon them) and their teachings are not mere regional phenomena. They represent an interconnected, singular, consistent, and coherent effort by God to guide humanity and demonstrate His divine judgment on Earth as proof of the forthcoming Judgment Day for all mankind. The Quranic views on this scheme of things appear to be perfectly supported by non-religious historical sources and, more importantly, by the Old and New Testament.

Let us now move forward and analyze the Quran's perspective on Rasools. We will explore what the Quran says about this subject and why its explanations are morally, intellectually, and rationally sound. Additionally, we will examine how certain signs in our reality appear to support the Quran's assertions.

1 – Why Does God Communicate Through Prophets and Messengers Instead of Directly Communicating with Everyone?

Before we move forward, let us briefly discuss the rationale the Quran presents for why God communicates with humanity through Prophets and Messengers instead of direct communication.

The Quran, in Chapter 42, Verse 51 and in many other locations, states that God communicates with people in three ways.
1) By instilling thoughts and messages to the mind
2) Direct communication through speech
3) Through Angels who give God's message as revelation

According to the Quran, the direct means of communication—either through God speaking Himself or through angels bringing revelation—are used only for individuals who are Prophets and Messengers of God on specific missions. I always wondered, why does God need to do that? Why not speak directly to everyone? The Quran provides an answer that makes rational sense and is supported by what we understand about our reality.

Although we will discuss in detail what the Quran says about human purpose later, it's important to note here that one of the most crucial aspects of our purpose is the freedom to choose whether we want to perform good or bad deeds (Quran 2:256). According to the Quran, to provide this absolute freedom, God, angels, and their realm have been hidden from us (Quran 2:210, 6:8, 6:158, 15:7, 25:22, 26:4, 16:28, 32:12).

Hence, God communicates indirectly with the masses through Prophets and Messengers, providing guidance to those who seek it while also maintaining freedom of choice.

But then, what about the Prophets and Messengers? If they communicate directly with the Divine, what becomes of their freedom of choice? The Quran states that one of the traits of those chosen to be Prophets and Messengers of God for specific missions was that they were the best in character among people (Quran 68:4). However, once made a Prophet or a Messenger, the stakes become ever higher because the invisible realm is partially or completely made visible to them, leaving little room for excuses. Once that realm is directly visible, the reward for good is doubled, but on the other end of the spectrum, if the Prophet or Messenger does something wrong, even in the slightest manner, the consequences are immediate, and the severity of consequences is doubled for them (Quran 17:75). It's akin to running a red light while knowing a sergeant is watching—you would be fined double the normal amount.

According to the Quran, God made direct contact with those He chose as Prophets (Nabis) and Messengers (Rasools) to communicate to the masses through them. These appointed figures are given access to the hidden realm, ensuring they are certain of who and what they follow, leaving no room for doubt. For everyone else, death is the moment when the invisible becomes visible, and the freedom to choose no longer exists (Quran 50:22).

Why Keeping the Divine Realm Hidden Makes Sense

If you do not believe in any God, just suppose for a moment that this entire framework involving God and our exercise of free will is true. Logically speaking, it would make sense for God, angels, and that entire realm to be concealed from us. Otherwise, how could we possibly possess the freedom to choose wrongly? Imagine living in the direct presence of such overwhelming beings like God and angels, facing immediate consequences for any misdeed—would anyone in their right mind dare to commit wrongdoing? The obvious answer is no. Human nature dictates that we do not break laws when we know an authority is watching and will impose consequences for violations. Therefore, if the concept of God and our freedom of choice is valid, it is reasonable for God and that realm to remain hidden from us, allowing us the absolute freedom to choose between good and evil.

Support for the Idea of Hidden Realms from Our Knowable Reality

For many of us, any idea from religion becomes more palatable when it is supported by science. Consider the following two statements:

1) God has concealed most of existence from us to preserve our freedom of choice.
2) Science informs us that we are unaware of what constitutes 96% of the universe—it remains invisible to us.

For someone with a skeptical mind like mine, the second statement might sound more palatable, even though it conveys a message similar to the first. The idea that God has concealed most of reality from us finds some parallel in our understanding of the universe. The matter and forces that constitute everything in the universe account for only about 4% of its total composition; the remaining 96% consists of elements that we cannot see, measure, or directly perceive. What appears to us as empty space is filled with substances about which we know nothing. We don't know what this substance is or where exactly it exists, but we are certain of its existence because we observe its effects on visible matter. This elusive substance is referred to by scientists as "Dark Matter" and "Dark Energy," with the term 'Dark' emphasizing our complete lack of understanding about its nature. Thus, according to science, most of existence remains unseen, undetectable, and unknowable to us.

A word of caution: I am not suggesting that dark matter and dark energy are realms of God and angels. Rather, I am merely pointing out that the religious notion that God has hidden most of existence from us finds some support in our current scientific understanding.

Let us now turn to the Quran's extraordinary accounts of the Rasools.

2 - In the Beginning, All Humans Believed In One Same Truth

To fully grasp the extraordinary nature of events involving Muhammad (PBUH), it is essential to start our exploration from where the Quran begins its narrative—with the inception of modern humans. I will delve into the Quranic account of the creation of Adam and Eve in greater detail later, and it might surprise you; it's not what most people expect. For now, let's focus on the Quran's assertion that at the dawn of humankind, everyone adhered to one same truth about God and divine accountability in the afterlife.

A Basic Sense of Right and Wrong Is Embedded Within Humans

I once believed that religion posited humans had no inherent knowledge of right and wrong, and that it was scripture that informed them of these concepts. This belief led me to question the validity of religious claims, especially when considering morally upright individuals who do not follow any scripture. Contrary to this, the Quran asserts in 91:8 that a fundamental sense of right and wrong is intrinsic to humans. This assertion explains the presence of morally good people who do not adhere to any scripture. The idea that a basic sense of morality is innate aligns with the common human tendency to label actions as right or wrong, even though definitions of these terms may vary. Those lacking this moral sense or who exhibit a severe distortion in their sense of right and wrong are often labeled as insane, psychopaths, or sociopaths.

First Humans Were Contacted Directly by the Divine

According to Quran 2:31, the initial group of humans received direct communication from the divine, clarifying their origin and purpose. Thus, equipped with an inherent moral compass and explicit divine instructions, the first humans were fully aware of the Divine Truth. The Quran further states that whenever humanity strayed from this truth, God dispatched Prophets and scriptures to remind people of this guidance and to rectify any distortions that had emerged (Quran 2:213).

This truth, as outlined in various Quranic verses, encompasses belief in one supreme God, angels, an afterlife, judgment in that afterlife based on the moral choices made in this life, and a consequential good or bad outcome in that judgment based on the life lived in this world.

The Quran Explains the Existence of So Many Different Religion

The Quran explains the existence of many religions and mythologies by stating that over time, people began to deviate from the truth for various reasons, such as mutual animosity and worldly benefits, leading societies to indulge in paganism and idol worship (Quran 2:213; 25:18). People started worshiping Jinns and angels alongside God, creating mythologies around them by attributing sons and daughters to the divine (Quran 6:100; 34:41). According to the Quran, all of humanity originally knew the basic truths about God and existence; they were on the path of monotheism but gradually shifted towards polytheism and idol worship.

Support of Quran's Idea from Our Knowable Reality

In its stories of Rasools, the Quran asserts that all humanity was on the path of truth before divisions arose. Essentially, the divine book suggests that all Abrahamic faiths, and indeed most of the religious beliefs, are offshoots and mutations of a single truth. This makes sense because human beings tend to divide over beliefs, even if the foundation of those beliefs is unanimously agreed upon. Consider Muslims, for example. Muslims have the Quran, which they unanimously accept as the final book of God that clearly explains all matters related to beliefs, yet Muslims are divided into numerous sects with vastly differing views.

On the other hand, a competing hypothesis—mainly from non-religious circles—suggests that human beings started off as a clean slate and gradually began to invent spirits, gods, and an afterlife to explain their existence and make sense of death and the mysterious reality around them.

Which hypothesis is true? The one presented by the Quran or the competing one? Anatomically modern humans have been around for about 200,000 years. Unfortunately, we cannot use a time machine to go back and discover what the earliest humans thought about the divine. Additionally, there are no written records older than about 5,000 to 7,000 years ago, when writing was invented.

Many academics who assert that humanity began with paganism and idol worship base their argument on archaeological findings like statues and icons of gods and goddesses discovered in the ruins of many ancient societies. However, before the invention of writing, what kind of archaeological footprint could pure monotheism possibly leave? The answer is none. In pure monotheism, there are no idols, icons, or symbols to worship, which archaeologists could unearth to conclude that a particular society practiced monotheism. Monotheism would not leave any footprint in the absence of writing.

So, is there anything in our knowable reality that can provide us with a clue to help us decide if the Quranic claim that all humanity initially shared a single belief is true or not? Yes, there is.

Similarities in Beliefs - A Reason to Believe in the Quran's Claim of Single Origin of Truth

There exists a strange, broad conceptual similarity in religious ideas among societies across the globe—societies that have absolutely no apparent reason to share these similarities, except for the possibility that these concepts might originate from a single source. As we discussed earlier, nearly every human culture, with very few exceptions, has had concepts of God or Gods, angels, and an afterlife.

> *Religion – the belief in supernatural beings, including gods and ghosts, angels and demons, souls and spirits – can be found throughout history and in every culture ... Every known human culture has creation myths, with the possible exception of the Amazonian Pirahã people, who also lack number words, color words, and social hierarchy.*[23]

Digging deeper in this direction, the Quranic claim gains more support. The Quran states that all humans initially knew the truth, which according to the Quran includes the existence of one God, an afterlife, accountability in that afterlife, and the reward of Paradise or punishment of Hell based on one's conduct in this world. Now, let's examine which cultures around the world have held similar beliefs.

What follows might seem like advanced academic research, but it is actually very basic research by a layman over the internet. You can open Google and search for phrases like "Religious beliefs of ancient cultures" and you will find most of what I am quoting on the first page of the search results. It is extremely important to note here that there is a vast variety of opinions and counter arguments from history experts on the matters I will discuss below, but I am only sharing with you an oversimplified view of things—a broad, general, simple understanding of things which a layperson will get when skimming through easily available material on this matter.

Firstly, let us discuss the major world beliefs of relatively recent times before we move to lesser-known and more ancient ones.

All of us are familiar with the Abrahamic religious tradition—Judaism, Christianity, and Islam. Although they differ in details, they all teach the same basics: There is one God. Humanity has an enemy from another life form commonly referred to as Satan, who has also been called "The Deceiver" in the Old Testament, the New Testament, and the Quran, who tricks humankind into committing evil deeds. There is divine accountability after death. In the afterlife, there is a good place (Heaven) and a bad place (Hell) for everyone, depending on how you conducted matters here on earth.

Zoroastrianism, preached by Zoroaster in Persia, taught the exact same principles, calling the one God "Ahura Mazda" and the devil "Angra Mainyu" or the "Evil Destructive Spirit". There is divine accountability after death, resulting in a permanent good or bad outcome based on the life led in this world.[24]

Hinduism also teaches similar core principles. A morally good or bad life determines a positive or negative outcome after death, through reincarnation, ultimately leading to Moksha/Nirvana or liberation. Although there isn't a singular devil figure, Hinduism includes the concept of Rakshasas—evil demons capable of taking various forms. While Hinduism is largely seen as a polytheistic religion today, the concept of a single God still exists in its scriptures. Consider the following verses from Hindu texts:

> *Before this world was manifest, there was only One existence, One existence without a second. - Chandogya Upanishad - Chapter 6, Section 2, Verse 1*

> *To what is One, sages call by many names. - Rigveda - Book 1, Hymn 164, Verse 46*

> *He cannot be seen, neither above, nor across, nor in the middle. He is beyond grasp. There is no image true to His form. His name is glory itself. The senses cannot perceive Him. The mind cannot comprehend... His form is not visible. The eyes cannot see Him. But those who know Him as abiding in the heart—through their hearts and minds—become immortal. - Svetasvatara Upanishad - Chapter 4, Verse 19*

Now let's check out some lesser-known and more ancient beliefs.

Native Americans: Generally, Native Americans are known to worship one chief God and also seem to believe in angels. Thomas Harriot detailed his understanding on the matter in these words:

> *...the Indians believed that there was one chief and great God, which has been from all eternity, but when he decided to create the world, he started out by making petty gods, to be used in the creation and government to follow.[25]*

The Anishinaabeg, a group of indigenous tribes that are among the oldest inhabitants of North America, believe in the One God, referring to it as the Gitche Manitou or "The Great Spirit." Other Native

American tribes also refer to the single chief God as Manitou or "Great Spirit." Anishinaabeg view themselves as people ordained to live on the righteous path by their Creator, a concept similar to the "Straight Path" prescribed by the Quran. Among the Anishinaabeg and other Native American tribes, life must be led with good morals and values to ensure souls reach the spirit world—a good place—or the underworld, which is not a very good place. There is also the concept of a "Trickster" or "Deceiver." Such figures are not always seen as bad by Native Americans because they often end up teaching good life lessons to the people.

"The Nanabozho" [26] is the Deceiver for the Anishinaabeg [27], whose goal is always to create problems for the people.

China: Not much is known about ancient Chinese beliefs before 2000 BC, but there is evidence that people worshiped one supreme God called "Shangdi." The Supreme God was also referred to as "The Jade Emperor" in certain parts of China. There is also a concept of hell called "Diyu," where souls are taken to atone for sins, and then there is the Heavenly Realm or Tian.[28]

The Chinese have their own version of Satanic forces—called the Mogwai. In present times, many Chinese associate the term with certain spirits of their ancestors who are vengeful for some evil that was inflicted on them during their lifetime. However, ancient Chinese believed that Mogwai are evil beings who wish to harm humans and aim to tempt humans to do evil things.[29]

Aboriginals: For many tribes of the Aboriginals, Baiame is the Supreme Creator Sky God, and there is also belief in spirits of nature and spirits of their ancestors who they believe created everything. There is also a vague concept of heaven. They believe that post-worldly death, the soul must reach the "Land of the Dead," where entry seems to be dependent on how much the person participated in certain rituals in life or how well the mortuary rites were performed. So, although extremely vague, the concept of One God, Afterlife, and a good or bad consequence (being able to reach the land of the dead or not) is present, along with a notion that certain duties performed in this life will dictate one's destiny in the afterlife.

The ancient Aboriginals believed that everything was created by the creators during the Dreamtime—a period before anything in our world existed. The creators also instructed humans on how to live to reach a good place after death. During the Dreamtime, the creators formed men, women, and animals, established the laws of the land, and dictated how people were to behave towards one another. They set the customs for food supply and distribution, rituals of initiation, ceremonies of death (which are required to be performed so that the spirit of the dead travels peacefully to their spirit-place), and the laws of marriage.[30] The trickster figure also exists; the ancient Yolngu people believed that "Bamapana" is the trickster and deceiver who causes discord among humans.[31]

Ancient Egypt: Many deities were considered supreme gods and worshiped in ancient Egypt, with each dynasty often venerating its own supreme deity.

The supreme god of the first dynasty, "Ptah," bears a striking resemblance to the traditional concept of a monotheistic god. Ptah is described as the eternal uncreated creator of everything, the begetter of the first beginning, the one who listens to prayers, the lord of truth, and the master of justice.[32]

The concept of the feather of Maat also existed, stating that after death, individuals are presented for accountability before the divine. Their hearts are measured against the feather of truth and justice, determining whether the souls of the departed would successfully reach the paradise of the afterlife.[33]

Yoruba Religion in Africa: Known to have existed for thousands of years, the Yoruba religion includes the concept of a supreme god called Olorun or Olodumare, and the concept of angels, referred to as Irunmole. Followers of the Yoruba religion strive to achieve perfection and find their destiny in Orun-Rere (the spiritual realm of those who do good and beneficial things). As per an article on britannica.com:

> Generally speaking, African religions hold that there is one creator God, the maker of a dynamic universe. Myths of various African peoples relate that, after setting the world in motion, the Supreme Being withdrew, and he remains remote from the concerns of human life.[34]

Many African religious belief systems include the concept of a "Deceiver" or "Trickster" who, despite often being portrayed as evil, is sometimes considered good. Regardless of moral alignment, the role of someone who deceives and tricks to achieve their goals is prevalent in many ancient African belief systems.

According to the Encyclopedia Britannica,

> The trickster is a prevalent type of mythic character in African mythology. Tricksters overturn convention and are notorious for pursuing their insatiable appetites and shame-less lusts, even at the price of disaster.[35]

Norse Mythology: Not much is known in detail about the beliefs of the ancient Scandinavian people, but they appear to have had a vague concept of a Supreme God whom they called Odin.

Norse heaven is known as "Valhalla" described as "the hall of slain warriors, who live blissfully under the leadership of the god Odin."[36]

And there is the concept of Hell known as Niflheim referred to as a "cold, dark, misty world of the dead…. a place into which evil men pass after reaching the region of death."[37]

The trickster figure is also present and is called "Loki". He is not mentioned as particularly good or bad but his main aim was always to create chaos.[38]

Greek Mythology: Zeus is the supreme god for the ancient Greeks. Elysium is the paradise to which heroes, on whom the gods conferred immortality, were sent. The "Underworld" is the ancient Greek version of hell. There is also the character of the Trickster, known as "Prometheus"—the Supreme Trickster. -41 Prometheus commands Dolos, the spirit of deception, along with Pseudea, the spirit of lies.[42]

Although the details of the beliefs and mythological stories from the above-mentioned cultures are vastly different from one another, they all share broad, general conceptual similarities—such as the concept of one Supreme God or Creator, an afterlife, and moral consequences in that afterlife based on one's actions in this life. Additionally, there is often the figure of the Trickster or Deceiver, an entity mainly intent on misleading humans and tempting them into committing wrongful deeds. Why do cultures across the world share these similarities in ideas? The very existence of such concepts in almost every human society suggests a common origin, as there appears to be no other reason why nearly every human culture would independently develop these concepts. Nothing in our psychology or external environment indicates that all humans were destined to think in this specific direction and to develop such ideas to explain reality. For me, this supports the Quranic claim of a singular message that has deteriorated over hundreds of thousands of years into varied religious beliefs and mythological stories, which, despite their differing details, retain broad conceptual similarities.

3 – Nabis (Prophets) of God Are Sent to Humankind

The Holy Quran advances the narrative, explaining that when humanity began to stray from the truth, God reached out to righteous individuals from various nations, dubbing them "Nabi" or "Prophet of God."

These appointed prophets were tasked with guiding people back to the truth and rectifying any distortions that had emerged (Quran 2:213).

Vague Concepts of Prophets of God Throughout Human History

The Holy Quran posits that all of humanity was familiar with the concept of God's Prophets, but most Prophets were rejected by their people and did not garner any notable worldly following (37:71-72). This claim aligns with historical observations that, on a conceptual level, humanity has indeed been familiar with the idea of individuals in touch with the divine to guide humankind. Hence, we see concepts like Shamans, Rishis, and Sages across all human cultures. However, there are sparse records of specific personalities who were messengers of God, with few exceptions like the Sages of Hinduism, Prophet Zoroaster of Zoroastrianism, and the Prophets from the Abrahamic tradition.

According to the Quran's narrative, once humanity strayed from the truth, God sent Prophets to nations, most of whom were rejected. Accepting or rejecting a Prophet's message carried no worldly consequences, as divine accountability for each individual is to be carried out after death on the "Day of Judgment."

After the Prophets, God sent Messengers who were not only sent to guide people but also, accepting or rejecting them carried profound worldly consequences.

This brings us to our main topic of focus—the concept of a Rasool of God!

4 - The Rasools (Messengers) of God

For a detailed discussion and references pertaining to the messengers of God, and specifically Muhammad (PBUH) as a messenger of God, please refer to the following playlist on the YouTube channel "Ghamidi Center of Islamic Learning."

(Playlist titled: "Response to 23 Questions - Itmam e Hujjat - Javed Ahmed Ghamidi")

Nabi (Prophet) and Rasool (Messenger) are Two Different Offices

A "Rasool" literally means a Messenger or an Emissary. All Rasools are Nabis, or Prophets of God, meaning they receive direct communication from God. However, the Quran makes a distinction between the two offices of Nabi and Rasool (Prophet and Messenger), as it employs these two terms distinctly. The Quran states:

> *Whenever I (God) sent a Rasool (Messenger) or a Nabi (Prophet) before you (O Muhammad) - he recited my revelations to people... (Quran 22:52)*

Muslim scholars acknowledge that the terms "Nabi" (Prophet) and "Rasool" (Messenger) refer to two distinct offices. Scholars such as Ibn-e-Ashoor and Zamakhshari have discussed how a Nabi does not bring any new book or laws, whereas a Rasool brings a new book and laws from God. However, this distinction presents a problem because, although the Quran identifies Jesus as a Rasool, Jesus stated that he followed the law of Moses and did not introduce any new divine laws. Maulana Maududi, addressing this issue, concedes that even though, according to the Quran, Nabi and Rasool are different statuses, there is ongoing debate among Muslim scholars about the exact differences, and no conclusive answer has yet been reached.

In this regard, scholars such as Amin Ahsan Islahi and Javed Ghamidi have accurately identified what a Rasool of God truly represents according to the Quran. These scholars have conducted extensive work in this area in their literature. For me, understanding the correct concept of a Rasool of God is the master key to correctly grasping most of the key concepts of Islam.

Correct Concept of the Messenger of God - God's Divine Court of Judgment on Earth

According to the Quran, a Nabi is a Prophet, someone who delivers God's message to the people. Some prophets receive books from God, which are meant to serve the purpose of settling disputes about religion among people after the Nabi dies (Quran 2:213). Accepting or rejecting a Nabi carries no worldly consequences. However, a Rasool is a Messenger - accepting his message or unjustly rejecting his message will carry very profound worldly consequences for the addressees of the Rasool. The Quran states:

> For every nation there is a Rasool. Once their Rasool comes to them – judgment is passed on them in all fairness and they are not wronged even in the least manner. (Quran 10:47)

> I (God) do not punish a society until I send among them a Rasool. (Quran 17:15)

> Your Lord does not punish a society until He sends a Rasool to the main city of that nation – who recites to them God's message and revelations. (Quran 28:59)

According to the Quran, all societies to which Rasools were sent, each had their own set of evils prevalent among them, but the reason for worldly punishment was their rejection of God's Rasool sent to them. (Quran 16:112-113; 69:10; 64:5-6).

This resolves a longstanding question for me. As I mentioned earlier, I used to wonder if, when God punished individuals on Earth for their sins—such as in the flood of Noah or the rain of fire and stones on the people of Lot—why doesn't God punish people in modern times for their sins, especially in cities where sin has been openly preached and practiced for centuries? The Quran solves this puzzle by clearly stating that, generally, people will be judged for their sins on the Day of Judgment. However, the crime of rejecting a living Rasool (Messenger) of God carries worldly punishment for those who are the immediate recipients of that Rasool's message.

Some scholars have argued that the judgment or punishment mentioned in these verses is not worldly punishment; instead, it refers to reward and punishment on the Day of Judgment. However, the context of these verses does not support this idea. For example, in verses 48 and 49 of chapter 10, as cited above, it becomes clear that the punishment being discussed is definitely worldly punishment, because in these verses when people asked that when will this judgment come to pass, Muhammad (PBUH) is told to say that each nation has a pre-ordained time frame or an interlude, and once this time is over, the judgment is imposed upon them. Specifically, in Surah al-Hijr, verse 4, it is stated that societies are allotted a preordained time before the proclaimed judgment is inflicted upon them. Furthermore, Muhammad is told in various passages, including Surah al-Ra'ad verse 40, al-Ghafir verse 77, and Yunus verse 46, that God may show him some aspects of this judgment during his lifetime and reveal other parts after his death. These revelations clarify that the judgment discussed in the Quran, particularly concerning the recipients of the message, is a worldly one. This implies that among the immediate recipients of the message, those who reject and persecute the messenger will certainly face punishment on the Day of Judgment, but they will also endure punishment here on earth. Many traditional scholars, including Zamakhshari, Bayzaavi, and Abu Hayaan, concur that the judgment mentioned in these verses pertains to worldly judgment and regard the opposing view as secondary.

The role of God's Messengers, or Rasools, is succinctly summarized in Surah Ibrahim, verses 13 to 15, and Surah al-Anbiya, verses 6 to 9. These verses illustrate that the Rasools presented their messages to their communities but were unjustly rejected and faced threats and persecution. Consequently, divine judgment was imposed on those rejectors, resulting in the salvation of the Rasools and their followers, while those who opposed them faced elimination.

Rasools not only bring punishment for the deniers, but they also bring worldly rewards for their followers. The Quran states in 7:96 that those who accept Rasool's message are rewarded in this world. Furthermore, in 14:14, the Quran asserts that once the enemies of the Rasool are eliminated, those who accept and support the Rasool are granted worldly rewards in the form of authority on Earth.

Hence, there is worldly punishment from God for the deniers and persecutors of the Rasools and a reward for those who accept and support the Rasool.

5 - The Kind of People the God of the Quran Has Issues With and Why It Makes Sense

Rejecting a Rasool of God carries worldly punishment for the immediate audience of the Rasool. This fact raised a question in my mind. If I happen to be among the immediate addressees of a Rasool, will God punish me if, despite lending a sincere ear to the Rasool, I don't accept the Rasool's message for very justified reasons—for example, if some aspect of the message didn't make moral or rational sense to me? The Quran says no! Let me explain.

The Quran insists that for the immediate addressees of the Rasool, God makes the truth clear beyond all doubt. To achieve such clarity, God employs various means. For instance, the impeccable personality and character of the Rasool, along with his profound arguments, leave no room for any valid counterarguments. Moreover, the Rasool is granted miracles, and external political and military circumstances unfold in a way that supports his claims, adding further credence to his message. Consequently, through the power of arguments, the character of the Rasool, miracles, and supportive external events, an environment is created where the truth becomes unmistakably clear to the Rasool's immediate addressees. Those who deny it are typically motivated by unjustifiable reasons. For example, they may reject a Rasool due to negligence or because they perceive the message as contrary to their worldly benefits, desires, traditions, or ego.

The Quran proclaims that you will not be punished as long as your intentions are sincere and genuine, and until you wrongfully and unjustly reject a Rasool's message. This is clearly stated in the following verse:

> Your Lord would never destroy a society until He sends to its capital a Rasool...He does not inflict punishment unless its people become Zalimooon - (meaning people who knowingly and deliberately persist in wrongful and unjust behavior and deeds) (Quran 28:59).

In the Quran, in verses 9:70 and 14:45, God states that societies to which messengers were sent were destroyed when the people "wronged their own selves." This term refers to when people commit wrongdoings while fully aware that their actions are incorrect.

Furthermore, in the Quran 40:5, God states that those who became subject to God's punishment among the addressees of Rasools were those people who "Wajadaloo bil Batili," meaning they rejected truth for unjustified and false reasons.

Similarly, lying and arrogance are unacceptable to God. The Quran contains many instances where God declares that arrogance is not acceptable. For instance, in Quran 40:60, it is proclaimed that those who reject God's message due to arrogance will be doomed. Additionally, the very first verse where God addresses the first humans indicates that prophets and messengers will come to guide them should they deviate from the truth. Here, people are instructed not to "Kazzaboo" (lie about their misunderstanding of the message) and not to "Wastakbaroo" (arrogantly refuse to accept what they know deep down as truth).

Muhammad (PBUH) further clarifies what "Takkabur," or arrogance, means in a Hadith:

> *Arrogance is refusing to accept something you know as truth*
> *and to look down upon people (Sahih of Muslim, No: 91).*

The God of the Quran takes significant issue with individuals who recognize the truth from God yet reject it for unjustified reasons. Let us examine some examples from the Quran where God condemns people for dismissing His message, despite knowing deep down that it indeed represents Divine Truth.

The Quran, in 27:14, states that Pharaoh and his people rejected Moses despite being deeply convinced in their hearts that he was sent by God.

The Quran proclaims that the Meccan polytheists were aware of God's blessings upon them, yet they acted ungratefully and denied His message (Quran 16:83).

The God of the Quran proclaims about a segment of Jews and Christians among the immediate addresses of Muhammad (PBUH): "Those people to whom I (God) have given scripture (Jews & Christians) recognize this Prophet as they recognize their own children, but a group of them knowingly hides the truth" (Quran 2:146).

Some among the People of the Book (Jews and Christians) of that time are also condemned for "knowingly hiding the truth" (Quran 3:71).

Quran 6:28 states that the people of hell will be those who used to "hide the truth" during their worldly life.

The Quran 7:9 states that on Judgment Day, the losers will be those who "wrongfully rejected" God's guidance—or rejected God's guidance for unjustified or wrongful reasons.

The Quran 47:32 specifically calls out those who oppose God and His Messenger after "guidance has become clear" to them.

In the Quran, 27:14, those people are condemned whose hearts are convinced of the truth regarding God, but they still deny it wrongfully and arrogantly.

Who is a Kafir?

The primary term used in the Quran for those who reject God's messengers is "Kafir," which broadly means someone who denies or covers up the truth. In the Quran, individuals are called Kafirs or Deniers specifically if they have openly declared their rejection of the message delivered by Muhammad (PBUH). However, the term Kafir encompasses more than just denial. It also connotes ungratefulness and arrogance, reflecting a deeper significance in its usage within the Quran.

The word "Kafir" is derived from the root K-F-R, which was used by Arabs in pre-Islamic times to describe farmers who covered seeds in the soil—essentially burying them. Much like how farmers conceal seeds in the ground, the term "Kafir" also refers to a person who hides the truth, someone who denies the truth while knowing deep down that it is indeed the truth.[44]

Hence, a Kafir is someone who denies the truth but also someone who hides the truth. In other words, it implies a person who refuses to accept the truth for unjustified reasons.

The Quran clearly states that through a Rasool, God makes the truth unequivocally clear to His immediate addressees. Once this clarity is achieved, those who reject the Rasool do so for unjustified reasons and thus become eligible for God's punishment. Let us consider a few examples of specific unjustified reasons the rejectors of the Rasools used in response to God's message.

1) The Quran condemns those who reject God's verses without even trying to understand them (Quran 27:84).

2) Refusal to accept the truth unless God speaks directly to the elite of society (43:31).

3) Refusing to accept the truth because it contradicts one's worldly benefits and desires (53:29, 5:48).

4) People who refuse to listen and do not sincerely use their intellect and reason (67:10, 8:22).

5) Refusal to accept the truth because it contradicts their traditions or ancestral beliefs (14:10, 7:70).

6) Refusal to accept the truth based on reason, instead demanding supernatural explanations (6:124, 17:89-93).

7) Refusing to accept the truth based solely on reason because the messenger is merely a human with no supernatural abilities (21:1-3, 17:94, 25:7-8, 14:10).

8) The refusal to accept the truth because it is followed only by the poor and weak (26:111, 13:27).

9) Some segments of Jews are condemned for not accepting Muhammad (PBUH) as a Prophet of God, solely because he did not belong to their nation (Quran 2:87-90).

The entire Quran is filled with verses discuss reasons which God deems unjustified for rejecting His message.

It makes Sense for God to Punish Rejecters

Suppose the entire scheme of the Quran regarding God's Rasools is true; it is both rational and morally justifiable that people should be punished for rejecting God's Rasool for the unjustified reasons mentioned in the Quran.

A Brief Note on Branding Others as Kafir

Only God knows what is in the hearts of people! Since prophets and messengers are directly in touch with God, they are told directly by God about whoever is rejecting the truth for unjustified reasons.

According to the Quran, Muhammad (PBUH) is the last Prophet and Messenger of God. After him, we cannot declare anyone as a Kafir because we are unable to look into someone's heart to determine the precise reason why they are rejecting the divine message. Perhaps that person was exposed to a distortion of the truth, rather than the actual truth—which is quite possible considering the numerous, often contradictory interpretations of Islam. It is also possible that the person is rejecting the truth because the arguments presented have not satisfied them morally, intellectually, or rationally. Additionally, they might be facing such significant struggles in life that they cannot spare sufficient time and energy to seek out the truth. So, in a nutshell, we cannot ask God directly or look into a person's heart to determine if that individual is rejecting a message for sincere reasons or for unjustified reasons.

God communicated directly with Muhammad (PBUH) and his immediate followers. After Muhammad (PBUH), the determination of who is a Kafir and who is not will only be made on the Day of Judgment. Therefore, all those who reject Islam today are simply non-believers and cannot be branded as Kafirs.

I hope that, so far, the Quran's narrative of Rasools is making as much rational and moral sense to you as it did for me.

6 - Noah (PBUH) - The First Rasool

The story of Prophet Noah (PBUH) is mentioned in numerous places throughout the Quran. I will use only a few verses to support my points.

The Holy Quran does not attribute a specific timeline to Noah (PBUH), but the way the Quran discusses him suggests that he was the first Rasool sent to his people (Quran 4:163; 14:9). Noah (PBUH) opposed the polytheism and idol worship prevalent in his nation, calling his followers to worship one God and seeking moral reformation. The chiefs of Noah's (PBUH) nation dismissed his message, disregarding logic and reason (Quran 71:5-7). They also ridiculed him with objections such as questioning how Noah could be sent by God without possessing supernatural powers, or why only the poor and lowly followed him if he were truly sent by God (Quran 11:27; 23:24; 26:111). They even threatened to stone Noah (PBUH) to death if he did not cease his preaching (Quran 26:116). According to the divine law concerning His Rasools as outlined in the Quran, Noah's (PBUH) entire nation was eradicated by a flood due to their opposition and persecution of God's Rasool. The few followers who accepted and supported Noah's (PBUH) message were rewarded by being saved on a boat and later granted authority over the land (Quran 11:40; 26:119-120; 7:64; 10:73).

The Quran does not specify the exact location of Noah's (PBUH) nation and it also does not specify a timeline for the events concerning Noah (PBUH) or his nation, yet it distinctly states that Noah's (PBUH) flood was not a global event but a regional one intended to eliminate the rejecters among his immediate audience. I will delve into this point more thoroughly later. For the moment, the question arises: can we scientifically or historically confirm whether Noah (PBUH) truly existed, and if a regional flood wiped out his people? There is no scientific method available to either confirm or refute these claims.

But there is hope. The Quran makes a very intriguing claim about Noah's (PBUH) story, which might provide evidence that there is some truth to the Quran's account of Noah (PBUH).

God says in the Quran that the story of Noah (PBUH) was preserved by Him in collective human memory and was made to be "a sign" and "a remembrance" for later generations of humankind (Quran 25:37; 69:12; 37:78). Even though the Quran narrates the stories of many

Rasools after Noah, it makes this particular claim only about Noah's (PBUH) story. Indeed, this is a very strange claim. So, is the story of Noah (PBUH) present in our collective human memory? Yes, it is.

Noah's (PBUH) story is indeed present in numerous cultures across the globe, which seems to support the Quranic claim. These stories vary in detail but share general conceptual similarities, suggesting a common origin. This specific claim of the Quran about Noah's (PBUH) story is intriguing and lends more credence to the idea of the Quran's divine origin, because Muhammad (PBUH) could not have possibly known that from China to India, and all the way to North America, Africa, and Australia, almost all cultures have a flood story with broad similarities.

We know that Noah's (PBUH) story is present, with minor differences, in Islam, Christianity, and Judaism. Let's analyze a few cultures across the globe and their flood stories.

Analysis of Flood Stories Present in Almost All Cultures Across the World

Native American Flood Stories: The story of Waynaboozhoo and the Great Flood asserts that either God or the Great Spirit, displeased with humanity, sent a vast flood to eradicate them. A man named Waynaboozhoo survived by constructing a raft and subsequently remade the earth.[45]

Norse Flood Story: The earth is flooded with the blood of a giant killed by God Odin. Only a "Frost Giant" survives with his wife on a boat and repopulates the earth.[46]

Chinese Flood Story: A few children do a favor for the thunder god who, in return, warns them of an impending flood. He provides them with a gourd to use as a boat for their escape. The occupants of the gourd are saved from the flood by the thunder god and they repopulate the earth.[47]

Hindu Flood Story: A man named Manu did a favor for a fish which, according to some versions, was an avatar of the god Vishnu. After Manu saves the fish, it transforms into a deity and informs him that humanity will be destroyed by a flood. Manu is instructed to build a boat. He survives the flood and later repopulates the earth.[48]

Greek Flood Story: The god Zeus became angry with humanity and sent a great flood to wipe it out. Zeus saved a man named Deucalion and his wife, who later repopulated the earth.[49]

Flood Story of Ancient Mesopotamia: In the Epic of Gilgamesh, the great gods in the heavens decide to flood the earth and destroy humankind. One of the gods shares this plan with a man named Utnapishtim and tells him to build a boat to save himself. Utnapishtim follows the instructions and constructs a boat. Along with some fellow humans and a variety of animals, he boards the boat. A great flood came and annihilated the land. Utnapishtim, his wife, and their few followers were saved and blessed by the god Enlil.

According to the Sumerian flood myth, "the human race, which the gods had created to do their work, became so numerous and noisy that the god Enlil sent a flood to destroy it. However, another god, Enki, wanted to save King Ziusudra (King Atrahasis in some versions). Forbidden by Enlil to warn the king directly, Enki spoke to the king's reed house instead. The king overheard the warning, built a boat, and saved his family and a collection of animals."[50] [51]

Egyptian Flood Story: The Egyptian flood narrative involves the god Ra and his daughter Sekhmet. Ra sought to eliminate humanity after they became rebellious against him and sent Sekhmet to accomplish this. After Sekhmet had unleashed substantial death and destruction, the gods flooded the earth with wine to intoxicate her, thereby halting her rampage. This allowed the survivors to begin life anew.[52]

Flood Story of the Hawaiian People: The flood story of the native people of Hawaii bears a striking resemblance to the story of Noah; the man in the story even shares Noah's name, specifically called Nu. In this narrative, God commanded Nu to build a boat. Nu and his family are saved, while humanity is destroyed by a flood.[53]

African Flood Story: Many ancient tribes in Africa had their own flood stories, with remarkable similarities to that of Noah. One example is the flood story of the Maasai tribe.

According to the flood story of the Maasai, there came a time when humanity had become so corrupt that God decided to cleanse the earth with a flood. There was a righteous man named Tumbainot. He was commanded by God to build a boat and place some animals and his family onboard. They were saved from the flood.

I have highlighted examples from cultures around the world to establish the authenticity of the Quran's claim that God embedded the story of Noah (PBUH) in collective human memory. I find this remarkable that the Quran narrates stories of many Rasools, but it specifically claims that Noah's (PBUH) story serves as a remembrance for all humankind. This claim proves to be very accurate, as Noah's (PBUH) story appears in some form in almost every human culture, with very few exceptions.

As an aside, for those who doubt the divine origin of the Quran, consider its account of Noah's story (PBUH). The Quran remarkably claims that Noah's narrative is recognized in cultures worldwide, not just in Arabia or neighboring regions. This raises an intriguing question: how could Muhammad (PBUH) have possibly known about the global pervasiveness of Noah's story? It's a thought-provoking point.

So far, in my opinion, whatever the Quran states in its account of the Rasools seems plausible and backed by evidence. Let's continue exploring the Quran's narrative of the Rasools.

7 - Phase 1 of God's Plan Regarding Rasools: Individual Rasools

After Noah, the God of the Quran initiates what I call Phase 1 of God's plan regarding Rasools, in which individual Rasools were sent to various nations (Quran 10:47; 17:15; 28:59). The Quran mentions some Rasools, but others remain known only to God (Quran 25:38; 14:9).

It appears from the Quran that individual Rasools were sent to different nations as humanity spread across small settlements. As humanity progressed into the era of nations and civilizations, Phase 2 of God's plan was initiated. In this phase, individual Rasools were replaced by nations tasked with practicing and preaching God's message. For this purpose, the progeny of Abraham (PBUH) was chosen by God. While there is no specific timeline for Abraham's (PBUH) existence, Biblical scholars generally place him around 4,000 years ago, which coincides with humanity's transition into the age of civilization.

Historical Verification of Rasools Before Abraham

Before moving forward, let's address a common question: Can we historically verify that individual Rasools appeared in all nations before Abraham? Unfortunately, due to the limited recorded history of about 5500 years, there is no way to historically ascertain whether individuals arrived in all nations worldwide claiming to be Rasools or Messengers of God, or if nations were destroyed for unjustly rejecting their Rasools.

Why Does the Quran Mention Only Specific Messengers from the Middle East?

The Quran while stating that Rasools were sent to all nations before Abraham, mentions stories of very few specific Rasools (Saleh, Hudd, Lot, etc.) and Quran says that the reason for mentioning these specific Rasools and their stories is that the immediate audience of the Quran (Arabian Polytheists, Jews, and Christians) were already familiar with these stories. (Quran 54:4).

8 - Phase 2 of God's Plan Regarding Rasools: Raising Nations from Abraham's Progeny

According to the Quran, there are two phases in the story of Rasools. In the first phase, individual Rasools (Messengers) are sent to their nations (Quran 10:47, 17:15, 28:59). In the second phase, Messengerhood is made exclusive to a select group of people, and through these Messengers of God, nations are raised to practice and preach God's message to the world. For this purpose, God chose the progeny of Abraham (PBUH) (Quran 29:27; 3:33).

Abraham (PBUH), a Rasool of God sent to his people, was rejected and persecuted (Quran 29:24). However, Abraham (PBUH) was saved, and his people were destroyed. The Quran does not specify a timeline for Abraham (PBUH). Additionally, Abraham was given another mission. As the starting point of Phase 2 of Rasools, two nations would be raised from his children—one through Isaac (PBUH) and one through Ishmael (PBUH). These nations would practice and preach God's message to the world.

Why Quran's Two-Pronged Approach to Rasools Makes Sense?

The Quran's two phases, along with the roles of Rasools, make sense considering human society has evolved in two main stages. Initially, individual Rasools were sufficient for delivering God's message when humanity consisted of small tribal settlements. For the majority of its existence, up until around 5 to 6 thousand years ago, humanity was primarily made up of small tribal villages and towns. However, as the age of civilization dawned, the scope of God's work expanded. It became a sensible approach for God to raise entire nations to keep His message vibrant in an era when humanity was transitioning from small settlements to kingdoms and empires.

First Nation from the Offspring of Isaac (PBUH): Moses (PBUH) and the Exodus

Isaac's (PBUH) descendants lived in the Canaan area, and they migrated to Egypt, where the Biblical and Quranic story of Joseph (PBUH) unfolded. The children of Isaac (PBUH) were enslaved by the Egyptians and were not yet tasked with any divine duty of practicing and preaching God's message to the world as a nation. That divine mission would commence with the onset of Moses (PBUH)!

Moses (PBUH) is identified as God's Rasool to Pharaoh and his people. God's law manifests through Moses (PBUH). He is assured that he and his supporters will prevail over those who oppose him (Quran 28:35), and that the Israelites will be saved and made leaders of the land (Quran 28:5). While the Israelites accept Moses as a Rasool, he faces rejection from Pharaoh. Those who reject the Rasool, persecute him, and fight him - that is, Pharaoh and his people - face divine punishment (Quran 8:54). In contrast, those who accept the Rasool and support him, namely the Israelites, are saved and rewarded by God, as He granted them kingdom and authority on earth (Quran 7:129; 7:137; 5:21).

The details of this divine mission are mentioned in the Book of Deuteronomy 20:1-20, where the Israelites are informed that they have been granted the land of Canaan and its surrounding areas. They are instructed to cleanse the land of all pagan beliefs and dedicate it exclusively to the practice and preaching of the religion of one God. For this purpose, all pagan nations in Canaan are expected to vacate the area or face absolute and total destruction. The presence of pagan nations among the Israelites is viewed as a threat to the all-important divine mission, as it jeopardizes the purity of the monotheistic message that the Israelites are meant to practice and preach to the world as a nation on behalf of God.

The Controversial Biblical Order and Its Justification

The Biblical command to annihilate the pagans in Canaan is often perceived as cruel and unjustified. However, when viewed in its historical context, it can be understood differently.

1. The Israelites generally adhered to a strict moral code of war, offering peace to their enemies before engaging in battle. If peace was rejected, only armed men could be fought and killed, while women and children had to be spared (Deuteronomy 20:10-14).

2 . Canaan was the area given to the Israelites as a land where they could establish themselves as a nation with the sole mission of practicing and preaching God's message to the world. Only in the case of Canaan did God command the complete annihilation of all pagans who did not leave. The reason for this was that their presence among The Israelites posed a severe threat to the purity of God's message—and understandably so! Picture this: events were unfolding in a world where polytheistic pagan beliefs and practices predominated, while only a small group of Israelites upheld monotheism. Now, if the God of Abraham's doctrine holds true, consider the apocalyptic significance of the mission to be the sole custodian of God's true message in a world riddled with false beliefs. Reflect on the responsibility of preserving the purity of God's message through many future generations, and the duty of proclaiming it worldwide for centuries to come. In this context, if pagans were allowed to reside among the Israelites, there would be a very real risk that over years and decades, these pagans and their beliefs could gradually infiltrate and blend with the true message of God, bringing with them mythologies and practices deemed immoral by God. Thus, it makes sense for God to decree that all pagans in Canaan be annihilated if they do not depart.

Archeological Evidence of Joseph *(PBUH)*, Moses *(PBUH)* & the Exodus:

Contrary to the belief that there is no physical evidence of Joseph (PBUH), Moses (PBUH), or the Exodus, the documentary "Decoding the Exodus" by Simcha Jacobovici, produced by James Cameron, presents compelling archaeological proof of their existence. This evidence challenges the notion that there is no historical basis for these figures and events. Additionally, the Old Testament is not only a source of divine wisdom and laws but also contains a historical record preserved by the Israelites about their past, and it should be regarded as a substantial source of Jewish history.

Israelites As a Nation under Moses (PBUH):

Under the leadership of Moses (PBUH), the Israelites were transformed by God into a nation. For the first time, divine laws were issued to govern societal matters. This nation was being groomed by God to practice and preach His message to the world (Quran 28:5). This is corroborated by our living history—the Israelites have stood as flag bearers of monotheism for thousands of years, preaching to the world about their singular God's message, as mentioned in the Quran. They faithfully fulfilled this duty for a considerable period. However, over time, religious arrogance and moral decline began to emerge. In the Quran, extensive sections of chapters such as Surah al-Baqarah and Ale Imran detail how the Israelites deviated from the truth and compromised their duties to God, which is further supported by Surah Maryam, verse 59.

Jesus (PBUH) – the Last Rasool for the Israelites:

The Quran states that Jesus (PBUH) was a Messenger of God. He preached to the Israelites, condemning them for their severe arrogance, misdeeds, and violations of their covenant with God (Quran 5:78, among many other references, especially in Surah Maida). In the Bible,

Matthew 23 lays out Jesus's indictment against the religious leaders of the Israelites, who were destined to face God's judgment on earth through Jesus (PBUH). Many of the Israelites rejected Jesus (PBUH), and some even sought to kill him. According to God's law concerning His messengers, those who reject and persecute the messenger become subject to divine punishment. In Matthew 24:32-41, Jesus (PBUH) foretells this impending punishment.

I want to pause here for a moment and again mention how remarkable it is that Biblical stories are in complete sense and seem to be in absolute harmony with the Quran's depiction of Rasools as God's judgment on Earth.

Let's continue.

In Matthew 24:32-41, Jesus (PBUH) declares that those persecuting Him will not die before they witness God's worldly punishment. He proclaimed that, akin to the time of Noah (PBUH), God's wrath would be unleashed on His immediate audience. However, not all would be wiped out; some would be killed while others would be left behind. The punishment came at the hands of Romans who destroyed Jerusalem in 70 AD, approximately 10 to 15 years after Jesus's (PBUH) departure. They killed nearly half of the Bani Israel and took the remainder captive, fulfilling Jesus's (PBUH) prophecy. Imagine the miraculous nature of his claim: Jesus (PBUH) foretold that the people who persecuted and rejected him would still be alive to witness God's punishment—a punishment in which half would be killed and the other half would survive. And it came true! This event further establishes that in God's design for Rasools, if the complete elimination of a nation is not necessary, then divine punishment is meted out through the hands of others to the nation that rejects the Rasool.

The Last Nation from the Children of Ishmael (PBUH): Muhammad (PBUH) - The Last Rasool of God

After approximately 600 years since ending the covenant with the descendants of Isaac for rejecting Jesus (PBUH), God chose to raise a new nation one final time. This nation would emerge from the descendants of Ishmael (PBUH), Abraham's second son. For this purpose, God selected Muhammad (PBUH) as His final Prophet and Messenger.

In many early Meccan chapters, such as Surah Qamar, Muhammad (PBUH) is told that he is a Rasool, just like those before him, and that the same fate will befall Muhammad's (PBUH) addressees as befell the addressees of previous Rasools (see also Quran 8:38).

Muhammad (PBUH) is also told that he is a Rasool, in the exact likeness of Moses (PBUH) (Quran 73:15). Being a Rasool in the likeness of Moses (PBUH) means that Muhammad (PBUH) has the exact same mission as Moses (PBUH), and everything that happened with Moses (PBUH) and the Israelites will come true for Muhammad (PBUH) and his followers. The Quran makes this point abundantly clear in almost every other chapter. To mention a few examples, the Quran claims that:

- Muhammad's (PBUH) enemies will be completely defeated (Quran 58:5; 58:20-21 among others).
- Those who support him will be formed into a nation who will be given authority on land (Surah Nur verse 55) and they shall be tasked with preaching God's message to the world (Quran 22:78).
- Just as Moses (PBUH) and his nation were given the area of Canaan to make it a center for the religion of one God and to cleanse it of all other religions, Muhammad (PBUH) was given the region of Hijaz to establish it as the new center for the monotheistic faith and to purify it from other religious ideologies (Quran 48:28; 9:33; 61:9). In this context, Muhammad

(PBUH), as reported in a well-known Sahih Hadith, pro-claimed that the Arabian Peninsula must be exclusive to the religion of one God.

لا يَجْتَمِعُ دِينَانِ فِي جَزِيرَةِ الْعَرَبِ

Two religions shall not co-exist in the Arabian Peninsula (Muwatta of Malik, No: 1862).

Before moving forward, it is important to remind ourselves that the teachings of the Messenger of God are intended for all humankind, though the Divine Worldly Judgment through Rasool applies primar-ily to his immediate addressees. With the historical context discussed earlier, the Quran introduces Muhammad (PBUH) as a religious guide from God to all people, and as a Rasool of God (Worldly Judgment of God) to the Arabs and surrounding areas (Quran 6:92; 42:7). Muhammad (PBUH) wrote letters to the rulers of Persia, Byzantine, Ethiopia, Negus, Bahrain, Egypt, Yemen, and Sham, which precisely defined the exact jurisdiction of God's judgment on Earth.

Important Note About Muhammad's (PBUH) Letters to Kings

We discussed initially that, according to God's law regarding Rasools, God clarifies the truth to a Rasool's immediate addressees not only through arguments and reasoning but also through the personality of the Rasool and by orchestrating external events in a manner that appears to support the Rasool's claims. These factors combine to compel the immediate addressees of the Rasool to give him serious consideration.

The letters that Muhammad (PBUH) wrote to several kings are readily available online. These letters contain an invitation to Islam and include a warning that rejecting the invitation of a Rasool of God will subject the kings and their armies to divine punishment. The kings were aware of the developments in Arabia—they knew that Muhammad (PBUH) claimed to be a worldly judgment of God for his immediate addressees and were also informed of Muhammad's (PBUH) complete victory in Arabia. Despite this knowledge, when some of the kings outright rejected his invitation without attempting to listen or understand, they became subject to divine punishment for wrongfully rejecting the message of a Rasool of God, as per the laws of Rasools outlined in the Quran.

Moreover, Maulana Maududi, in his Tafheem ul Quran, has extensively commented on Surah Tawbah, detailing how Muhammad (PBUH) engaged with people in neighboring empires for years before sending letters to their kings. He provides detailed accounts of how Muhammad (PBUH) repeatedly sent delegations and how, in some instances, members of these delegations were murdered. Therefore, it wasn't the case that the kings were oblivious to Muhammad (PBUH) and his teachings—they were well aware of what was happening in Arabia. To understand in detail how rejecting Muhammad's (PBUH) letters subjected the kings and their armies to divine judgment, please watch the video titled, "Response to 23 Questions - Part 84 - Itmam e Hujjat - Javed Ahmed Ghamidi" on the YouTube channel of "Ghamidi Center of Islamic Learning."

In essence, all of Arabia and the surrounding areas to which Muhammad (PBUH) sent letters became the realm for God's worldly demonstration of judgment, to be carried out through the last Rasool of God.

The Quran 9:52 proclaims that divine judgment will be inflicted, either through natural disasters or by the swords of Muhammad's (PBUH) followers. As previously discussed while talking about Jesus (PBUH), if the elimination of an entire nation is not required, then divine punishment comes through the swords of people.

The Quran states that if divine punishment is to be inflicted through the swords of Muhammad's (PBUH) companions, then two types of divine punishment can be administered to his immediate addressees: the death penalty or, as suggested in the Quran (39:26 and 58:20), a life of subjugation and humiliation.

In Hadith literature, Muhammad (PBUH) explains in the context of Quran 9:29 that, for his immediate audience, God's punishment for rejecting and fighting a Rasool would be inflicted by the swords of his companions (Musnad Abd bin Humayd, No: 545).

Muhammad (PBUH) himself instructed his companions that, according to God's law with messengers, God would inflict His punishment not only in Arabia but also upon all neighboring kingdoms and empires to which he had communicated the divine message through letters (Sahih of Bukhari No: 2941).

Muhammad is clearly told in the Quran that some of this divine judgment will be imposed through him, and some of it will occur after his passing (Quran 13:40; 40:77; 10:46; 43:41-42).

All of the above is a detailed roadmap in the Quran of what was to happen to Muhammad (PBUH) and his immediate addressees. The 23 years that followed Muhammad's (PBUH) initial claim of Prophethood saw events unfold exactly as foretold by the Quran. Let us discuss these 23 years briefly. I will only mention the generally accepted parts of history, avoiding the details that are often debated and disputed among religious scholars and historians.

- Muhammad (PBUH) preached God's message for many years in and around Mecca. Some people accepted his message while others rejected it. Soon, the entire city of Medina accepted Muhammad's (PBUH) message, and he became the religious and political leader of Medina.
- Because not all people rejected God's Messenger, and many accepted him, with many more willing to consider God's message sincerely, God's punishment would not come through natural

disasters aimed at completely annihilating a society. Instead, it would come through the swords of the people. This time, those inflicting God's punishment would be the Messenger and his followers.

- Those who were not merely rejectors of God's Messenger but also chose to actively fight and persecute him were immediately punished by God through defeats in battles—the Battle of Badr, to be specific. According to the Holy Quran, the Battle of Badr was God's way of eliminating the chiefs of Mecca who chose to fight against God's Messenger. Almost all of the main leaders from Mecca who opposed Muhammad (PBUH) were killed at Badr (refer to Surah Anfal for further details).

- Those who simply rejected the teachings, without actively opposing God's Rasool, were given due time. According to the Quran's law regarding Rasools, every nation is allotted a period before a worldly judgment is declared upon them (Quran 15:4). Another reason for delaying judgment was that, as the God of the Quran proclaims, many individuals in Mecca and surrounding areas were inclined towards accepting God's message; hence, a temporary reprieve was granted (48:25).

- During the reprieve, all those who accepted God's message were instructed to identify themselves as Muslims and migrate to Medina before divine punishment was proclaimed. The command to migrate was emphasized to such an extent that, apart from the poor and the weak, those who refused to migrate without a justified reason were threatened with hell by God (Quran 4:97-98).

A Brief Clarification of a Hadith Related to Inheritance

It is important to mention a hadith that is perfectly explained when viewed from the perspective of God's judgment through His Rasool, Muhammad. The hadith reads:

A Muslim may not inherit from a disbeliever or a disbeliever from a Muslim (Sahih of Bukhari, No: 6764 and Sahih of Muslim, No: 1614).

If the aforementioned narration is considered a permanent directive, it results in a contradiction. Muslim men can marry Christian and Jewish women. Why, then, is marriage permissible but inheritance not?

It seems that Muhammad (PBUH) made the aforementioned statement during a period when Muslims were instructed by God to fully separate from and disassociate themselves from disbelievers before divine judgment was enacted upon them. This directive was a temporary measure specific to that particular situation and was not intended as a permanent policy.

Let's continue:-

Then finally, there came a time when God proclaimed that those who were rejecting God's message were doing so for unjustified reasons. Two kinds of punishment were proclaimed.

1) For all those who were polytheists, God proclaimed that the truth had been made completely clear to them through the Messenger of God, and they persisted in their actions for unjustified reasons. Associating partners and equals with God is considered the ultimate act of treason against Him. Consequently, these polytheists were sentenced to death by the God of the Quran, and Muslims were commanded to kill them unless they surrendered to God's authority (Quran 9:5).

2. Associating partners with God is the ultimate act of treason against Him, and therefore, God decreed the death penalty for polytheists unless they reformed their ways. However, among the rejecters of Muhammad (PBUH) were also Jews and Christians. These groups are referred to as "People of the Book" in the Quran—people to whom God provided scripture.

According to the Quran, Jews committed their own offenses against God, such as persecuting His messengers and altering His guidance, but they did not commit the ultimate betrayal of associating partners with God. Hence, the Quran describes them as those who have earned the displeasure of God (Quran 1:7). Christians, even though they believe in the trinity, still uphold the belief in one God and justify their belief in the trinity as a belief in a single God. Therefore, they are seen as having made a mistake rather than committing the ultimate treason of polytheism (Quran 1:7). Consequently, Jews and Christians were spared the death penalty and instead were subjected to a life of humiliation and subjugation under Muslims, as mandated in Quran 9:29 (refer to Surah Tawbah for more context).

Thus, the Quran fulfilled its promise that for those who reject God's final Messenger, punishment would come at the hands of Muhammad's (PBUH) companions, leading to either a humiliating life or a humiliating death for the rejectors.

Clarification on a Hadith Concerning Conflict with Non-Muslims

It is within this specific context—a Rasool serving as God's judgment on Earth for his immediate companions—that Muhammad (PBUH) declared on various occasions that he had been ordered to fight people until they accepted God's message. Consider the following Hadith as an example:

> I have been ordered to fight people until they accept that no one has the right to be worshipped except God and if they accept that ... then their life and property is sacred for us and we will not interfere with them..." (Sahih of Bukhari, No: 392 and 387).

The above Hadith should not be considered a directive for all

Muslims to follow at all times. According to Quran 2:256, there is expressly "no compulsion in matters of religion." Generally, those who reject God's message will be judged by God on the Day of Judgment if their rejection was due to sincere reasons, such as the message not making enough sense in the manner it was presented, or for wrongful reasons, such as ego or worldly gain. Muslims are instructed not to impose anything on non-Muslims regarding religious beliefs in this world. However, in the unique circumstance where a Rasool of God is present in the world, the aim of God is to demonstrate judgment worldly. Hence, He clarifies truth beyond all reasonable doubt through the power of argument, the impeccable personality of the Rasool, external geopolitical events, and miracles. After a pre-ordained period, God identifies those who reject His message for wrongful reasons and punishes them in this world.

Clarification about a Hadith Concerning the Killing of a Non-Believer

Another Hadith is perfectly explained when viewed from the perspective of the punishments ordained in Surah Tawbah.

Muhammad (PBUH) is reported to have judged in a case that a believer should not be killed for killing a disbeliever (Sahih of Bukhari, No: 6517).

If interpreted as a permanent policy, this hadith poses a problematic situation because it contradicts every injunction of justice the Quran has ordained—an unlawful murder is a crime, regardless of the religion of both the murderer and the victim. Then, why did Muhammad (PBUH) say this? When the Hadith is viewed through the lens of the Quran, it appears Muhammad (PBUH) may have made this statement around the time when the death penalty was announced for idolaters. Hence, from the perspective of the Quran, it seems that Muhammad (PBUH) was suggesting that if any Muslim killed one of the polytheists, then he shall not be given the ultimate punishment because the death penalty has already been issued against the polytheists as divine punishment for rejecting and persecuting a Rasool of God.

In other words, if the death penalty has already been issued against a certain person and someone else kills that person, then the killer will not receive the ultimate punishment for this killing.

Let's continue our discussion of how the Quran's claims about Muhammad (PBUH) as a Rasool of God came true.

- Just like Moses (PBUH) and the Israelites, Muhammad's (PBUH) companions were groomed by God into a nation, similar to Bani Israel before them, with a promise to practice and preach the religion of one God (Quran 2:143).
- Just as Canaan was purged of all other religions and given to Moses (PBUH) and the Israelites, the Arabian Peninsula was purged of all other religions and given to Muhammad's (PBUH) followers to exclusively practice and preach the religion of one God.

But the story continues.

In his role as a Rasool of God, Muhammad (PBUH) sent letters to kings. Were these kings, as recipients of correspondence from a living Rasool of God, not subject to God's punishment? Indeed, they were! These kings and their armies became subject to the Quran's law concerning Rasools.

Remember how Muhammad (PBUH) was told in the Quran that he might see some parts of the judgment while other parts might occur after his passing? That's exactly what transpired. Once God's judgment was complete in Arabia, Muhammad (PBUH) passed away. The kings who dismissed Muhammad's (PBUH) letters faced divine punishment. Within 15 years of Muhammad's passing, the consequences of rejecting a Rasool of God befell these rulers. These kingdoms miraculously fell into the hands of Muhammad's (PBUH) immediate companions. Hence, those who rejected the living Rasool of God were defeated not just in Arabia, but on a global scale and those who supported him were made rulers of almost half of the civilized world, just as promised in the Quran, 24:55.

This miraculous victory of the Arabs over global superpowers was not due to any military might or prowess they possessed; in fact, this victory was God's miracle and the worldly reward of "Authority on Earth" mentioned in Surah Nur Verse 55, destined for the supporters of God's Rasool as promised in the Quran. Indeed, the Arab Bedouins were militarily extremely inferior and inexperienced compared to their neighbors.

Professor of Islamic History, Carole Hillenbrand, writes:

> *Much ink has been spilt on the phenomenon of the Islamic conquest, but few firm conclusions can be drawn...It seems unlikely that the Arabs possessed military superiority over their opponents. Certainly, they had no secret weapon, no new techniques ... they were also unfamiliar with how to fight naval engagements.*[56]

The ease with which the superpowers of the time fell before primitive desert dwellers, who possessed no significant military expertise, was so miraculous that it continues to stun experts and historians even today.

Andrew Louth writes:

> *The speed with which the eastern provinces of the Byzantine empire succumbed to the Arabs remains to be explained by historians.*[57]

Historian Barnaby Rogerson writes:

You have to remember, that the two great superpowers were the Byzantine empire [Eastern Roman empire] and Sassanid Persia...they were the dominant powers. If you're putting it in a modern parlance, it's a bit like the Eskimos taking on the United States of America and Russia.[58]

You may compare Muhammad (PBUH) to figures like Osman Ghazi, who founded the Ottoman dynasty, or to Alexander the Great or Genghis Khan of Mongolia, arguing that they too claimed divine destiny to conquer the earth and professed to have dreams and visions of glory that came true. However, Muhammad's (PBUH) case is entirely distinct.

Muhammad (PBUH) didn't just mention a one-off dream; Muhammad's claim was that his God had laid down in detail the entire sequence of events that would unfold, with things unfolding exactly as he said, down to the minutest detail. The Quran states each and every detail beforehand on how divine judgment through the Rasool would unwind, and it occurred exactly as mentioned, not just on a regional scale in Arabia but on a global scale.

Moreover, unlike figures such as the Osman Ghazi or Genghis Khan, who proudly boasted about their political, military, and strategic prowess, Muhammad (PBUH) asserted that he did not make decisions or act on his own will. Instead, he was merely executing instructions received from a higher being—instructions that often contradicted and overruled many of Muhammad's (PBUH) own decisions.

Another important point is that, unlike Alexander, Ottoman, and Genghis Khan, Muhammad (PBUH) and his followers had virtually no military expertise. This is what makes their case so unique. Imagine a group of people with little to no military skill proclaiming that they are guided directly by God, who will enable them to conquer half of the earth—and then they actually do end up conquering half of the world. If I were to witness such an event, it would be both a moral and rational obligation for me to seriously investigate what these individuals claim about God.

Muhammad's (PBUH) companions understood that their miraculous victories were not the result of their own military or strategic prowess. Instead, they recognized these victories as manifestations of God's laws specific to the Rasools. Consider the Battle of Yarmouk, for instance. This confrontation was pivotal between the Byzantine Empire and the Muslims—defeat meant losing everything. According to some modern estimates, the Byzantine Army numbered a massive 150,000 men, while the Muslim army had only 40 to 45 thousand fighters. With so much at stake and with such limited resources and numbers, the Muslim ruler Omar (RA) made a significant change. He removed the star commander Khalid bin Waleed (RA), who had been on a long winning streak, and replaced him with Abu Ubaida (RA). This decision served to remind the Muslims that their victories were not the result of their own skills or numbers, but rather manifestations of God's law specific to the Rasools. God was punishing those who rejected the message of His Rasool and rewarding the companions of Muhammad (PBUH) for supporting His messenger.

Muslims will Eventually Undergo Moral Deterioration, Similar to that Experienced by the Israelites

God established a covenant with the Israelites, stipulating that they would sincerely practice and spread His religion throughout the world—a duty they fulfilled for many centuries. However, they eventually declined morally to such an extent that God ended His covenant with them during the time of Jesus PBUH. In particular, Arab Muslims, and all Muslims in general, have now been tasked by God to sincerely practice and disseminate His true message to the world. The Quran is given to them as a guide, a book to be shared globally as God's teachings. Nevertheless, like the Israelites, Muslims will also face moral deterioration, and once this occurs, there will be no more Rasools to raise nations in carrying out God's work, as Muhammad (PBUH) is the last Rasool. Hence, the judgment day will befall humankind. Muhammad (PBUH) predicted this eventual deterioration of Muslims. Take the following Hadith for example:

Muhammad (PBUH) is reported to have said:

> You would tread the exact same path as was trodden by those before you inch by inch and step by step so much so that if they had entered into the hole of a lizard, you would follow them in this also -- the companions of Muhammad (PBUH) asked: Oh God's Messenger, when you say 'those before us', do you mean Jews and Christians? He said: Who else! (Sahih of Muslim, No 6448).

Recap of the Quran's Scheme of Things Regarding Rasools

The summary of our discussion so far is as follows: According to the Quran, every human is innately aware of God and possesses inherent knowledge of right and wrong. Originally, God communicated directly with the first group of humans, revealing our origins and purpose. Initially, all humanity followed the correct path. However, as deviations occurred, God sent Nabis (Prophets) to steer humanity back to the truth. When these Prophets were predominantly rejected and humanity continued to deny the true God and Divine Judgment, by refusing to listen and disregard reason, Rasools (Messengers) were dispatched. These Messengers served as worldly demonstrations of Divine Judgment, affirming the existence of God and forewarning of the impending Judgment Day for all humankind.

A Rasool arrives in a society and spends years preaching God's message. The power of the arguments, the character of the Rasool, and miracles, combined with external events that support the Rasool's claims, all contribute to creating an environment where God makes the truth clear beyond all reasonable doubt for the Rasool's immediate audience. Then comes a time when God Himself proclaims worldly judgment on the immediate followers of the Rasool. At this point, those who accept the Rasool's message are saved and rewarded in this world, while punishment is proclaimed on the rejectors. If the elimination of the entire society is required, punishment comes through natural disasters, and if total elimination is not necessary, then punishment is delivered at the hands of people.

Individual Rasools were sent to various nations when humanity consisted of small settlements. As humanity transitioned into the age of nations and civilizations, these individual Rasools were succeeded by nations chosen to practice and preach God's message to the world. To facilitate this, Abraham's (PBUH) progeny was selected by God for the purpose of elevating these nations.

The first nation was raised through the descendants of Abraham's (PBUH) son, Isaac (PBUH). They inherited the land around Canaan, with a directive to dedicate it solely to God's religion and to entirely eliminate all other religions and their adherents. Under the leadership of Moses (PBUH), they received the law and were established as God's chosen nation with the mission to practice and spread God's true guidance across the world. They fulfilled this mission for an extended period until they began deviating from the truth. At this point, Jesus (PBUH), as the last Rasool to them, implored them to amend their ways and renew their covenant with God, warning that failure to do so would terminate their status as the chosen nation and lead to severe repercussions. Unfortunately, Jesus (PBUH) was rejected and persecuted by the Israelites, which, as a divine punishment, led to devastating consequences inflicted by the Romans.

Six hundred years after Jesus (PBUH), God raised another nation to uphold His message for the final time—this time from the descendants of Abraham's (PBUH) other son, Ishmael (PBUH). For this purpose, God chose Muhammad (PBUH) as His final Prophet and Messenger. In the entire context of the Quran's scheme of things regarding Rasools, our known history is a witness that, in the case of Muhammad (PBUH), things unfolded on a global scale exactly as claimed in the Quran. Additionally, all the Biblical stories about God's judgment on earth are through the likes of Noah, Lot, Abraham, Moses, and Jesus (peace be upon them all) make complete sense when viewed through the Quran's prism of God's law regarding Rasools. These narratives are not merely random instances of God unleashing His wrath on sinners; in fact, they are interconnected events in God's grand plan to raise nations that represent Him in the world and to provide the most significant worldly proof of Judgment Day, which will befall all of humankind in the hereafter.

The fulfillment of the Quran's claims regarding the Messengers of God is a compelling reason why it is crucial for everyone to earnestly explore the Quran as a serious contender for divine truth from God.

5A – Resolving Problematic Concepts through Quran's law of Rasools

Several problematic issues are resolved when Islam is viewed through the prism of God's law alongside the teachings of the Rasools. I have already discussed two issues that were resolved: the inheritance rights of non-Muslims and the punishment for a Muslim murdering a non-Muslim. Now, let us explore three more issues that are addressed when viewed through the prism of the Quran's laws in conjunction with the Rasools.

1 - Punishment for Apostasy

A vast majority of Muslims believe in divinely ordained punishment for those who leave Islam, often interpreted as death penalty. This belief is rooted in a Hadith where Muhammad (PBUH) is reported to have said:

Kill those who change their religion (Sunan of al-Nisa'i, No: 4059; 4061 and 4062).

This hadith appears to be reinforced by the Ridda Wars, in which Caliph Abu Bakr waged war on tribes that renounced Islam following the demise of Muhammad (PBUH).

The Hadith seems to contradict the Quran, which states in 2:256 that there must be no compulsion in matters of religion. Moreover, various verses in the Quran discuss the issue of leaving Islam (e.g., Quran 4:137; 2:217, and 3:86-90) and mention no worldly punishment for this act. Why, then, does an authentic Hadith from Muhammad (PBUH) seemingly order the killing of those who change their religion, and why did Abu Bakr wage war on those who renounced their faith after Muhammad (PBUH)?

When we mistakenly approach the Quran through the lens of the Hadith, and consider the Hadith an independent source of Islam rather than an explanation of the Quran, such contradictions emerge. How can the Quran unequivocally state that there must be no compulsion in matters of religion, yet some Hadiths suggest executing people for changing their religion?

This problem is instantly solved when we adopt the correct approach of understanding Hadith through the prism of the Quran, recognizing that Hadith is not an independent source of Islam but contains explanations of the religion given in the Quran and Sunnah. Let me explain.

There are three crimes for which the Quran authorizes the death penalty:

1) Murder
2) Crimes that wreak havoc on Earth by harming someone's life, property, or dignity include armed robbery, terrorist activities, kidnapping, and rape (Quran 5:32).

3) Rejection of a Rasool by an immediate addressee carries worldly punishment. The death penalty or the punishment of subjugation is authorized for the direct addressees of a Rasool if they reject or persecute him. (For reference, see earlier discussion on God's Law of Rasools and verse 33 of Surah 5 of the Quran (5:33)). The Hadith refers to people from among the immediate audience of Muhammad (PBUH) who are guilty of rejecting a Rasool's message after accepting it.

When viewed in the context of the crimes for which the Quran authorizes the death penalty, it is evident that there is no permanent punishment for anyone who chooses to leave Islam. The individuals Muhammad (PBUH) addressed were specifically those in his immediate audience, whom God had already decreed would face the death penalty if they rejected His last Rasool. In the case of the tribes against whom Abu Bakr waged war, they too belonged to the immediate audience of God's last Rasool. Their rejection of the Rasool after his death subjected them to divine punishment, in accordance with God's laws concerning His messengers. Thus, punishment on matters of faith is an act of God's worldly judgment, limited to scenarios where a Rasool of God is present among the people. This type of punishment was specific to the immediate addressees of the Rasool and does not pertain to later Muslims. According to the Quran, Muhammad (PBUH) is the last Messenger of God—there will be no other Rasools and, consequently, no further instances of God's worldly judgments. Therefore, no one after Muhammad (PBUH) and his companions has the authority to punish anyone on matters of faith. Consider this example:

Among Muhammad's (PBUH) immediate audience, divine judgment was proclaimed against polytheists and those who fought and persecuted God's Rasool; they were subjected to the death penalty unless they accepted God's message. This acceptance was their singular path to avoid God's punishment. Specifically, if any of these individuals renounced Islam afterward, the waiver would end, and they would once again be subject to the divine punishment originally ordained for them. Thus, this Hadith specifically addresses only those immediate addressees of Muhammad (PBUH) who were subject to God's worldly judgment through a Rasool. This Hadith does not apply to anyone else other than the immediate addressees of Muhammad (PBUH)—God's last Rasool.

2 - Fighting Non-Muslims for Their Faith

Another apparent contradiction is resolved when Islam is understood through the law of God, applicable only when a Rasool is among the people. The Quran proclaims complete freedom in matters of religion (Quran 2:256). Yet, on another occasion, the Quran instructs Muhammad (PBUH) to fight those polytheists who have breached their treaty with Muslims until they accept Islam. Additionally, the Quran directs Muhammad (PBUH) to battle Jews and Christians until they embrace Islam or agree to pay a tax as a sign of humiliation and subjugation (Quran 9:29).

Similarly, numerous Hadiths appear to contradict the concept found in Quranic verse 256 of Surah 2, which states that there must not be any compulsion in matters of religion. Consider the following Hadith, for example:

> I have been ordered to fight people until they declare that there is only one God and Muhammad is God's messenger and establish prayer and give the obligatory charity (Zakat)... (Sahih of al-Bukhārī, No: 25).

When viewed through the lens of God's law alongside the Rasools, it becomes clear that these commandments are not intended as an eternal policy for Muslims regarding non-Muslims. Instead, they are orders to inflict divine punishment solely on the immediate recipients of a Rasool of God's message.

The Quran states that whether it was the flood during Noah's (PBUH) time, the punishment of the nations of 'Ad, Thamud, Abraham (PBUH), and Lot (PBUH), or the Roman conquest of the Israelites during Jesus's (PBUH) era, or the battles fought by Muhammad (PBUH) and his companions against the people of Arabia and surrounding regions, such worldly punishment in matters of faith is specifically a consequence for rejecting a living Rasool of God. This punishment is limited to those who directly confronted a Rasool and cannot be extended to others. Consequently, for everyone outside the immediate audience of a Rasool, all matters of faith will be judged by God on the Day of Judgment. After Muhammad's (PBUH) departure, Muslims are only permitted to convey God's message to non-Muslims; they are not allowed to use force or fight them over matters of faith.

3 - Islam Will Prevail Over All Other Religions

The Quran proclaims that "God's religion (Islam) will prevail over all other religions" (Quran 9:33). When seen out of context, this statement might appear to be a global prophecy, which many militant organizations idealize to fulfill. However, when viewed through the prism of God's law and His messengers, it becomes clear that this prophecy was specific to Muhammad's (PBUH) addressees. A messenger's addressees are judged in this world—the opponents are completely defeated, only God's messenger, his followers, and God's message prevail over all the opposing forces and beliefs. Therefore, this prophecy of Islam prevailing over all other ideologies was specific to Muhammad's (PBUH) addressees and was fulfilled exactly as prophesized.

The complete context of verse 9:33 makes it clear that God is addressing the immediate followers of Muhammad (PBUH) rather than issuing a global prophecy for all future times. The verse explicitly states that God has sent His Messenger with the religion of truth and has fulfilled His promise to make this Messenger and the religion of truth prevail over all other ideologies of the polytheists of Mecca and Arabia, who were Muhammad's (PBUH) primary opponents. Below, I will share the complete verses with their context.

> *They wish to extinguish God's light with their mouths – but God will ensure that His light is perfected, no matter how much the disbelievers dislike it. Indeed, it is God who has sent his Messenger with guidance and religion of truth – making it prevail over all other religions even though the polytheists are dismayed by it. (Quran 9:32–33).*

Similarly, another verse, Quran 48:28, is often cited as predicting that Islam will prevail over all other religions and that the entire world will either become Muslim or live under Muslim subjugation in the end times. However, when this verse is read in context, particularly from verses 20 to 30, it becomes evident that it specifically addresses the Meccans, informing them that they will be defeated and that Islam will prevail over them.

I presented the aforementioned information to emphasize that the sayings and actions of Muhammad (PBUH) and his companions are more comprehensible when viewed through the lens of God's law regarding Rasools as explained in the Quran.

5B - Muhammad's Personality & Predictions about Him - Two Additional Factors Add Credence to His Message

The Quran's scheme of Rasools, particularly how things transpired with Muhammad (PBUH) as a Rasool, provided compelling reasons for me to consider Islam seriously as a contender for divine truth. However, two additional aspects, in my opinion, lend further credence to Muhammad's (PBUH) message:

1) The personality of Muhammad (PBUH)
2) The prophecies about Muhammad (PBUH) in earlier scriptures

Let me explain each briefly.

1) Personality of Muhammad (PBUH)

A Honest and Truthful Man

Before Muhammad (PBUH) declared himself a Prophet of God, he gathered the people and asked if they would believe him if he said an army was coming from behind a mountain to attack them. The people responded affirmatively, stating that they had always found him to be an honest and truthful man (Sahih of al-Bukhari, No: 4770, 4972).

No Evolution of Thought

Every eminent scholar in military, political, economic, or social fields exhibits a clear evolution of ideas and thoughts throughout their life. This evolution, however, is notably absent in the case of Muhammad (PBUH). It appears to be a sudden phenomenon at the age of 40 when Muhammad (PBUH) declared that he was contacted by God. Following this, he began to recite the Quranic texts, marked by their poetic and linguistic brilliance, encompassing deep religious, political, and social discussions and proclamations, along with astute, flawless military decisions and strategies. This absence of evolution is mirrored in the Quran; there is no alteration in the fundamentals of its message or its arguments from the first day to the end, despite the rapidly changing external environment over the 23 years of its revelation. Let me elaborate further.

There is always an evolution of thought or talent in an individual. Shakespeare didn't become the renowned playwright we know from the first day. Similarly, Gandhi's ideology evolved over time. Muhammad (PBUH) presents a unique case in our known history because there was no apparent evolution of religious, political, or social thought in his life. He also never displayed any significant interest or ability in poetry. His life, until the age of 40, showed no signs of these influences, yet the Quran, with its rich content spanning religious, social, political, legal, and poetic themes, appears as an unexpected phenomenon in his life. This fact strongly supports the hypothesis that Muhammad was not the author of the Quran.

No Interest and Background in Seeking or Preaching Religious Knowledge

When the Quran provides information about Muhammad's (PBUH) personality, it can be trusted as accurate. The Quran was recited to an audience who knew Muhammad (PBUH) very well. Had the Quran presented any false information about Muhammad (PBUH), it would have been contested by those immediate listeners. The Quran informs us that Muhammad (PBUH) had no prior interest or background in seeking or preaching religious knowledge. Verse 86 of Surah 28 in the Quran states that Muhammad (PBUH) was not expecting any revelation, nor was there any effort on his part to seek religious enlightenment or divine knowledge.

In this context, it is crucial to address a popular story that portrays Muhammad (PBUH) as a seeker of divine knowledge. This tale tells of Muhammad (PBUH) periodically retreating to the Cave of Hira to engage in mystical meditations. I will delve deeper into this later, but it is important to clarify initially that Muhammad (PBUH) did not visit the Cave of Hira to seek religious enlightenment or to perform mystical exercises. The well-known story of Muhammad's (PBUH) enigmatic meditation in Hira is based on a Hadith with a single chain of narrators. Moreover, this Hadith is not a direct quote from Muhammad (PBUH) himself. Ibn Ishaq, one of the earliest biographers of Muhammad (PBUH), includes only a small portion of this narration and disregards the rest. Regarding the first revelation, Ibn Ishaq presents another narration that contradicts the widespread story of Muhammad (PBUH) engaging in mysterious mystical meditations in the Cave of Hira. Instead, he offers the following version of events:

Many in Arabia followed a primitive version of the Abrahamic religion called "Deen-e-Hanif," which Muhammad (PBUH) also adhered to. Practices such as fasting during Ramadan and engaging in "Aitekaaf," which involves fasting and worshiping in seclusion, were common traditions in this religion. During this period, Muhammad (PBUH) left the idol-worshiping city of Mecca to retreat into the mountains with his family for Aitekaaf. Many others followed this practice with their families as well. Thus, Muhammad (PBUH) was not engaging in mysterious meditations in search of divine truth and enlightenment; rather, he was observing a typical ritual of the Deen-e-Hanif, like many others. In his 40th year, while engaged in this ritual worship, the angel Gabriel appeared to him for the first time. I will discuss this incident in detail later, but for now, I want to clarify that Muhammad (PBUH) participated in the standard ritual worship activities of the monotheistic religious tradition prevalent among his people without actively seeking religious knowledge or enlightenment through mysterious meditations in caves.

Furthermore, according to verse 16 of chapter 10 of the Quran, Muhammad (PBUH) informs his immediate addressees that he has lived his entire life among them before receiving the revelation; he never discussed the matters that the Quran addresses. Therefore, it was common knowledge among Muhammad's (PBUH) immediate audience that he had no background in religious preaching or in seeking religious knowledge before he proclaimed to have received a divine revelation..

No Interest or Background in Poetry

The Quran (36:69) informs us that Muhammad (PBUH) had absolutely no interest in poetry and was never known for listening to or reciting poetry. However, the Quran itself is one of the finest poetic masterpieces of the Arabic language.

The poetic style of the Quran is so powerful that it influenced one of Arabia's greatest poets, Abu Aqil Labid ibn Rabiah ibn Malik al Amiri, to convert to Islam. Labid's poem was among the "Mu'allaqat," the seven greatest poems of the Arabic language, which were displayed outside the Kaaba in a sort of poetic Hall of Fame. He was particularly impressed by the style of Surah Al-Kawthar, which ultimately led him to embrace Islam.[60]

The poetic magnificence of the Quran is a well-established fact. Its structure is so poetically refined that it stands unique as a voluminous book which can be easily memorized by children as young as seven years old, or even younger. This ease of memorization extends even to those who do not understand Arabic. Every year, thousands of children in Muslim countries successfully memorize the Quran by heart within a year.

So, in light of what we discussed, Muhammad (PBUH) was generally known to be a truthful man. He had absolutely no background in seeking or preaching religious knowledge, yet the Quran engages in profound religious discussions. Additionally, there is no evolution of thought in the ideas discussed in the Quran, and there is complete consistency of thought and ideas throughout its 23 years of revelation. Moreover, Muhammad (PBUH) had no interest or background in poetry, yet the Quran remains one of the most remarkable literary works in the Arabic language. All these factors add more substance to the possibility that the Quran is not the product of Muhammad's (PBUH) own mind.

Did Muhammad Persuade Others to Come up with the Quran for Him?

One might argue that perhaps Muhammad (PBUH) commissioned someone else to write the Quran; however, this is highly unlikely. For Muhammad (PBUH) to have others write the Quran, he would have needed two teams: one consisting of world-class experts in religious knowledge, particularly in Abrahamic faiths, and another made up of supremely skilled poetry experts. Considering the consistency of the ideas in the Quran and the poetic language used throughout, he would have required the services of these teams from the very beginning, enduring throughout the 23 years of the Quran's revelation. Notably, there is no historical evidence to suggest that Muhammad (PBUH) had access to such teams. In fact, during the initial years, he was primarily a solitary preacher with only a few followers, and his early group of companions were not recognized as experts in these fields.

2) Predictions about Muhammad (PBUH) in Earlier Scriptures

Prophecies about Muhammad (PBUH) in the Bible

The Quran does not present Muhammad (PBUH) as an isolated figure; instead, he is depicted within a continuum of earlier divinely inspired prophets and messengers. What makes Muhammad's (PBUH) case particularly interesting is that there are prophecies in the Bible—both in the Old and New Testaments—which, when considered together, appear to align remarkably with Muhammad's personality and mission. Let us briefly explore some of these.

Old Testament - Book of Deuteronomy 18:18

God tells Moses (PBUH) and his people:

I (God) will raise up a Prophet like you (Moses) from among their brothers (from among the brother of Israelites) and I shall put my words into his mouth and that Prophet shall tell them all that I command. Anyone who will not listen to the words which the Prophet speaks in my name, I myself will hold accountable for it.

So, God informed the Israelites that a Prophet would arise not from among them but from their brethren, a tribe closely related to them. This Prophet, in the exact likeness of Moses (PBUH), would deliver God's message to his immediate audience. Those who rejected him would face God's judgment here on earth. As we have previously discussed in detail while exploring the laws in the Quran regarding Rasools, Muhammad (PBUH) hailed from the brethren of the Israelites, specifically from the descendants of Ishmael. The Quran affirms that he is a Prophet in the likeness of Moses (PBUH), delivering God's message to his contemporaries. Those who rejected him faced divine judgment here on earth, as per God's law regarding Rasools..

One could argue that the aforementioned verse predicts the coming of Jesus (PBUH). However, this interpretation is not viable, as Jesus (PBUH) was from the nation of the Israelites, whereas the prophecy suggests that the foretold individual would belong to a tribe or people who are the brethren of the Israelites. Moreover, the person prophesied will be a prophet similar to Moses—meaning that everything that transpired for Moses and his nation will occur for him as well. He will introduce new divine laws, lead an army, gain earthly authority, and have his nation appointed as custodians of God's religion to fully practice and preach God's message to the world. None of these events transpired in the case of Jesus. Furthermore, when we examine the New Testament, it appears that Jesus himself predicts the arrival of someone after him who closely aligns with the figure described in Deuteronomy 18:18.

New Testament - The Book of John

In 1 John 2:1, Jesus (PBUH) is referred to as a "Paraclete" or a "Comforter." In the subsequent verses, Jesus (PBUH) predicts the coming of another "Comforter" apart from himself and says:

And I will pray to the Father, and he shall send you another Comforter...(John 14:16).

Jesus further explains:

Indeed, I tell you the truth—it is important for you that I go away, for if I do not go away, the Paraclete (Comforter/ Counselor) will not come... (John 16:7-8).

I have much more to say to you, more than you can now bear. But when he, the Spirit of truth, comes, it is he who will guide you into all the truth. He will not speak on his own; he will speak only what he hears, and he will tell you what is yet to come (John 16:7-13).

Other prophets in the Bible are referred to as "Spirit" (1 John 4:1-3). Since Jesus (PBUH) was a human being, and other human beings were referred to as Spirit, it is entirely reasonable to believe that the term "Spirit" in the aforementioned verses refers to a human being.

When considered together, both Moses (PBUH) and Jesus (PBUH) appear to predict the arrival of an individual from a people related to the brothers of the Israelites. This individual will speak the literal words of God and be a prophet akin to Moses (PBUH). This description aligns closely with Muhammad (PBUH). As a descendant of Ishmael, Muhammad (PBUH) and his people are considered brethren of the Israelites. He spoke God's words, preserved in the Quran, and served as a prophet in the likeness of Moses (PBUH). Like Moses, he introduced a new divine law. Through Muhammad (PBUH), God raised a nation to practice and preach His message to the world, granting them significant authority on earth, much like Moses and his people.

3 - Muhammad's Prediction in Hindu Scriptures

The Quran states that prophets of God were sent to all nations before prophethood was exclusive to the descendants of Abraham (PBUH).

Hindus assert that their religious texts are over 5000 years old, a time-line some scholars associate with the probable era of Abraham (PBUH). It is therefore plausible that, before prophethood was limited to the progeny of Abraham, God inspired prophets in the Indian subcontinent. As previously discussed, Hinduism incorporates the concept of Rishis or Sages, divinely inspired holy men who imparted divine knowledge to people. From a Quranic perspective, it is conceivable that the Vedas and other Hindu scriptures were originally divine revelations, retaining fragments of divine truth despite thousands of years of interpretations and reinterpretations.

Within these scriptures, there is a passage where I believe a divinely inspired Prophet of God predicted the coming of Muhammad (PBUH). Over the course of hundreds or even thousands of years, these predictions may have evolved into the concept that God Vishnu will incarnate as a human and confront evil in the final age. Let's explore these predictions. While I believe they foretell the coming of Muhammad (PBUH), you are free to form your own opinion.

At this point, I want to acknowledge the information I got from the public speeches of Dr. Zakir Naik on this particular subject. Although I may disagree with some of Dr. Naik's ideas and interpretations, his commendable work in highlighting predictions about Muhammad (PBUH) in non-Abrahamic scriptures has greatly assisted me in my research.

For references pertaining to all points discussed below, please see the following:

- Bhagwata Purana - Khand 12, Adhyay 2, Shloka 18-20: Kalki will be born among the chiefs of the city of Shambhala in the house of VishnuYas - Kalki will ride a horse with a sword in his hand - he will defeat the enemies and be helped by angels.
- Kalki Purana Chapter 2 Verse 15 - Kalki will be born on 12th of Madhav month to VishnuYas and Sumati.

- Kalki Purana Chapter 2, Verses 4, 5 and 7: Kalki will be born among chiefs of Shambhala to VishnuYas and Sumati - He will take on evil forces with the help of 4 companions and angels will assist him on battlefield.
- Kalki Purana Chapter 3 Verse 1 - Kalki will receive knowledge on a mountain - will migrate to north and come back.

There is a person called Kalki Avatar in Hindu tradition who is known as the last of a series of avatars and will come in the last age of mankind to take on evil. I will mention the prophecies and draw parallels with Muhammad (PBUH) and let you draw your own conclusions.

1) Kalki Avatar will be born to a man named Vishnuyash and a woman named Sumati.

"Vishnuyasha" is a Sanskrit term that can be translated to mean: "Vishnu" means God, and one of the meanings of "Yash" is "glory," "honor," and it also means "to strive for." Thus, "Vishnuyash" refers to someone who strives for or honors God Vishnu, or perhaps represents the glory of God Vishnu. Muhammad (PBUH) was born to Abdullah, and the name "Abdullah" signifies someone who worships God.

"Sumati" is a Sanskrit term which can mean devotion or benevolence. Muhammad's (PBUH) mother's name was Amina, which means devoted, faithful, and the one who is safe.

(Vishnuyasha, and Sumati, translated from Learnsanskrit.cc)

2) He will be born in a village called Shambhala.

Shambhala, according to the New World Encyclopedia, is a Sanskrit term meaning "a place of peace."[61]

Muhammad (PBUH) was born in Mecca, which the Quran refers to as "the city of peace" in Chapter 95, Verse 3. Even before the advent of Islam, Mecca was known as a city of peace because various Arab tribes annually visited this city for their religious pilgrimage. No violence was permitted within Mecca.

3) *Kalki will originate from the clan of the city's chiefs and will be born in the house of Shambhala's chief*

Muhammad (PBUH) belonged to the Quraish tribe, the chief tribe of Mecca. He was born in the house of Abdul Muttalib, the chief of Mecca and the Quraish tribe, in the presence of his son Abu Talib, Muhammad's (PBUH) uncle.

4) *Kalki will be born on 12th of the month of Madav to Vishnuyas and Sumati.*

Muhammad is said to have been born on 12th Rabiul Awwal.

5) *He will ride a horse and will carry a sword. He will bring people from darkness into light, ushering in the age of truth (Satya Yuga). He will have four friends who will help him. Angels will assist him on the battlefield.*

Muhammad (PBUH) rode a horse with a sword and brought people from the darkness of ignorance into the light of Divine guidance. He was succeeded by what Muslims call "The 4 Rightly Guided Caliphs or Successors," who were Muhammad's (PBUH) very close companions, namely Abu Bakr, Umar, Uthman, and Ali [may God be pleased with them all]. The Quran proclaims on multiple occasions, such as in Quran 3:125, that angels were sent to help Muhammad (PBUH) and his followers on the battlefield.

6) *Kalki will gain wisdom on a mountain, then migrate northward before returning.*

Muhammad (PBUH) received his first revelation in the Cave of Hira on a mountain. He migrated north to Medina from his hometown of Mecca, returning triumphantly less than a decade later.

7) Kalki Avatar means The Final Avatar or the Antim Rishi.

Muhammad (PBUH) is referred to as the final Prophet of God—the last Messenger of God (Quran 33:40; Jami' al-Tirmidhi, No. 2272).

To summarize our discussion, there are specific prophecies in other scriptures, aside from the Quran, that appear to predict the arrival of Muhammad (PBUH). Considering these prophecies along with what we've discussed, I have become deeply interested in what the God of the Quran has to say about existence and my purpose within it. At this point in my journey, I wanted to evaluate whether the Quran offers moral, ethical, and rational coherence and whether it provides satisfactory answers to my existential questions. If it does, combined with the evidence we've reviewed, the Quran would become a strong contender for divine truth in my view.

CHAPTER 6

WHAT DOES THE GOD OF THE QURAN WANT FROM ME AND DOES IT MAKE SENSE?

My life was going splendidly well: I had fame and wealth, and I was busy diving into all the diverse endeavors the world had to offer. In the face of the more urgent indulgences of life, things like religion and God often seemed boring and secondary in importance. However, this thought would profoundly unsettle me: when death approaches, the most crucial aspect will be whether I found a reasonable answer to the question of God and the afterlife, and whether I lived my life according to the demands of those answers.

In the back of my mind, I couldn't let go of the thoughts about Muhammad (PBUH) and the miracle of his mission as a Rasool of God. I could not remain undecided because imagine if Muhammad (PBUH) was right and he truly was contacted by God, THE GOD—the uncreated fundamental reality that created everything else - the same God who contacted Jesus, Moses, Abraham (PBUT), and countless others!

What if there truly is divine accountability after death, resulting in a permanent good or bad outcome for me? Imagine if all of this is true and how terrifying it would be if I lived negligent of this truth. Imagine the sense of utmost horror I would feel when death comes!

I needed to make up my mind conclusively about this matter. It was essential to explore Muhammad's (PBUH) message in detail and assess whether it made sufficient rational and moral sense for me to determine whether his message is from God or not.

The miracle of Muhammad's (PBUH) mission as a Messenger of God compelled me to explore his message in detail. On my journey to thoroughly investigate Muhammad's (PBUH) message, the next logical step was to analyze what the God of the Quran expects from me and why - and more importantly, what I need to do to succeed in divine accountability. I wanted to determine if these demands were morally, ethically, and rationally sensible. If they were not, then perhaps Muhammad's (PBUH) mission was an extraordinary anomaly in our known history with no divine connection. However, if the content of Muhammad's (PBUH) message is morally, ethically, and rationally sound, then, coupled with the miraculous nature of his mission as a Messenger of God, I would run out of reasons to reject Islam. Consequently, I would find myself in a position to genuinely acknowledge Muhammad (PBUH) as indeed contacted by God, affirming the truth of Prophets, Messengers, Angels, Scriptures, and Divine Accountability.

I needed to investigate further and see what the God of the Quran expects of me and whether it makes sufficient sense.

What I am about to share with you is not a product of any scholarly venture into the scriptures. No! It is the result of a simple yet focused exercise—a one-time reading of the Quran, with relevant material from Hadith literature readily accessible online.

Let us also revisit our discussion about the sources of Islam and how to analyze them.

- The Quran is the preserved record of divine communication to Muhammad (PBUH), revealed over a period of 23 years. This revelation marked the event of God unleashing His final earthly demonstration of Divine Judgment.
- The Sunnah represents the actions within Islam.

These two are the primary sources of Islam, which were transmitted from Muhammad (PBUH) to an entire generation of his immediate followers, numbering more than a hundred thousand. These followers, in turn, passed them down en masse to their descendants, continuing all the way to the present.

- Hadiths—historical information about Muhammad (PBUH)—and historical accounts of the companions of Muhammad (PBUH) must be understood in the context of the Quran and Sunnah, as they provide explanations and applications of the religion contained therein. Hadiths are individual reports about the words and actions of Muhammad (PBUH), which were recorded decades after his passing.

Also, at this point, I would like to express my gratitude once more to Mr. Javed Ahmed Ghamidi. From him, I have learned a great deal not only about the Rasools of God and the sources of Islam but also about the principles governing divine accountability on Judgment Day, which I will discuss in detail now.

Let us move forward.

We shall now discuss two topics:

Firstly, we shall discuss the criterion for success in divine accountability as explained in the Quran, which is truly universal and transcends all religious identities.

Secondly, we shall discuss the specific actions Islam encourages us to take to achieve maximum success in divine accountability.

The Criterion for Success in Divine Accountability as Explained in the Quran is Truly Universal and Transcends All Religious Identities

As a young teenager, I was told that the criterion for divine accountability was simple: Muslims go to heaven and non-Muslims go to hell, regardless of their moral conduct. Contrary to this, the Quran transcends earthly religious divisions and establishes a truly universal criterion for salvation on Judgment Day, applicable to all of humanity, regardless of their religious identities. Let me briefly explain this criterion. However, before we delve into this universal criterion, we need to familiarize ourselves with some fundamental Quranic concepts.

There is one central theme in the Quran that is reiterated on nearly every other page: We are all created by God, and after we die, God will resurrect us and hold each person accountable for the life they led in this world, resulting in a permanent good or bad outcome. The purpose of humans is to save themselves from the bad outcome by leading a righteous life and qualifying for Paradise—a perfect and eternal place of absolute peace, happiness, pleasure, and contentment. This is the main message of the Quran.

It is a prevalent idea among Muslims that only those who identify themselves as Muslims will go to Paradise, and they often cite Quran 3:85 as the main verse supporting this belief. The verse states:

> *Whoever seeks and desires for a way other than Islam—it*
> *shall never be accepted from them on the Day of Judgment*
> *(Quran 3:85).*

This posed a dilemma for me: if this verse truly implies that only those who identify themselves as Muslims can enter Heaven, what about morally upright non-Muslims who lead righteous lives and sincerely adhere to the teachings of their respective religions that they genuinely believe to be true and divine? Many individuals lack the time to explore different religions, as they are engaged in time-consuming, intensive work just to meet their families' basic needs. Will they be condemned to hell simply because they did not identify as Muslims? Additionally, a person born into a Muslim family is more likely to die a Muslim compared to someone born outside of this faith. This suggests that a person's divine salvation is heavily influenced by their birthplace. It appears unfair because if God determines that a person is born into a non-Muslim family, that individual is from the outset placed at a significant disadvantage in comparison to someone born into a Muslim family, particularly concerning the qualifications for entering Paradise.

When I investigated in detail, I found that Quran 3:85, when studied in context, does not, in fact, state that only those who identify as Muslims will go to Paradise. I shall explain this matter in more detail later in this section. The Quran as a whole negates the idea that only those who identify as Muslims will go to Paradise. Instead, the Quran establishes a universal criterion for entering Paradise, and whoever fulfills that criterion will go to Paradise, regardless of their religious identity. To understand the criterion for eternal salvation, we must comprehend two very important concepts explained in the Quran.

In my early teen years, I was taught that according to various religions, humans lacked the concept of God and morality, and it was religious scriptures that introduced these concepts to humankind. Contrary to this idea, the Quran asserts that a basic awareness of God and a fundamental sense of right and wrong are inherent in human nature. This innate knowledge of God and morality forms the basis on which we will all be held accountable, regardless of the religion or culture into which we were born.

Awareness of God Is Within Us

The Holy Quran asserts that all humans possess an innate under-standing of their creation by a higher power. Specifically, Quran 7:172 proclaims that all humans inherently know about God. The Quran describes a testimony that all souls affirmed regarding their creator before entering this world. This innate awareness of being created by a mighty power predisposes us to believe in God.

This makes sense because, as we discussed before, almost all human cultures, with very rare exceptions, have believed in God or gods.

Moreover, numerous studies imply that human beings possess a strong tendency toward belief in a powerful entity. Among many stud-ies supporting this hypothesis, I wish to highlight one of the latest, involving 57 researchers who conducted over 40 separate studies across 20 countries, representing diverse cultures. This research concluded that humans seem predisposed to believe in God or gods and an afterlife. One finding of the study is that children under five years old are par-ticularly inclined to believe in an all-knowing supreme being.

Project Co-Director Professor Roger Trigg, from the University of Oxford's Ian Ramsey Centre, says:

> This project suggests that religion is not just something for a peculiar few to do on Sundays instead of playing golf. We have gathered a body of evidence that suggests that religion is a common fact of human nature across different societies. This suggests that attempts to suppress religion are likely to be short-lived as human thought seems to be rooted to religious concepts, such as the existence of supernatural agents or gods, and the possibility of an afterlife or pre-life.[62]

So, even if many of us become agnostic or atheist later in life after exposure to different ideologies and influences from our environment and experiences, it appears that in our early years, we are naturally predisposed to believe in a higher power. It seems as though we are born with an innate sense of God, just as the Quran proclaims. Even in today's world, where atheism is gaining ground, most people continue to believe in some form of God, gods, or a higher power. This demonstrates that something within our nature inclines us toward such beliefs.

Awareness of Right and Wrong Is Within Us

The Quran states that apart from an innate sense of being created by a higher power, human beings are also instilled with a sense of right and wrong (Quran 91:8). This single verse answered an age-old question for me: Why do morally good people exist who don't believe in any religion or scripture?

The Quran once again appears to offer a perspective that resonates. All rational humans possess a sense of right and wrong, along with a general understanding of what is considered good and bad. For instance, throughout history, humans have recognized that injustice and oppression are detrimental, whereas truthfulness and honesty are virtuous. Historically, even when individuals have engaged in oppressive acts, they have attempted to justify their actions by appealing to a perceived greater good. For example, many conquerors have rationalized their brutal military campaigns with the noble aim of achieving global peace. Similarly, various cultures have engaged in the appalling practice of human sacrifice, justifying it with the noble intent of appeasing their gods to ensure a prosperous harvest for their tribe. While our definitions of right and wrong may vary across cultures and evolve over time, and there have been instances where brain damage has altered an individual's moral perception, the core fact remains: we all retain an inherent mechanism that discerns right from wrong, generally understanding what is good and bad.

Even most criminals and psychopaths usually retain an intact sense of right and wrong. They understand that injustice, oppression, and unlawfully harming someone's life, dignity, or property are wrong. They grasp this understanding because, although they may commit crimes against others, they themselves would not wish to endure such harm. This universal criterion for distinguishing right from wrong is so clear within us that each one of us would readily identify wrongful actions if they were done to ourselves. The Bible lays out this criterion very clearly in a verse where Jesus (PBUH) reportedly warned about the universal mechanism through which justice will be administered on Judgment Day.

> With whatever judgment you judge, you will be judged; and with whatever measure you measure, it will be measured to you (Matthew 7:2).

Before we discuss the verse about the universal criteria of judgment, we must analyze five very important principles that govern divine accountability on Judgment Day.

Some Principles That Govern Divine Accountability

1 - Tests Are Not Equal for Everyone

For a long time, I harbored an unanswered question: If there is a God who will hold humanity accountable, will an educated and wealthy individual with ample leisure be judged in the same manner as a poor laborer who spends nearly all his time earning a living, with scarcely any time to ponder existential questions? Similarly, how does the judgment compare between someone raised in a morally sound environment and another brought up in deprived circumstances? According to the Quran 6:165, people are not judged equally. Each person will face judgment based on what they have been granted in their worldly life, implying that the evaluation will consider their abilities, intellect, and circumstances.

2 - Perfect Justice Will Be Executed, and No One Will Be Wronged, Even in the Slightest

Another very important principle explained in the Quran is that on the Day of Judgment, no one will be wronged, even in the least bit (Quran 21:47). Such perfect justice will be executed that everyone, including those condemned for punishment, will acknowledge its perfection (Quran 39:75 - see Mustafa Khattab's note on the verse in his translation).

3 - You Will Only Get What You Want and Make an Effort For It

The Quran makes it clear that:

> *Each person (on the Judgment Day) will only have what they themselves strived for. Their effort will be fully analyzed and they shall be recompensed accordingly (Quran 53:39–41).*

The Quranic verses 17:18-19 also emphasize that those who prioritize worldly life over the afterlife will receive their reward in full in this world based on their capabilities and efforts. However, they will have no share in the afterlife. In contrast, those who seek success in the afterlife will receive their destined sustenance in this world, but their full reward will be granted in the afterlife. Essentially, the Quran teaches that while it is acceptable for those seeking God's blessings in the afterlife to strive for a better life in this world, it should not come at the expense of the hereafter.

Essentially, the God of the Quran is saying that each person will receive exactly what they have striven for. It makes sense.

4 - Small Sins Will Be Forgiven

Another very important principle of accountability is that if a person avoids major crimes and sins, the smaller sins will be forgiven. This is stated in the Quran 4:31:

If you avoid the major sins out of what you have been for-
bidden from – then I (God) will surely forgive your small sins
and admit you into a place of honor (Paradise).

5 - The Crucial Importance of Acting Upon What a Person Sincerely Believes to be the Truth - Even If It is a Mistaken Belief

The God of the Quran desires that people sincerely act upon what they genuinely believe to be the truth, even if they are mistaken in their beliefs. Sincerity in both belief and action is of utmost importance to God.

This principle is made clear in Quran 2:187. Let me briefly explain. In this verse, the Quran comments on a few companions of the Prophet (PBUH) who mistakenly believed that God had prohibited intercourse between spouses for the entire month of Ramadan, even during the night after breaking the fast. Despite this belief, these companions still chose to have intercourse with their spouses at night after breaking their fasts. The Quran clarifies that these companions were mistaken in holding such a belief and that a husband and wife are allowed to have intercourse during the nights of Ramadan after breaking their fasts. However, God also tells those companions who harbored the flawed belief that they were committing a wrongful deed by having intercourse with their wives, despite their sincere, yet mistaken belief that God had forbidden it. The principle is that if you genuinely believe God has prohibited something, then you shouldn't do it, even if you are mistaken in that belief. Here is the literal translation of the verse:

It is lawful for you to have sexual relations with your wives
during the night of the fast. They are your garment, and you
are theirs. God knows that you used to betray yourselves and
He mercifully relented and pardoned you. You can intimately
associate with your wives and benefit from the enjoyment
God had made lawful for you and eat and drink at night
until you can distinguish the white streak of dawn against

the blackness of the night; then (give up all that and) complete your fasting until night sets in. But do not associate intimately with your wives during the period when you are on retreat in the mosques (I'tikaf). These are the bounds set by God; do not, then, even draw near them. This is how God makes His signs clear to humankind so that they may stay away from sin (Quran 2:187).

Maulana Maududi commen⁵ on this verse in his Tafseer Tafheem-ul-Quran:

Although there was no categorical ordinance in the early days prohibiting sexual intercourse between husband and wife during the nights of Ramadan, people generally assumed that this was not permissible. Despite the feeling that their action was either not permitted or was at least disapproved of, they did at times approach their wives. Such a betrayal of conscience can encourage a sinful disposition. God, therefore, first reproaches them for their lack of integrity, for this is what was objectionable. As for the act itself, God makes it clear that it is quite permissible. Henceforth they might engage in sexual intercourse as a perfectly lawful act unencumbered by feelings of guilt.

The above-mentioned instance clearly shows that the Quran encourages people to act upon what they sincerely believe to be divine truth, even if they are mistaken in their beliefs. However, it is important to remember that the Quran also expects individuals to always be open and attentive to discussions about God and religion that appear to be logical, and to judge these matters on their merits, setting aside all biases when examining information about God and religion. We must also keep in mind that on the Day of Judgment, genuine and sincere mistakes will be forgiven, but deliberate negligence and the failure to accept the truth for wrongful reasons will not be tolerated.

Universal Criterion for Divine Accountability

Now that we have discussed some precursor ideas, let's turn to the verse where the Quran explains the three main principles of divine accountability that will be enacted on the Day of Judgment. Quran 2:62 states:

> *Whether you are a Believer (in Muhammad (PBUH)) or a Jew or a Christian or a Sabian – anyone who believes in God, believes in the Day of Judgment and lives a righteous life with good deeds will find their reward secure with God and they shall have nothing to fear on that day (Day of Judgment).*

According to this verse, all humans must respond to the guidance instilled within them and do the following, regardless of whichever religion they are born into or identify with:

1) All human beings must respond to their inner awareness of God and strive to live in acknowledgment of being created by a higher power.
2) All humans must seriously ponder the prospects of being accountable to a higher power. Essentially, God and divine accountability must become significant concerns for everyone. Sincere efforts must be made to live with a constant awareness of God and the prospects of divine accountability.
3) Humans must use their sense of right and wrong with utmost honesty, expressing and acting on what they sincerely perceive as good and right, while avoiding what they sincerely perceive as evil and wrong.

Where does Islam fit into the picture? To understand this, we must comprehend some basic concepts.

What Is Islam?

As we discussed earlier, the basic knowledge of God, as well as the concepts of right and wrong, are embedded within humans. Additionally, God directly contacted the first humans and communicated the details of this inner knowledge to them. This detail includes explanations of who our Creator is, what the Creator wants from us, and what we need to do in life to fulfill our purpose (see Quran 7:11-25 and Quran 2:31-38). When humans corrupted this guidance over time, God sent Prophets and Messengers to correct these corruptions and provided scriptures so that people could have a criterion to judge what is truth and what is a corruption of truth (Quran 2:213).

This divine guidance, as stated in the Quran (42:13), is the same that was given to the first humans, extending through Noah, Abraham, Moses, Jesus, and Muhammad (Peace be upon them all). The Quran maintains that this divine truth has remained constant throughout time. Other religions, such as Judaism and Christianity, are considered divisions and mutations of the singular message conveyed through all Messengers and Prophets (Quran 42:14; 6:159).

Islam is the only divinely ordained way of life that ensures maximum success in divine accountability (Quran 3:19). The word "Islam" in Arabic means "to surrender," signifying that a "Muslim" is someone who surrenders to God and divine truth.

Rejecting Islam or "Divine Truth" for Unjustified Reasons: A Terminal Crime

There are certain significant crimes that threaten a person's salvation on Judgment Day, even if that person lived life mostly in accordance with the criteria stated in Quran 2:62. Suppose a person was living his life in accordance with the criteria explained in 2:62, this individual lived his life acknowledging creation by a higher power and feared being answerable to that authority while sincerely following the moral compass within. However, he ended up unlawfully murdering an innocent person. According to the Quran, such crimes have the potential to nullify all the value of his beliefs and deeds, leading to eternal doom on Judgment Day (Quran 4:93). Just like murder and other severe crimes, rejecting the divine guidance sent through a Rasool for unjustified reasons, or showing criminal negligence toward it, is similarly a grave offense. It threatens salvation on Judgment Day despite leading an otherwise moral life, as it is akin to rebellion against God.

Since Muhammad (PBUH) is the final source of guidance from the divine, everyone will be asked about their response to Muhammad's (PBUH) message once it reached them. Did they pay heed to it? If not, why? Did they listen and reject it? If so, why? Did they listen and accept it? If so, why? These are the questions expected concerning the divine guidance as explained in the Quran.

Again, a reminder—each individual will be questioned based on their abilities and circumstances. Genuine mistakes will be forgiven, and only those who reject God's message for unjustified reasons will be punished. For instance, if I realize something might truly be from God and I reject it because it conflicts with my ego, desires, biases, interests, or those of my tribe or nation, that counts. Maybe I had the free time and intellect, yet I was simply negligent towards the message of God even though it reached me from different sources in ways that raised questions in my mind that needed answers. Nevertheless, I was so distracted by the world that I didn't make any effort to resolve these doubts. If that's the case, it could indeed be seen as rebellion against God, and it seems fair that such behavior would have adverse consequences if there truly exists a God who will hold everyone accountable.

Genuine Mistakes Will Not Be Punished

As we discussed earlier, if someone makes a genuine and sincere mistake regarding divine truth, they will be forgiven. For example, in the

Muslim world, Islam has become quite complex with many ideological divisions. What if someone encountered not the divine truth but a distorted version that did not seem morally, rationally, or ethically sound? Or if someone simply lacked the time to explore different ideologies while struggling with basic survival? Such individuals would be regarded as having made a genuine mistake and would be forgiven for not accepting the Quran as divine truth or Islam as the divinely ordained way of life. They will be judged based on the criteria in Quran 2:62, which takes into account their awareness of God, their understanding of right and wrong as inherent within them, and how they lived their life according to this basic knowledge.

According to our inner sense of right and wrong, endowed by God, punishing a genuine mistake is unjust. For instance, if it is established that Person "A" killed Person "B" due to a genuine mistake, then Person A should not be punished for murder, or at the very least, the punishment should be significantly less severe than that typically meted out for murder. The Quran supports this notion, stating that genuine mistakes are not treated like deliberate crimes. For example, God declares in the Quran that He only punishes individuals when they wrong themselves or knowingly commit a wrongdoing. For details on how God forgives genuine mistakes and only inflicts punishment for rejecting His message for unjustified reasons, please refer to the section where we discussed "Unjustified Reasons for Rejecting Rasools."

Explanation of Quran 3:85

This verse is often presented as evidence from the Quran, suggesting that only those who identify themselves as Muslims will enter Paradise, and no one else. However, this belief appears to completely contradict the universal criteria of salvation explained in detail in the Quran, as we discussed earlier.

When understood in its proper context, Quranic verse 3:85 does not suggest that only those who identify as Muslims will enter Paradise. In fact, the verse communicates that if someone becomes aware that Islam is the divinely ordained way of life, but they choose another path despite this knowledge, then that choice will not be accepted by God. The context here is important: it addresses those who have recognized that Muhammad (PBUH) is truly a Messenger of God and that Islam is the divinely mandated way of life, yet they have abandoned Islam for reasons that, according to the God of the Quran, are unjustified. Let us consider the verses:

> Whoever seeks/desires a way other than Islam, it shall never be accepted from them, and on the day of judgment, they shall be among the losers. How can God guide those who choose to disbelieve after they believed and acknowledged that the Messenger is indeed saying the truth after receiving clear proofs? God does not guide such wrongdoing people (Quran 3:85-86).

Hence, when seen in context, the verse suggests that if someone becomes aware that Islam is indeed the divine truth but, despite knowing this, chooses another way of life, it will not be accepted on Judgment Day. This makes sense. To know that a way of life is from God yet reject it in favor of another is akin to rebelling against God. If there truly is a God, then it is justified that such an action should be punished by Him.

Then one might ask: If people can attain salvation without knowing the divine truth brought by Messengers, then why bother telling them?

Divine Truth Delivered by Messengers: A Test for Humanity

According to the Quran, the very purpose of our worldly existence is to test individuals in every aspect, conclusively revealing their moral standing. Our response to divine guidance provided through the

Messengers of God serves as a mechanism to assess our moral fiber. For those who accept the divine truths delivered by these Messengers, part of their test involves the integrity and sincerity with which they seek to understand, implement, and propagate these truths. Those to whom this divine truth is imparted face a moral examination in how sincerely they react to it. Therefore, both the sharer and the recipient of the divine truth are morally tested through this process.[63]

Summary of the Quranic Criteria for Salvation on Judgment Day

The entire paradigm of judgment as explained in the Quran presents a truly universal message that transcends all religious identities tied to this world. On the Day of Judgment, everyone will be individually held accountable by God based on the kind of life they led. Success in this accountability will secure a permanent dwelling in Paradise, whereas failure will lead to punishment. Every human being, irrespective of the country or culture they are born into or the religion they are raised in, will be judged based on the following criteria: given their abilities and circumstances, the extent to which a person nurtured their innate awareness of a higher power, and how sincerely and honestly they utilized their sense of right and wrong. Furthermore, everyone will also be questioned about their response to the divine truth delivered through Muhammad (PBUH) if it reached them. Genuine and sincere mistakes will be forgiven. Minor sins will also be forgiven. However, deliberate negligence or wrongful and unjustified behavior and actions will be punished.

Human beings are not merely physical and emotional creatures; they are also intellectual and moral beings. The Quran states that all human beings are undergoing a test—a test of ethics, morality, and character. How you respond to the guidance within you in matters of your daily life, and how you react to the guidance from external sources, are mechanisms to fully demonstrate the kind of moral person you are.

The Quran's criteria for divine accountability on Judgment Day resonated with me, and I could not find any moral or rational objections to it.

Now, the question arises: What does the God of the Quran want me to do to succeed in this test and be granted the blessings of Paradise?

Things Islam Wants from Us for Success in Divine Accountability

Islam is the divine truth sent by God through prophets and messengers. It provides a specific roadmap for individuals to ensure maximum success in divine accountability on Judgment Day..

1 - Tazkiya: Self-Purification - The Sole Aim for All Humans

According to the Quran, the primary goal of every human being is to "purify" themselves; the more purified you are, the more successful you will be on Judgment Day (Quran 87:14, 91:9-10). The entire Quran is filled with instructions that demand people cleanse themselves of all kinds of moral impurities.

> *Those people will be successful who Purify themselves (Quran 87:14).*

> *Successful indeed is the one who purifies his soul, and doomed is the one who corrupts it (Quran 91:9-10).*

2 - Monasticism is Not Permitted; We Must Engage with the Testing Mechanism of the World

When we think of an ideal religious person, many of us might envision monasticism or monkhood—a life characterized by renouncing worldly pursuits to devote oneself entirely to acts and rituals of worship in seclusion. But does the Quran advocate for this way of living? No! In verse 57:27, the Quran addresses the practices of Christian monks, where the Almighty states:

As far as Monasticism is concerned – they made it up because I (God) did not ordain it for them – they made it up to make God happy and (even though it was something they made up themselves) most of them did not observe it sincerely – but I (God) still gave some blessing to those who were faithful but indeed most of them were rebellious (Quran 57:27).

According to the Quran, this worldly life is a test established by God to select individuals for Paradise, an eternal world perfect for those who are morally good and righteous. In this worldly test, the God of the Quran desires humans to fully engage with their lives to demonstrate conclusively where each of them stands morally. This is why the Quran provides detailed moral instructions relating to all aspects of life. For example, the Quran offers moral guidelines on being a good son or daughter, spouse, businessperson, neighbor, ruler, judge, warrior, and more.

Prohibiting monasticism makes sense because if this world is a test and the God of the Quran wants us to take this test, then monasticism is akin to refusing to take the test by walking out of the examination hall.

When it comes to the concept of this world being a test, there are two very popular objections that need to be addressed before we move forward:

Answering Popular Objections

1 - If God Knows Everything - Why Does He Test People?

This is a popular question that we need to address briefly here.

Firstly, a word of caution: the nature of time, the exact nature of God, and the exact dynamics of how God can know the future yet not control it—such matters are not fully comprehensible to us at this time. The Quran warns against attempting to understand the exact nature of things that are beyond our observation and complete comprehension in this life. Specifically, Quran 3:7 states:

> *God is the One who has revealed to you this Book – part of this book is very clear to understand and this is the main part of the book and the foundation of the book – while the other part of the book is "Mutashabihaat" - (meaning things that are analogies, parables, or ideas whose true understanding is not possible for us right now). Those with deviant hearts insist on finding the true meaning of these verses (the Mutashabihaat) and seek to cause discord through this. Only God knows the true meaning of these verses.*

So, keeping the above instructions in mind, it is clear that people are tested in this world not for God to determine their moral standing, but rather for individuals to understand their own morality before judgment is passed upon them. According to the Quran, God does not judge based on His knowledge of the future. Instead, judgment is passed based on an individual's actions and deeds (Quran 67:2).

It makes moral sense because if God were to pass down judgment solely based on His knowledge without giving everyone a chance to demonstrate their actions, then any of God's self-aware sentient creations, equipped with sense of justice and morality, can rightly raise this objection on Judgment Day—that they were not even given a chance to prove themselves. Indeed, justice demands that a person be given an opportunity to demonstrate their capabilities before passing judgment on them.

2 - Could God Have Achieved His Goals Without Testing Individuals?

Could God have achieved His objective of selecting individuals for His Paradise without employing a testing mechanism? For instance, God could have simply created those who would have entered Paradise and instilled in them the knowledge of how they reached Paradise without initiating this extensive scheme of testing or subjecting people to this ordeal. Possibly. However, consider the perspective presented in the Quran, which states that God created countless trillions of free-willed sentient beings—humans, jinns, angels, and others unknown to us—all endowed with a sense of right and wrong, and a sense of justice. Perhaps this was the most optimal method to select the residents of Paradise while upholding all aspects of justice, ensuring that all sentient beings with free will are morally satisfied with the justice administered by God. The Quran asserts that on Judgment Day, everyone will testify to the perfection of the justice executed by God (Quran 39:75).

How to Achieve Tazkiya or Self-Purification?

Let us move forward and discuss what the God of the Quran specifically wants me to do for self-purification, or Tazkiya, in this world to achieve maximum success on Judgment Day.

The entire Quran is filled with moral instructions, and this is probably the easiest part of the Quran to understand. I will try to summarize the Quran's roadmap on how to purify oneself and the areas in which one is expected to make efforts for this purification.

To put it very simply, the Quran's ultimate aim is to encourage humans to morally purify themselves in two main areas: their relationship with God and their relationships with each other.

In pursuit of moral purification in our relationship with God and with others, the Quran instructs us to adhere to specific guidelines regarding bodily cleanliness and the cleanliness of the food we consume. This makes sense. In fact, it is common sense that our overall bodily hygiene and the types of food we eat profoundly affect our psychology.

So, in light of our discussion so far, the Quran's roadmap for self-purification can be divided into four main categories::

1) Purification of the Body.
2) Purification of Food.
3) Purification of one's concept of God and one's relationship with Him.
4) Purification of one's moral being, especially in the context of one's interaction with other human beings.

The more effort one puts in the categories mentioned above, the more successful one will be on Judgment Day. The principle of the Quran is that every person will only get what they made an effort for.

> *Each person (on Judgment Day) will only have what they themselves made an effort for. Their effort will be fully analyzed and they shall be recompensed accordingly (Quran 53:39-41).*

Let us briefly discuss these 4 points.

1 - Purification of the Body

A clean body contributes to a clean mind, and body cleansing rituals serve as reminders of the need to cleanse the mind and soul as well.

The Quran emphasizes the importance of maintaining bodily cleanliness, mandating followers to perform ritualistic cleansing before each prayer. It states in various verses, including Quran 2:222 and 9:108, that God desires for people to continually ensure their cleanliness. Additionally, the Quran requires followers to bathe and thoroughly cleanse themselves after being exposed to impurities, such as bodily fluids or blood from intercourse or menstruation (Quran 5:6). Muhammad (PBUH) also instituted additional cleansing practices as part of the tradition of the Prophets, or Sunnah. These practices include the circumcision of male infants, removal of pubic and armpit hair, and trimming of mustache hair, among others.

Bodily cleanliness and the cleanliness of one's surroundings hold such importance that Muhammad (PBUH) very clearly proclaimed:

Cleanliness is half of faith (Sahih of Muslim, No: 0432).

2 - Purification of Food

What we eat affects us not only physically but also psychologically, emotionally, and spiritually. For instance, until recently, American Marines were required to drink cobra blood during their training to evoke feelings of aggression and ferociousness.

The Quran appears to trust in divinely endowed human nature and does not provide a detailed list of specific foods. Instead, it states a general principle that its followers must only consume herbivores and abstain from eating carnivores (Quran 5:1). This guideline is aimed at nudging human temperament toward benevolence, as herbivores are captured without aggressive efforts, and consuming their meat does not invoke ferocious or savage tendencies in one's psyche and mind.

Killing animals is forbidden in Islam except for self-protection or for food. The allowance to take an animal's life for sustenance is a significant aspect of Islam, intended to invoke feelings of extreme gratitude among humans. Muslims are obligated to recite the 'Takbeer' before slaughtering an animal for food. This invocation consists of a few lines thanking God for permitting the act of taking an animal's life, thereby granting humans the culinary and nutritional luxury of meat.

Note: If you have a lingering question about why God allows the killing of animals for food or sacrifice, I have addressed this question in detail in the Question/Answer Section of the book.

Let's continue.

Any land carnivore that hunts for food is forbidden in Islam, as stated in the Quran (5:1). This is why pig meat is specifically prohibited by name in the Quran, as well as in older scriptures. The pig has long been a source of confusion; it is an omnivore, meaning it consumes both plants and meat, and it is an animal with hooves like herbivores, yet it hunts and eats like a carnivore. Consequently, the pig is deemed a carnivore by the Quran and is specifically named as forbidden to eat.

On the other hand, all animals caught from the sea are permitted (5:96), with no distinction between carnivores or herbivores. This permission is primarily because, unlike the process of catching carnivores on land, humans usually exert no aggressive and ferocious efforts to attain most sea animals—it is a relatively passive process. For this reason, the Quran allows hunting fish even for a person who is wearing Ihram and on the pilgrimage to Mecca, while hunting on land during the pilgrimage journey is forbidden.

The Quran ordains that any meat on which God's name is not invoked, or if the meat is slaughtered in the name of false gods or anyone else apart from God, then it should not be consumed. This makes sense—if one aims to maintain their relationship with God on the right footing and direct all their emotions and feelings solely towards One God, then it is logical to avoid such meat.

Other things that the Quran deems impure include blood and animals that have died of natural causes or accidents, or killed by other animals (see Quran 2:173, 5:1, 5:3, 6:121 and 16:115 for details).

The Quran instructs its followers to avoid mind-altering substances and maintain a sober mind to make sound decisions in life. For this reason, it prohibits all intoxicants. Hence, anything that induces a high is forbidden, and one cannot consume such substances in either small or large amounts. These substances include alcohol, marijuana, cocaine, meth, and heroin, among others (Quran 4:43).

3 - Purification of One's Concept of God and One's Relationship with God

This section can be divided further into 4 parts:

- a) Take matters concerning God very seriously and sincerely.
- b) The concept of God needs to be correct and purified from all kinds of conceptual impurities.
- c) Love, loyalty, devotion, and obedience must be directed strictly toward one God, with absolutely no partners or intermediaries.
- d) Ritual Worship: Physical expressions of one's love, loyalty, devotion, and obedience to God.

Let us briefly discuss these points.

a) Take Matters about God Very Seriously and Sincerely:

A single reading of the Quran by a lay person makes it abundantly clear that God expects humans to consider existence with utmost seriousness and continuously contemplate the larger questions of life. The Quran anticipates that an individual will sincerely pay attention to what is considered worthwhile in the context of God and evaluate matters based on their merit. If some information about God appears to be true, then the Quran expects one to surrender to the truth, even if it contradicts one's own desires, biases, prejudices, or worldly benefits. The God of the Quran wants people to take matters concerning the divine very seriously and, most importantly, with sincerity.

It makes sense. As I explained at the beginning of the book, it is criminally negligent not to make at least one serious effort in life to find reasonable answers to existential questions.

b) The Concept of God Needs to Be Correct and Purified from All Kinds of Conceptual Impurities:

The Quran makes significant efforts to emphasize the importance of having the correct concept of God. This is logical since the purpose of Islam is to cultivate one's relationship with God, and to have a sincere relationship, one must truly understand who they are relating with.

Another reason why the Quran goes to great lengths to present what it deems as the correct concept of God is that, according to the Quran, the concept of God has been greatly distorted by many religions across the world, and the Quran aims to correct these distortions. Let us briefly analyze some key points that the Quran explains about God in this regard.

i) The Exact Nature of God:

What exactly is God? What constitutes the fundamental ultimate reality that is conscious, intelligent, and omnipotent? What is it made of? How can it exist eternally and be infinite? Is it energy? Is it light? Unfortunately, the Quran declares that we cannot comprehend the exact nature of God. The God described in the Quran exists beyond space and time (Quran 57:3) and is so entirely unique that nothing in existence can serve as a parable or analogy to grasp its true essence (42:11 & 112:4)—it is neither light nor energy but something beyond these concepts. This perspective from the Quran is logical. Let me explain.

We are creatures constrained to think within the parameters of space and time. Therefore, if there exists a reality beyond space and time—be it God or something else—it follows that there can be no analogy or parable to accurately represent it. No matter how diligently we try, we are fundamentally unable to visualize, conceptualize, or understand the exact nature and dynamics of such a reality at any level.

However, all hope is not lost. Even though we cannot understand the exact nature of God, as described in the Quran, we can certainly grasp this infinite phenomenon of God on a limited scale. God is infinite and unlimited, yet we share some limited attributes with the Divine. Through these attributes, we can begin to comprehend the nature of God. We learn from the Quran and other scriptures that God is a someone, not a something—a conscious, sentient being who experiences happiness and love, shows displeasure, communicates, and possesses a sense of right and wrong as well as a sense of justice.

Now, some may argue that we are attributing human qualities to God. However, from God's perspective, these are actually Divine attributes. According to the teachings found in the Quran (15:29), when Divine attributes like life, consciousness, intelligence, emotions, aesthetics, and a sense of right and wrong are transferred to inanimate matter, it becomes humans and all other life around us. So, which of these two perspectives do we regard as true? Are we assigning human characteristics to God, or do we, as humans, embody divine attributes? Unfortunately, this isn't a question that can be scientifically proven or disproven; therefore, it fundamentally relies on belief. Consequently, everyone is free to analyze the available evidence and form their own conclusions. I am sharing my perspective in this book, which is that after reviewing what I consider evidence, I have concluded that it is more logical to believe that it is indeed divine attributes that, when transferred to varying arrangements of inanimate matter, result in life, consciousness, intelligence, the capacity for emotion, and our moral existence.

Now, we shall discuss some extremely important concepts that the Quran clarifies about the Oneness of God.

C) Love, loyalty, devotion, and obedience need to be directed strictly to One God with absolutely no partners or intermediaries

The extreme emphasis on the absolute Oneness of God: This is the central theme of the Quran and something that is emphasized from all angles on every other page of the Quran.

The Quran states clearly and very passionately that God is One - and this Oneness can be divided into two categories

1) Physical Oneness of God - God did not originate from anything, nor did anything originate from God: Quran 112:3 states that God neither begets nor is begotten, meaning it is incorrect to believe that God came from something, or that God transforms into something material. This assertion refutes various concepts, for example:.

- The Christian belief that Jesus (PBUH) was God manifested in human form is contradicted by this statement. Similarly, any religious notion suggesting that God assumed a human or material form on Earth is also negated.
- The Meccan pagan belief that angels are the daughters of God—implying they are made of the same substance as God, who manifested Himself as angels—is refuted.
- Even among Muslims, there is a prevalent idea that the entire universe is part of God - meaning God has manifested Himself materially in the form of the Universe and everything within it. However, this concept is negated by the Quran. The correct understanding, according to the Quran, is that the Universe is the creation of God but not a material manifestation of God Himself..

2) There are absolutely no partners or associates of God when it comes to God's decisions about running the affairs of existence: There is a prevalent idea among many religions that, although there is a Creator

God, there are other gods who make decisions regarding the affairs of existence. For example, in Hinduism, the creator God is Brahma, but it is the gods Vishnu and Shiva who manage the affairs of existence. This pattern is similar in many other polytheistic religions.

Even within Islam, there exists a tradition that states there are humans, both dead and alive, who are so pious that God grants them the authority to make decisions on His behalf. These individuals are known in this tradition as Ghaus, Abdal, and Qutub.

The Quran negates any ideas suggesting that anyone shares in God's authority. While the concept of angels exists within the Quran, their sole jurisdiction is to implement God's decisions. The Quran is unequivocally clear that all creation powers and decision-making authority belong solely to God, with no one else sharing in this authority. Numerous verses underscore this vital principle; for instance, Quran 7:54 states:

> *All power of creation and all authority of command belongs solely to God alone.*

Furthermore - Quran 18:26 says:

> *God does not share his command and authority with anyone at all*

3) The Quran preaches the need to have a direct relationship with God without any intermediaries: In this regard, the Quran makes three things absolutely clear.

   a) Humans need to direct their primary emotions of love, loyalty, devotion, and obedience strictly toward God alone.
   b) God hears everyone directly.
   c) Everyone needs to place their trust solely in God and no one else.

Let us discuss these things briefly.

a) Humans need to direct their primary emotions of love, loyalty, devotion and obedience strictly to God alone: Worship means that one directs extreme feelings of love, loyalty, devotion, and obedience to someone. The Quran proclaims that the primary purpose of humans is to worship God (Quran 51:56).

Does this verse suggest that humans are destined to engage eternally in ritual worship of God? Not at all. The verse simply implies that humans should make God the primary object of their love, loyalty, devotion, and obedience. All these emotions directed towards anyone else should be secondary. Many verses in the Quran address this topic, but I want to share some specific ones here. Quran 2:165 states:

> *And there are those who venerate others alongside God and love them with the kind of love that should only be directed towards God alone - but those who truly believe in God love God the most.*

Quran 40:65 says:

> *There is no one worthy of worship except God alone – hence, call solely upon God alone with sincere devotion.*

Having anyone or anything that holds equal stature to God, attributing partners or associates to Him, or performing acts and rituals of worship for anyone or anything other than God are considered Shirk, or "Associating Partners with God." The Quran identifies Shirk as the ultimate sin that will not be forgiven (Quran 4:48). Previously, we discussed that a genuine mistake will be forgiven. So, if someone commits Shirk because they were never adequately exposed to true guidance, then perhaps it could be considered a sincere mistake and forgiven. However, if someone was properly exposed to true guidance but was negligent towards it, or if they engaged in Shirk for other wrongful reasons such as ancestral belief, personal or tribal interests, or due to ego, then according to Quran 4:48, Shirk is a crime for which there is absolutely no forgiveness.

It makes sense, as Shirk is indeed the most immoral act one can commit—it represents the ultimate betrayal toward God. Let me explain:

If I discover a phenomenon as extraordinary as God, who not only caused me to be born out of nothing but also sustains me and offers me eternal paradise for being righteous, then this God should be the center of all my worship. My only true relationship is with this God, and all of my other relationships—such as those with my parents, siblings, spouse, children, and friends—are determined by God, for He decided where I was born. If God had chosen to place me in another time and location, I wouldn't even know the people in my life whom I hold near and dear. If I find out that such a God exists, then it would indeed be the most immoral act and the greatest injustice if I were to hold anything or anyone else equal in love, devotion, obedience, and loyalty to this God—whether it be another person, another deity, or even my own self-interest, desires, or ego.

Strict obedience to one God serves another very important purpose: If Paradise is to be a perfect place, complete subservience to a single supreme authority is necessary. Otherwise, conflict and disharmony will arise. Consequently, there can be absolutely no room for any violation of this supremacy in any way. Therefore, if someone is found guilty of the crime of Shirk on Judgment Day, it makes sense that this person would be denied citizenship in Paradise.

b) God hears everyone directly: Quran 2:186 proclaims that God hears everyone directly and there is no need for any intermediary - the verse says:

> *(Oh Prophet), When people ask you about Me (God) - tell them that I am near to them - I hear their prayers when they call upon Me.*

Another verse, Quran 40:60 says:

God has proclaimed that: 'Call upon me, I will respond to you.'

Quran 50:16 goes to extreme lengths to highlight how close God is to everyone by stating that:

It is God who created Humans and He fully knows even the whispers of their souls and He is closer to them than their jugular vein.

c) Everyone needs to put all their trust solely in God and no one else: The Quran, in various places, emphasizes that humans should place their trust solely in God. Let us examine some examples:

God - there is no other Master besides Him. Believers must put all their trust only in God, and God shall ensure He helps them from where they never even expected. Anyone who puts their trust in God - then God will be enough for him (Quran 64:13).

... and trust only in God. God loves those who put all their trust in Him. If God supports you, no one can harm you, and if God forsakes you, no one can be of benefit to you. Hence, the believers must put all their trust only in God (Quran 3:159-160).

All matters are controlled by God. You shall worship God alone and put your trust only in Him. God is never unaware of whatever you do (Quran 11:123).

In light of our discussions thus far, it's clear that the God of the Quran wants us to understand that absolutely no one shares any kind of power with Him or authority with Him. Humans need to direct all their emotions and practices of worship solely to One God. The Quran also proclaims that God is very close to humans. He directly hears everyone, and humans need to put all their trust in God. All these factors imply that every individual needs to have a direct relationship with God.

There is a prevalent practice of venerating and worshiping certain holy personalities within some segments of Islam. We need to briefly analyze this practice in light of the Quran before moving forward, as it is important to address this matter in the section where we discuss the Quran's emphasis on developing a direct relationship with God without any intermediaries or associates.

i) The Prevalent Practice of Venerating and Worshipping Saints and Holy Personalities

Having a skillful teacher who instructs you in God's religion is no doubt beneficial. However, a popular practice exists within some segments of Islam that involves venerating holy personalities, whether deceased or alive. Devotees often subject themselves to serving these figures and dedicate sacred rituals of worship to them. For instance, they pray to these figures, perform ritual acts of worship, distribute food in their honor to please them, conduct animal sacrifices, and carry out charitable deeds in their name. People engage in these practices for various reasons, which I will outline below. Additionally, I will explain how the Quran refutes these reasons.

ii) Worship of Dead or Alive Holy Personalities for Prayer Acceptance

People venerate saints and holy figures, whether deceased or living, because they believe God is too holy and exalted for ordinary humans to approach directly. Hence, these saints and holy personalities will listen to their prayers and get them accepted by God.

This is contrary to the Quran's very clear teachings I mentioned above that God is extremely close to everyone. He loves each person more than anyone else. He hears everyone directly. People need to put all their trust in God - meaning people need to have a direct relationship with God and need to pray directly to Him.

Secondly, the fundamental purpose of Islam is to cultivate one's relationship with God. This purpose is utterly compromised if one believes that God is out of reach, while dead or alive saints and holy personalities are the ones who hear prayers and ensure they are accepted by God. Consider this: If one assumes that God neither hears nor cares to listen to their prayers, but believes instead that a specific saint, dead or alive, does listen and can intervene to have those prayers accepted by God, who then becomes the focus of their love, loyalty, devotion, and obedience? The answer is clear: the specific holy personality who is perceived as reachable and caring enough to listen. A significant and unfortunate outcome of this belief is that, knowingly or unknowingly, God is relegated to a secondary position.

Apart from the points mentioned previously, the Quran specifically prohibits any form of worship directed toward saints or holy personalities. In one particular verse, the Quran addresses certain groups of Jews and Christians who practice venerating their holy figures. The verse states:

> They take their Rabbis/Priests and Monks as Lords along-side God - and also Messiah son of Marry - even though they were commanded to dedicate all of their worship solely to One God (Quran 9:31).

iii) Worship of Dead or Alive Holy Personalities to Get Closer to God

Another justification given by some individuals who venerate both deceased and living holy personalities is that serving and venerating these figures will bring one closer to God. The rationale is that since saints and holy personalities are very close to God, and God loves them, serving these personalities and worshiping them will make God pleased and draw one closer to Him.

This idea stands in direct opposition to the Quran's teaching that emphasizes developing a direct relationship with God without intermediaries. Moreover, the Quran explicitly states that the way to draw closer to God or to be loved by Him is through mindfulness and awareness of Him. The more attentive and conscientious one is in following God's commandments in their daily life, the more beloved they are to Him. This principle is clearly articulated in the following Quranic verses:

> The friends of God will have nothing to fear nor shall they grieve. They are those who are sincerely faithful and mindful of God (Quran 10:63).

> Surely, the most respected and noble person in the sight of God is the one who is the most righteous and the most God-conscious among you (Quran 49:13).

So, the Quran negates the idea that one needs to serve holy personalities or worship pious people to get close to God. Instead, the Quran proclaims that the more righteous and God-conscious you are, the dearer and closer you are to God.

The Quran explicitly prohibits the practice of worshiping holy personalities in the hope of getting closer to God. Quran 39:2-3 asserts:

> It is I (God) who has revealed this book (Quran) with Truth - so worship God alone with sincere devotion and no one else. Indeed - devotion is due solely to God alone. As for those who venerate others alongside God saying: 'We venerate them only so they may bring us closer to God' - surely God will judge them for what they say and God does not guide those who lie and disbelieve (Quran 39:2-3).

In this context, a particular verse often cited to justify the practice of venerating holy personalities to get closer to God requires clarification, despite the Quran's explicit disapproval of this practice. The verse in question is Quran 5:35, which states:

> *Oh Believers! Be mindful of God and seek "Waseela" or "Means" to get closer to Him and struggle in His way so you may be successful.*

Many among those who wish to forcefully justify the worship of holy personalities to get closer to God argue that the word "Waseela," used in this verse and literally translating to "Means" or "Ways," implies that one should venerate holy personalities as a "Means" to get closer to God. This interpretation is a significant stretch and in complete contrast to the Quran's overall teachings on this matter, particularly Quran 39:2-3, which clearly does not approve of the practice of venerating holy personalities to get closer to God. The verse in question, Quran 5:35, simply states that one should seek ways or means to get closer to God—ways such as being mindful of God, doing good deeds, morally purifying oneself, and performing rituals of worship.

iv) Worship of Dead/Alive Holy Personalities So They Can Intervene on a Person's Behalf and Save Them on Judgment Day

It is crucial to address a prevalent concept in Islam known as "intercession." Commonly, it is believed that if an individual venerates Prophet Muhammad (PBUH) or another deceased or living holy personality, then, should that individual be condemned to hell by God on Judgment Day, the Prophet (PBUH) or the respective holy personality will intervene and rescue them from hell. According to the Quran, this concept is entirely incorrect.

All control on Judgment Day belongs solely to God. It is He who decides who will be punished in hell and who will be admitted to heaven. Additionally, it is God alone who determines whether to allow intercession for someone and by whom the intercession is to be made. The following verses from the Quran discuss the concept of intercession. I will mention some specific ones below to elucidate this concept.

Verses pertaining to the concept of intercession include 6:70, 6:51, 32:4, 39:43-44, 2:255, 10:3, 19:87, 20:109, 34:23, 43:86, and 21:26-28 and 74:46-48.

Let us analyze some specific verses.

The following verse clearly states that all matters regarding intercession will be decided by God alone.

> *All Intercession belongs to God (39:44).*

The following verse from the Quran clearly states that it is solely God who decides if a person should be saved through the means of intercession.

> *No intercession can benefit anyone except for someone for whom God allows (Quran 34:23).*

The following verse indicates that God will determine whose testimony is permitted, and the individual testifying will speak only the truth.

> *On that day (Day of Judgment), no intercession from anyone will be allowed except from someone whom God allows and whose words are true and pleasing to God (Quran 20:109).*

Thus, considering all the verses about intercession in the Quran, the accurate Quranic understanding of intercession is that for those condemned to Hell by God, no intercession will be accepted from anyone. (Refer also to the following verses for further clarification: Quran 7:73, 74:46-48).

However, for those individuals who are neither exceedingly virtuous for heaven nor exceptionally wicked for hell, it is God who decides to save a person from Hell. He chooses someone to step forward and provide a truthful testimony about that person, allowing God to spare them based on this account.

Therefore, I must emphasize again that the concept isn't that God will condemn a person to hell while someone else saves them. The accurate understanding is that God decides to save a person and utilizes good testimony as a means to confer additional merit on that individual in order to save them.

The flawed idea of intercession is prevalent among Muslims; it suggests that God will condemn a person to hell, yet some holy personality will save them. This concept contradicts the clear injunctions of the Quran, and it has another catastrophic implication. As discussed earlier, if I believe that a certain holy personality is listening to my prayers and having them accepted by God, then my primary feelings of worship will be directed towards that holy personality, not towards God. This issue parallels the flawed concept of intercession. If I believe a certain holy personality will save me in case God condemns me to hell, then my primary feelings of love, loyalty, devotion, and obedience will be directed towards that holy personality and not towards God.

There are some Hadith narratives in which Muhammad (PBUH) is reported to have said that he will be allowed to intercede for some people. From the Quranic perspective, this means that on the Day of Judgment, if God chooses to save a person from punishment, in some cases, Muhammad (PBUH) will be allowed to give a favorable testimony on their behalf. This will then become the means for their salvation. It is important to understand that the concept is not that God will condemn someone to Hell and Muhammad (PBUH) will intervene to save them. Rather, the idea is that God will decide to save a person and use Muhammad's (PBUH) testimony as the means to do so.

d) Ritual Worship – Physical Expression of One's Love, Loyalty, Devotion, and Obedience to God

Once the true concept of God is understood and accepted, and the correct relationship with God is established, Islam then lays down the divinely approved method of expressing one's devotion in that relationship—and one very important part of this expression is ritual worship.

A human being's relationship with their Creator is expressed through acts of worship such as prayer and fasting. These acts establish one's relationship with the Divine on the right footing and serve as reminders of God, contributing to the cleansing of the soul by acting as deterrents to one's tendency to deviate from the path of righteousness.

One can rightly argue that an entity such as God deserves a lifetime of full-time worship every minute of the day—hence, God Himself has sanctioned the bare minimum quantity of ritual worship in Islam, called Farz.

Farz rituals of worship are the compulsory amount of worship rituals. If someone identifies as a Muslim yet does not perform the most basic Farz prayers, then this will be considered a very serious transgression on Judgment Day.

After fulfilling the obligatory farz prayers, individuals are free to engage in as many voluntary acts of worship as they wish to draw closer to God.

In terms of purifying one's relationship with God, Islam mandates a correct concept of God, emphasizing His singularity in every aspect and the absence of any partners sharing His authority. Islam also encourages the development of a direct relationship with God, explicitly without intermediaries. It prescribes certain compulsory and voluntary rituals of worship as physical expressions of one's love, loyalty, devotion, and obedience to God.

Let us move to the last of the four main tasks that Islam expects people to undertake.

4 - Purification of One's Moral Character, Particularly in Interactions With Other Human Beings

As far as character, ethics, and morality are concerned, the Quran aims to mold its followers into good, righteous, sincere, honest, merciful, just, charitable, and humble human beings. I find myself completely agreeing with this aspect of the Quran's teachings because the values Islam aims to inculcate are not just Islamic or religious values, but the highest values found in all human societies and cultures throughout time.

The Quran is filled with ethical and moral guidelines; however, I will share a few selected ones with you. The God of the Quran expects you to become:

1) Someone who is a peacemaker and a well-wisher to all and holds no malice for anyone - someone who tries to make peace even if they are wronged (Quran 41:34).
2) Someone who controls anger and forgives others (Quran 3:133-134).
3) Someone who can lawfully take revenge for being wronged but instead chooses to forgive (Quran 16:26).
4) Someone who, in a situation where they have to turn away a pauper, does so very lovingly and gently (Quran 93:10 & 17:28).
5) Someone who doesn't follow up charity with reminders of their generosity and hurtful words (Quran 2:262-263).
6) Someone who is just even towards their enemy (Quran5:8).
7) Someone who doesn't mock or make fun of others or calls them by hurtful nicknames and doesn't dig up flaws in other people (Quran 49:11).
8) Someone who is humble, avoids arrogance at all costs, and never becomes a boastful person (Quran 31:18).

9) Someone who does not seek self-glory or personal exaltation (Quran 28:83).

10) Someone who walks very humbly, and even when ignorant people speak hurtful words, he responds with gentleness and peace (Quran 25:63).

11) Someone who is extremely kind and generous towards parents, relatives, the needy, and the orphans (Quran 17:23-34).

12) Someone who is extremely honest and fair when dealing with others (Quran 17:35).

13) Someone who does not show reluctance when required to fight against oppression and persecution (Quran 4:75)

14) Someone who does not use curse words or insulting words for other people's religion and gods despite believing that they are false (Quran 6:108).

15) Someone who doesn't gossip about others and backbite people (Quran 49:12).

16) Someone who does justice and speaks truth even if it goes against personal interests or the interests of one's family, tribe or nation (Quran 4:135).

Indeed, these values are universally recognized as the best a person can uphold. It is difficult for anyone to disagree with them. The Quran contains many verses that explain the moral dos and don'ts for human beings. I want to highlight a very special verse here because it outlines five categories of moral prohibitions, and all sins and crimes forbidden in Islam fall under these five main categories.

The Holy Quran, in Chapter 7, Verse 33, clearly states that there are only five categories of sins that God has forbidden for everyone, which are:

1) Any private or public sexual act or behavior outside the marriage between a man and a woman.

2) The Holy Quran forbids "Ithm." The Arabic word "Ithm" can imply two things: one meaning of the word is "sin," indicating that the verse commands people to avoid anything they consider sinful. The usage of this word in the verse also conveys another meaning— "injustice" or the curtailment of someone's rights. Therefore, the verse implies that people must refrain from committing injustices or denying others their rightful dues.

3) Wrongful transgression is prohibited, which means that people must refrain from committing any unlawful acts against another's property, dignity, or life.

4) Equating others with God.

5) Lying about God or speaking about Him without having certain knowledge.

The Quran outlines five major prohibitions in 7:33 that make perfect moral sense. These are the five big "don'ts" the Quran asks people to abstain from, encompassing all sins within these broad categories. For example, the Islamic prohibition of interest on loans falls into the second category, as it represents a form of economic injustice, while the moral commandments for men and women are categorized under the first.

I believe it is safe to assume that no one can have any justified objections to categories 2 through 5. It is indeed the right thing to do to abstain from what one genuinely considers a sin—to abstain from committing injustice—to abstain from unlawfully harming anyone's life, dignity, and property.

Furthermore, it is forgivable if someone refuses to believe in God due to rational and intellectual dissatisfaction with arguments about Him. However, I think we all agree that believing in God and then associating partners with Him without any justified reason is not a very good thing to do. Similarly, we can all agree that deliberately lying about anyone, including God, is not acceptable behavior.

The extreme emphasis on limiting sexual actions and behaviors within marriage: The first point discussed in Quran 7:33 raises a question for many: Why does God emphasize restricting all forms of sexual behavior to within the bounds of marriage between a man and a woman? I will provide a brief answer here and address the details further in the Question and Answer section.

The union of a man and a woman is a mechanism for bringing new human beings into this world. When a new human arrives, they require a tremendous amount of care starting from day one and continuing for at least 15 years or more. A human being is not merely a physical creature but also psychological, emotional, moral, and spiritual being. Consequently, the extensive care and nurturing a newborn requires must address all these aspects. A human needs physical, psychological, emotional, moral, and spiritual care and nurturing, directed towards enhancing their well-being in this life and crucially, in the hereafter. To fulfill this need, God has established the institution of the biological family unit, consisting of a biological male and a biological female united by marriage. As depicted in the Quran, God envisions a stable family unit that can provide long-term nurturing in all the aforementioned dimensions.

It makes sense; there is no better way than the stable family institution to provide the right kind of physical, psychological, emotional, moral, and spiritual nurturing to a newborn for more than a decade.

The prevalence and acceptance of sexual actions and behaviors outside of marriage represent some of the most serious threats to the institution of marriage. Therefore, the God of the Quran takes great lengths to emphasize the importance of restricting all kinds of sexual behaviors within marriage, and has indeed criminalized all forms of sexual activity outside of marriage.

We often view marriage from the perspective of the man and the woman, but God views marriage from the perspective of the child, who requires years of dedicated love, care, and nurturing in various aspects. This is so the child can develop correctly in relation to this world and the hereafter.

Another extremely crucial function of the family institution is to provide care for individuals as they reach old age. A stable family unit is the optimal mechanism for addressing the physical and emotional needs of the elderly. While nursing homes are a viable Plan B for many, and some individuals in developed countries might prefer them as their Plan A, it is quite evident—without needing to cite any research—that nursing homes cannot provide the same level of psychological and emotional fulfillment and care for the elderly that a stable family institution can provide.

For me, it makes sense. The normalization and prevalence of sexual actions and behaviors outside of marriage are bound to weaken the institution of marriage. If the goal is to protect and strengthen marriage and the family unit it begets, then it makes sense to strictly limit all kinds of sexual behaviors and actions within marriage. Exceptions aside, normally, a marriage stands on the pillar of sexual loyalty. If that is compromised, then the whole institution either becomes toxic and lifeless or completely falls apart.

Hence, if you engage in or promote any form of sexual activity or behavior outside of marriage—for instance, engaging in sexual activity outside of marriage or participating in media content that promotes sexually provocative images or dialogues—then you are directly waging war against the institution of the family, which God Himself created. Therefore, all forms of sexual activity or behavior outside of marriage are deemed as very serious offenses by God, carrying worldly punishments and severe consequences in the hereafter.

Divorce is permitted in Islam for both men and women; however, the God of the Quran encourages individuals to make every effort to maintain a stable family unit. The detrimental effects of toxic marriages on children are well-documented, highlighting the long-term, often irreversible, harm that children suffer from unstable family environments and the separation or divorce of their parents.

So, here is a summary of everything we discussed so far in this section:

To be favored by the Divine and enter paradise, the Quran wants me to earnestly and sincerely seek the truth about God and existence. It expects me to cultivate the right understanding of God and to dedicate all my love, loyalty, obedience, and devotion to God. The Quran wants me to keep myself clean, maintain purity in my food while avoiding intoxicants, and uphold my moral character by adopting the highest human values. I don't think I need to elaborate further on why I found nothing in these teachings of the Quran that I could disagree with.

Lastly, we need to briefly address the question: Does the God of the Quran permit me to fight and engage in armed conflict, and if so, under what circumstances?

Allowance of War in Islam

I have discussed the following ideas elsewhere in the book, but it is important to highlight them again in this section since we are discussing what exactly the God of the Quran expects of me to be successful in the hereafter.

When it comes to the use of force or violence, the Quran permits Muslims to engage in warfare or armed struggle for primarily two reasons.

1 - *Against those people who reject divine truth after it has become clear to them:* The Quran 9:5-29 instructs Muslims to confront the polytheists

until they embrace Islam. It also directs confrontation with Jews and Christians until they either accept Islam or agree to live under Muslim subjugation and pay a tax (Jizya) as a sign of this subjugation.

We have previously discussed that these verses pertain directly to the immediate audience of a Rasool of God. We explored how a Rasool of God not only brings guidance for all humanity but also serves as God's earthly demonstration of divine judgment for his immediate audience. A Rasool clarifies the truth to his immediate audience, and after a certain period, those who accept the Rasool's message are rewarded here in this world, while those who reject it face punishment in this world. When these verses are read in context, they refer to the divine punishment inflicted on the immediate recipients of a Rasool's message, whom God declared to be rejecting truth for wrongful and unjustified reasons.

Hence, these verses relate solely to Muhammad (PBUH), his companions, and his immediate contemporaries. They are not applicable to anyone following them. Therefore, Muslims are not obligated by God to fight non-Muslims for reasons of faith, to convert them to Islam, or with the intention of subjugating them. In fact, the Quran issues an eternal commandment that there shall be absolutely no compulsion in matters of religion.

> Let there be no compulsion in matters of religion now that truth stands out clearly from falsehood... (Quran 2:256).

2 – Fighting for self-defense and against oppression and persecution: The Quran permits Muslims to engage in combat for reasons of self-defense and against severe injustice, oppression, and persecution, particularly religious persecution. The verses that primarily address these directives include Quran 2:190-193, 22:39-40, and 49:9-10. These injunctions are universal and apply to all Muslims at all times. However, the Quran

also stipulates that such warfare can only be conducted under a lawful ruler. Quran 4:59 states:

> *Believers! Obey God and obey the Messenger and obey those who are put in positions of authority among you.*

I agree that there might be extreme exceptions where it could be morally justified to take up arms against an established authority or without the authorization of an established authority. However, as a general principle, Quran 4:59 clearly states that Muslims must obey the lawful rulers over them. This means that armed conflict can only be conducted under the authority of the established government.

In today's age, the accepted legal authority is the government of a country; hence, it would be correct to say that while acknowledging that there can be cases of extreme exceptions—as stated in the Quranic teachings, Muslims are permitted by God to fight for self-defense and against injustice, oppression, and persecution, but only under the authority of their country's government.

Keeping the above-mentioned points in mind, it is essential to answer two very important questions.

1 - Can any Muslim group fight other Muslims to enforce their own specific interpretation of an Islamic government system?

Answer: In light of our previous discussion - No! Muslims after Prophet Muhammad (PBUH) are permitted to take up arms only for self-defense, or against clear instances of injustice, oppression, and persecution, and even then, only under lawful leadership.

Moreover, the Quran issues a clear directive that in matters of collective affairs, Muslims should resolve matters through mutual consultation—not through force or armed conflict. Quran 42:38 articulates this principle with the following words::

... (True believers are the ones who) ... respond to their Lord, establish prayer, settle their collective matters through mutual consultation and donate from what I (God) have provided for them.

In light of the above verse, decisions on collective matters, such as the type of leadership that will lead a nation and the decisions to manage government affairs, must be made through public consultation.

The mechanism of mutual consultation can take various forms. For instance, during the time of Muhammad (PBUH), it involved a rudimentary form of consultation among key leaders from different tribes. In today's world, this consultation may manifest as Presidential or Parliamentary elections, or other methods allowing people to participate in collective decision-making through mutual consultation. Regardless of the form it takes, the Quran explicitly states that collective matters must be decided through mutual consultation, not through force.

2 - Can Muslim Governments Use Force to Implement Their Own Interpretation of Islam on Others?

Answer: According to Quran 22:41, a government of Muslims is indeed authorized to collect Zakat tax, summon Muslims to daily obligatory prayers, particularly the Friday prayer, and enact Islamic punishments for specific crimes explicitly mentioned in the Quran. However, does Islam empower Muslim governments to enforce their interpretations on issues like hijab, beard grooming, and gender segregation? Questions such as whether to wear a hijab, whether it should cover the face, whether to grow a beard and its required length, or whether men and women can study and work together arise. Can a Muslim government impose its own particular moral interpretations of Islam on such matters?

The answer is a resounding no! Let me explain briefly.

The phrase "Amar bil Maroof wa nahi anil Munkar" means "Call people to what is good and forbid them from what is evil." This directive is very popular and is often used as a justification for governments to enforce the wearing of head or face coverings on women and beards on men.

This instruction has been directed to Muslims in three main places in the Quran: in verses 3:104, 3:110, and 9:71.

There are three main points to understand in this regard:

1) The term "Amr," which signifies "to order someone to do something," is also employed in the Quran to mean "to invite someone to do something," as illustrated in Quran 2:169. Consequently, the verse suggests that if you hold a position of authority, such as in the police force, you are permitted to actively prevent people from engaging in wrongdoing. However, if you are an ordinary individual, your role is limited to advising and admonishing others

2) The words used in this verse for good and evil are "Maroof" and "Munkir." The very meaning of these words implies things that are commonly known as good and those commonly known as evil both from the perspective of Islam and from the perspective of universal human morality, these words do not imply that governments have an all-out sanction to impose their own interpretation of Islam on others in all matters. In fact, the verse suggests that governments can promote what is commonly known as good in a society, such as honesty, cleanliness, and kindness, while forcefully preventing what is commonly recognized as bad, including theft, dishonesty, fraud, robbery, unlawful violence, and injustice.

3) If a government chooses to enforce specific regulations based on Islamic teachings, it must have explicit authorization from the Quran. This means that for a government to impose a particular

mandate on its citizens, the directive must be clearly sanctioned by the Quran. For instance, the Quran authorizes governments to enforce the collection of Zakat (a form of almsgiving), to prevent acts of open adultery, and to administer appropriate punishments for those who engage in such acts.

In this context, if the Quran does not authorize a specific injunction of Islam to be enforced by a government, then it cannot be enforced by a government. For example, whether a woman should cover her head and face, or whether a man is obligated to have a beard, the Quran does not grant any government the right to enforce their interpretation of these matters on others. Everyone is free to pursue whatever interpretation they agree with.

Personally speaking, within the interpretation of Islam that I agree with, currently led by Mr. Javed Ahmed Ghamidi, men are not obligated to grow a beard, women are not required to cover their heads or faces (it is considered an optional good deed), and God has not decreed gender segregation at public gatherings. Additionally, the Quran does not authorize any government to enforce their interpretation of Islam on individuals regarding such matters.

CONCLUSION

In my quest to find satisfying answers to existential questions, science led me to believe in an intelligence underlying everything. Guided by the belief that any divine truth should be readily accessible, I explored the most prominent tradition of religion—the Abrahamic tradition. Within this tradition, I initially turned to the Quran because of its historical verifiability and technical robustness. Acquiring accurate knowledge about the sources of Islam allowed me to analyze it effectively. The personality of Muhammad (PBUH), his claim of being a messenger of God, and the unfolding events with him and his companions formed a compelling basis for believing that he might indeed have been conveying truths from the Divine. I endeavored to understand what the God of the Quran expects from me and whether it aligns with moral and rational principles. In this chapter, I share my findings from this endeavor.

In my early 30s, I reached a point in my life where it became apparent that Muhammad (PBUH) was truthfully relaying his contact with God, and the divine directives he conveyed made moral and rational sense to me. I found myself devoid of justifiable reasons to reject Muhammad (PBUH) and the message of the Quran. I had come to believe in the reality of God, angels, divine accountability after death, hell, heaven, prophets, messengers, and scriptures. This entire framework, I realized, was true!

But I still hadn't given in completely—I had some questions in mind, and before fully surrendering to the message of Islam, I needed to find reasonable answers to these questions. A message of acknowledgment needs to be stated here: Along with many other personalities, including mainstream Islamic scholars and even non-Muslim scholars, academics, and scientists, one of the main individuals who helped me have my questions answered was Mr. Javed Ahmed Ghamidi. I am grateful to God for making Mr. Ghamidi a resource for answering many of the problematic questions I had about Islam and existence in general.

I kept receiving morally and rationally satisfying answers to all of my questions until I had none left. I hold these answers to be true until they are challenged, as I remain open to being wrong. Hence, it was somewhere in early 2019 when I reached a point in life where all my existential questions were answered to a satisfactory level, and I realized I had no justified reason left to reject Islam as divine truth. This understanding led me to completely surrender to Islam, and I understood why Islam means 'to surrender' — because it indeed implies that one surrenders to divine truth when one realizes that it is divine truth.

In the next chapter, I will share with you some satisfying answers I found to important questions I had about Islam and existence.

CHAPTER 7A
QUESTIONS &
ANSWERS

Question 1: What is God Like?

What exactly is God? What is the precise nature of this fundamental ultimate reality that is conscious, intelligent, and capable of doing everything? What is it composed of? How can it exist forever and be infinite? Is it energy? Is it light? Sadly, the Quran proclaims that we cannot know the exact nature of God at this time. The God of the Quran states that He is beyond space and time (Quran 57:3), and so completely alien that nothing in existence can be used as a parable or analogy to comprehend His true nature (42:11 & 112:4) - so no, He is neither light nor energy - He is something beyond these things.

The Quran employs analogies to help humans understand aspects of the unseen realm such as paradise, hell, angels, and the soul. However, it clearly states that no analogy can fully encapsulate God—His true nature is completely beyond our comprehension.

It does make sense. If God created time and space yet transcends both, it means we can never fully imagine the true reality of God, because we are forced to think and comprehend within the framework of space and time. Everything in our reality exists in a specific place and form. As long as we are prisoners of space and time, anything outside these boundaries will be truly and absolutely incomprehensible to us.

Thus, according to the Quran, God is completely unlike anything else in existence. Although we can understand some attributes of God, we cannot comprehend His true nature as long as we exist in this limited worldly existence. Only on the day of judgment will we fully understand the truth about God's true nature.

Question 2: Why Did It Take God Billions of Years to Create the Universe and Earth, and What Was God Doing During Those Billions of Years Before?

Firstly, as we discussed earlier regarding the nature of time—time is a very fluid entity. Billions of years mean nothing to a photon of light, as it does not experience time. Similarly, as an object approaches the speed of light, time slows down for that object—hence, we should not impose our own perception of time on the universe or on God by asking such questions. Perhaps it took God only a fraction of a second to create the universe, while we perceive it as billions of years. The Quran addresses the issue of time being a relative concept and mentions that a day for God is not akin to the 24-hour day that we humans experience (Quran 22:47).

Secondly, the Quran presents a non-human-centric model of existence. Consequently, the God of the Quran has plenty of other matters to attend to beyond humans. For example, the Quran mentions a race of sentient beings that inhabit the entire universe and predate humans—this race, undergoing their own test of free will, is called the Jinn. The Quran notes that they were created well before humankind and are made of "smokeless fire" or "hot wind" (Quran 55:15 and 15:27). Accordingly, in the Quran's non-human-centric model, there were divine activities in the universe before the creation of humans.

Question 3: Why is Shirk (Associating Partners with God) Considered an Unforgivable Sin?

Shirk is considered an unforgivable sin primarily for three reasons:

1) When a person says that God has taken partners, they are lying about God because there is no reason within us or around us that can make one sincerely come to a conclusion that there is more than one God. In fact, Quran 7:172 states that an innate awareness of being created by a single God has been placed within all human beings. Even Atheism or rejection of God has some intellectual basis, but associating partners with God has absolutely no basis in anything. Hence, when one claims that God has taken partners, they are lying about God! This act of associating a lie to God is the greatest injustice one can do to God.

2) If I know that it is God who has created me out of nothing, sustains me, and offers me eternal Paradise, yet I give the same kind of love and loyalty to others that is due to God alone, then that is the greatest and deepest betrayal of God one can commit.

3) There is also a practical reason why Shirk cannot be forgiven. When you hold anything or anyone equal to God, it is akin to challenging the authority of God. It is like being in the army and pledging allegiance to two Army Chiefs, or being the citizen of a country and declaring that there are two or three presidents or prime ministers of that country—that is not acceptable. If Paradise is to be a perfect place, then there needs to be complete subservience to a single all-powerful authority, and any rebellion against this authority cannot be acceptable even in the least bit.

As previously discussed, genuine mistakes in belief might be forgiven. For instance, an individual may not have had sufficient exposure, or perhaps someone grew up in an environment that so distorted their intellect and morality that it became impossible for them to recognize the truth.

Question 4: Why Do We See Violence Among Animals, Experience Natural Disasters, Suffer From Horrible Diseases, and Face Birth Defects?

For a critical mind, it makes sense that man-made evil exists because God has granted humans freedom in this world as a test, and humans frequently misuse this freedom, causing harm to others. But what about natural disasters, horrible diseases, and birth defects? Why does God allow such pain and suffering to afflict people and animals? The short answer is that these are means of testing humans and providing lessons for us to navigate through this test.

For those who anticipated a world free from suffering—excluding that caused by humans—the Quran presents a starkly different reality. The world depicted in the Quran is fundamentally flawed and imperfect for living, yet it is perfectly designed for testing humans. In this world, human trials are conducted through prosperity, wealth, and comfort, as well as through pain, suffering, fear, and misery.

Secondly, human beings are meant to learn from the classroom of this world, and we learn everything by understanding its opposite—for example, we become aware of what kindness is when we encounter cruelty. That is why there is both perfection and benevolence, as well as imperfection and violence, in humans and in nature. Paradise is described as perfect, with no suffering. However, in this realm, for our testing and learning, there is a mix of benevolence and violence within us and all around us..

Question 5: Why Does God Allow the Infliction of Pain on Animals for Food, and What Is the Purpose of Animal Sacrifice in Islam?

This world is an imperfect one, designed to test its inhabitants; pain and suffering are among those imperfections. In contrast, the next world is perfect. In Paradise, all forms of food will be available without the need for killing or inflicting pain.

I'm not sure how relevant this point is in today's industrial age, but historically, killing an animal for food was a significant event aimed at igniting feelings of extreme gratitude, as it allowed for taking a life to attain a nutritional luxury and a culinary delight.

When I was not a believer in God, I discussed with my friend the brutality of God allowing the killing of animals for food and ritual sacrifices. I stressed the pain inflicted on the animals. However, my friend, a staunch believer, raised a point worth mentioning. He suggested that if God is merciful and has permitted the killing of certain animals, then He must have adjusted their pain thresholds so that they do not suffer excessively.

This struck a chord with me. It is known that many animals do not experience emotional pain as humans do. For instance, when the offspring of an animal is killed by another animal, there might be little to no display of sadness before the animal resumes its life. Elephants and a few other species are known to exhibit more significant emotional reactions to their dead, but only for a day or two before they move on as usual. If animals do not experience emotional pain as acutely as we do, then perhaps—and this is mere speculation—for those animals whose killing God has permitted, just like their emotional pain, their experience of physical pain might also be reduced.

There are times when I ponder why God couldn't devise a plan where He populates Paradise without any suffering. But then I remind myself that I am a mere being with limited knowledge. Imagine for a moment that you were God and had created billions and trillions of self-aware entities with a sense of justice and morality. Consider the trillions of parameters you would need to fine-tune to ensure all facets of justice, morality, and ethics are met for these billions upon billions of beings for eternity. Keeping all of this in mind, perhaps this was the optimal plan to satisfy all aspects of justice.

Will Animals Be Compensated For Their Suffering?

Firstly, animals do not possess a pronounced sense of right and wrong; therefore, they are not subject to any tests, which means there is no danger of hell for them. According to the Quran (81:5 and 6:38), animals will also be resurrected on the Day of Judgment. However, some hadiths state that animals will be turned to dust once God's justice is completely carried out. Meanwhile, other hadiths suggest that certain animals are creatures of Paradise. For example, there is a hadith in Sahih al-Jaami where Muhammad (PBUH) is reported to have told his followers to respect sheep and branded them as animals of Paradise (Sunan al-Kubra of al-Bayhaqi, No: 4357).

As far as the Islamic view on the animal afterlife is concerned, we understand from the Quran that animals will be resurrected on the Day of Judgment. Whether they enter Paradise remains unknown. Do some of them reach Paradise? This is uncertain. The appropriate way to consider animals within the divine scheme is to recognize that if any possess a sufficient level of consciousness to merit an afterlife, then they surely will have one.

Purpose of Animal Sacrifice in Islam

Millions of animals are killed every day for their meat; Islam has also permitted killing certain animals for food. However, there is also a ritual sacrifice of animals that occurs after the Hajj pilgrimage. A worldly benefit of this sacrifice is that millions of poor people receive free meat—a culinary luxury they might not have otherwise for long durations of time. But the religious significance of the sacrifice ritual is as follows:

A human being has various relationships in life, and there are rituals that exist to express one's love and devotion in these relationships. In Islam, the most important relationship one has is with God. Ritual worship is the expression of this relationship—for example, the ritual obligatory prayers and fasting. Hajj and ritual sacrifice are also acts of worship that are symbolic expressions to signify and represent one's willingness to sacrifice everything for God if needed.[64]

Question 6: Why Does God Need to Test People? Doesn't God Already Know?

Even though a teacher knows which students will pass and which will fail, he does not issue the final results based solely on his knowledge but allows the students to take the exam and demonstrate what they deserve.

According to the Quran, we have the freedom to make our own moral choices. Although God does not dictate or control these choices, He is aware of the decisions we will make—similar to how a teacher doesn't control the performance of the students but can predict how they will perform on the exams. Moreover, we humans experience time in a way that prevents us from seeing the future; however, any higher-dimensional being can perceive time in all directions. As three-dimensional beings, it is impossible for us to fully comprehend this. The concept that God does not control our actions yet knows the future is understandable in principle, even though we cannot fully grasp it because of our limited perception of time.

Question 7: Could God Have Still Achieved His Objective of Choosing People for His Paradise Without This Testing Mechanism?

For instance, could He not have simply created those individuals who would make it to Paradise and endowed them with the knowledge of how they achieved this without actually implementing the entire testing scheme and making people undergo these tests? It's possible. However, when considered from the perspective that, according to the Quran, God created many trillions of free-willed sentient beings—humans, jinns, angels, and others we do not know about—all endowed with a sense of right and wrong and a sense of justice, then perhaps this was the best possible way to select residents of Paradise while fulfilling all parameters of justice for all the sentient, free-willed beings in existence and those who will be born in Paradise for all eternity.

Let me give you an example of how a parameter of justice is met by this testing mechanism: In selecting the residents of Paradise, this test also serves the purpose of choosing its rulers. If God appointed certain humans as rulers of Paradise without implementing this testing mechanism, future residents could rightfully claim that these rulers, enjoying all the perks and powers of their position, should have physically undergone the process to demonstrate why they deserve this position rather than having it granted by God based solely on His foreknowledge while they did nothing to earn it. Hence, it is fairer for God to make decisions based on actions rather than solely on His knowledge of events.

Question 8: The Dual Nature of God - God is Not All Peaches and Cream!

The Quran depicts God as loving and forgiving to the righteous, but also as extremely capable of inflicting violence, torment, and punishment on the wicked and evil. Therefore, God is portrayed as both benevolent and loving, but also as violent and stern. This duality makes sense when considering nature. If God truly created nature, then it becomes clear that this God possesses the duality mentioned above, because in nature we find both love, beauty, and benevolence, as well as extreme violence and suffering.

Question 9: What is God's Law of Guidance?

A one-time layperson's study of the Quran reveals that God has established specific laws for guiding people. God has instilled within us a fundamental guidance that encompasses a sense of right and wrong and a sense of being created by a higher power. The more care you show for the guidance installed within you by listening to your inner conscience and making life choices accordingly, the more guidance you will receive. Conversely, the more you shun this guidance by engaging in wrongful actions and ignoring the voice of your inner conscience, the more misguided you will become. There will come a time when God will put a seal on your heart and mind, and then you will never be guided again.

God guides those who make a sincere, persistent, and serious effort to seek guidance while shunning moral pollutions such as arrogance and biases and are ready to analyze and accept things based on merit and reason. The more effort one invests in these aspects, the more guidance one receives. The Quran clearly states that those who persistently ignore God's signs and do not shun arrogance and biases reach a point where God allows them to remain misguided.

Question 10: What Does the Quran Mean When It Tells Husbands That Their Wives Are Like Their Farm Fields?

Quran 2:223 states that for husbands, their wives are akin to their farmland. Some critics interpret this verse as demeaning to women, suggesting it brands them as property for husbands to exploit. However, this parable is being misunderstood.

It is a beautiful parallel because, for a farmer, his entire existence is tied to his farmland. The farmer does not exploit the land but nurtures, protects, and sows seeds in it, working tirelessly day and night for its well-being and upkeep. The concerns of the farmland keep the farmer awake at night, worried. This parable serves to remind men of their duties to women, rather than giving them license to exploit them. This is why the verse continues to remind men that they should be mindful of God in their daily affairs and dealings.

Question 11: Was It Eve's (PBUH) Fault That They Ate From the Tree?

No! In nearly all instances where the matter of Adam and Eve (peace be upon them both) is mentioned in the Quran, it is stated that both made a mistake, rather than placing the blame on one over the other. However, there is one specific instance where the Quran appears to hold Adam (peace be upon him) more accountable for the mistake than Eve (peace be upon her). Quran 20:115 states:

> *I (God) gave a directive to Adam yet he forgot it - I (God) did not find him very determined and resolute in this matter.*

Question 12: Was Eve (PBUH) Created From Adam's (PBUH) Rib?

No! Regarding this specific issue, the Quran states:

> *O humankind - it is God who created you from one soul and from it created its mate...(Quran 4:1).*

Hence, the Quran seems to suggest that we are all descended from Adam (PBUH), and from either his soul or his species, God created Eve (PBUH). There is a Hadith in which Muhammad is reported to have said that Eve (peace be upon her) was created from Adam's (peace be upon him) rib.

O Muslims! I advise you to be gentle with women, for they are created from a rib, and the most crooked portion of the rib is its upper part. If you try to straighten it, it will break, and if you leave it, it will remain crooked; so, I urge you to take care of women (Sahih al-Bukhari, No: 5185; Sahih of Muslim, No: 3468).

If the attribution of this narration to Muhammad is accurate and he genuinely made this statement, then it's conceivable that he was creating a metaphorical parable using a woman and a rib to emphasize that women have a complex nature, and men should not attempt to forcefully shape them according to their expectations.

Question 13: What Is the Significance of Hadith of Gabriel?

If one wishes to understand what Islam is through key points, there sits the pinnacle of the most steadfast tradition across all Hadith literature, known as the Hadith of Gabriel. During the final months of Muhammad's (PBUH) life, an unrecognized man entered the mosque while Muhammad (PBUH) delivered a sermon. Given that Medina was a small community where locals were familiar faces, it was peculiar that nobody recognized him. Additionally, the man bore no signs of travel; he appeared remarkably fresh, clad in brand-new clothing. This stranger sat next to the Prophet (PBUH) and began asking questions about the faith. As the Prophet (PBUH) responded, the man nodded in approval of the answers, astonishing those in attendance. They wondered who this man could be to affirm the Messenger of God's explanations about their religion. Upon the man's departure, Muhammad (PBUH) revealed to everyone that this was Gabriel in human form, sent by God to elucidate their faith. Imagine that—God sent Gabriel in human form to simplify religious teachings through straightforward points! I want to share this hadith here because it is an excellent and perfect summary of the entire message of Islam.

Gabriel asked Muhammad (PBUH) - "What is Faith?" - he replied - "Faith is to believe in God, His Angels, the Meeting with God on Judgment Day, His Messengers and to believe in being resurrected on Judgment Day."

Gabriel asked - "What is Islam?" - he replied - "To worship God alone and no one else in the least bit - to offer prayers and to pay compulsory tax (zakat) and to observe fasts of Ramadan."

Gabriel asked further - "What is Ihsan (Perfection)?" - he replied - "To worship God as if you see Him and if you cannot achieve this state of devotion then you must remember that God sees you."

Gabriel asked - "When will the Day of Judgment be established?" - he replied "The answerer has no better knowledge than the questioner (meaning no one knows about the exact date) - but I shall tell you its signs:

1) When the slave gives birth to her master. (I agree with the opinion of Mr. Javed Ahmed Ghamidi that Muhammad (PBUH) said in a symbolic way that slavery as an institution shall be abolished in the world - which is a good thing.)
2) When Bedouin shepherds (Arabs) start competing in making tall buildings" (Sahih of Bukhari, No: 43 and Sahih of Muslim, No: 1).

It is noteworthy that both signs of Judgment Day foretold in this Hadith have materialized roughly in the same era: slavery was officially abolished globally in the UN Declaration of Human Rights in 1948, and Arabs began competing to construct tall buildings globally since the early 2000s.

Question 14: What Is Faith in the Unseen?

There is a common belief among Muslims that the Quranic term "Iman bil Ghaib" or "Faith in the Unseen" implies blind faith without reason.

This is not the case. The Quran emphasizes the use of reason on nearly every page.

Faith signifies trust in something based on evidence, while blind faith implies trust without any evidence. The Quran emphasizes faith, or trust, based on evidence. Faith in the Unseen refers to trusting in the existence of an unseen God and realm, grounded on available evidence.

Question 15: Why Is the Universe So Vast?

Quran 14:48 states that this present universe is the primordial form of the infinite, eternal world that is yet to form. To put it in very simplistic terms, it is the scattered raw material for the next world to come.

Question 16: Why is God Called Allah?

God, as referenced in the Quran, identifies Himself with two names: Rahman, meaning the Most Compassionate, and Allah, which translates simply to "God" in Arabic. Similar appellations are found for God in the Bible as well; for instance, the Hebrew word Elohim in Genesis 1:1-2:4a and the Aramaic word Eloi in Mark 15:34. Thus, whether it's Allah in Arabic, Elohim in Hebrew, or Eloi in Aramaic, all these terms in their respective languages mean "God."

The Quran, in Chapter 7, Verse 80, proclaims that all beautiful names can be attributed to God. Hence, God can be called by any beautiful name in any language, as long as it aligns with the attributes of God mentioned in the Quran.

Question 17: What Is the Importance of Knowing Our Limitations, and Can We Truly Understand the Reality of God, Angels, the Soul, and the World to Come?

For thousands of years, humanity has debated the true nature of the metaphysical but made no real progress. A consensus began to develop a few hundred years ago that humans should accept the limits of what they can know, let go of our focus on what is beyond the scope of our senses, and concentrate solely on understanding what we can objectively observe and measure. This acceptance of our limits led to the modern scientific revolution.

The Quran expects humans to accept the limits of what they can know and cautions people that the true nature of the Soul, Angels, the coming world, and the exact physical nature of God cannot be known by humans at this time, as they are beyond our observation and comprehension in this limited worldly life. The Quran calls verses that refer to such concepts as "Mutashabihaat," meaning things that are explainable only through parables and analogies. It cautions against trying to understand the true nature of Mutashabihaat in the following verse:

> God is the One Who has revealed to you ˹O Prophet˺ the Book, of which some verses are clear and they are the foundation of the Book – while others are Mutashabihaat (allegorical and ambiguous). Those with deviant hearts pursue the true meaning of these allegorical and ambiguous verses seeking ˹to spread˺ doubt through their ˹false˺ interpretations but none grasps their ˹full˺ meaning except God (Quran 3:7.)

Question 18: If the Quran's God is Universal, Why Do So Many Religions Exist?

Quran's God - A Global God

Typically, many religions portray God as being active exclusively within a particular area or culture. They often fail to address questions like: Why was God involved only in one part of the world for a specific culture and seemingly absent from the rest?

The Quran presents a universal God - a God who instilled guidance within humankind and then sent reminders, details, and corrections through Messengers to all societies. Finally, this God dispatched His Emissaries to all communities as earthly demonstrations of God's judgment before making the phenomenon of Prophethood exclusive to Abraham's lineage, with the purpose of raising nations to undertake God's work.

The Quran Explains the Existence of Other Religions

The Quran also accounts for the existence of all other religions. It states that other religions have emerged due to a combination of the following reasons:

1) Quran 2:213 states that all humanity originally followed the same religion, but over time, they began to differ due to mutual animosity.
2) Furthermore, the Quran states that people began to worship the Jinn, Angels, and pious individuals in their societies, as outlined in Quran 6:100, 34:40-41, and 9:31, inventing elaborate stories and mythologies around them.

Question 19: Why Did God Need to Send Scriptures Repeatedly?

Islam is not a new message of guidance; it is, in fact, the same message that has been provided to humanity since its inception. This message evolved and expanded to meet the needs of human cultural and societal evolution, and was finally completed in the 7th century. Consequently, the God of the Quran proclaimed:

> *This day, I (God) have perfected your religion for you and completed my favor upon you and have chosen Islam (Submission to the will of God) as a way of life for you [Quran 5:3].*

Question 20: What does Islam mean?

Islam is an Arabic word meaning "to surrender." Therefore, in its Quranic context, Islam signifies surrendering oneself to God and embracing the Truth.

Question 21: If Morality Can Only Be Derived From Religious Scriptures, Then Why Do Morally Good Atheists Exist?

There is a common criticism from skeptics of religion that questions the need for a religious book to be a moral person, asking why there are moral atheists if such a book is necessary. The Quran addresses this doubt by asserting that humans do not need a book to distinguish right from wrong, as this knowledge is inherently embedded within them (Quran 91:7-8). The scriptures given through prophets serve as reminders and elaborate on the moral guidance innate to every individual. They also offer divine direction in situations where the human moral compass has been corrupted.

Question 22: What Are Some Predictions in the Quran That Came True?

There are certain predictions made in the Quran about the immediate future that miraculously came true. These are some additional reasons why my belief in the credibility of the Quran is strengthened

a) In 615 AD, Khusru Parviz of Persia attacked the Byzantine (Roman) Empire and gained control of Syria, Palestine, and North Africa. He ransacked Jerusalem, set fire to the Holy Sepulcher, and destroyed numerous cities. The war concluded with a significant and clear victory for Persia, and the Byzantine Empire seemed doomed. However, the Quran immediately predicted that within a few years, the Byzantines would triumph against the Persians. It also foretold that on the same day, Muslims would rejoice over a victory granted to them by God. God describes this as a promise from Him that will surely come to pass (Quran 30:2-7).

This prediction was extremely risky because if it had not come true, then the entire case for the Quran being divinely inspired would have become doubtful.

Remarkably, nine years later, in 624 AD, the Byzantine Empire bounced back and won a decisive victory against Persia on the same day the Muslims won their first battle, the Battle of Badr, against the Meccan polytheists.

b) Quran chapter 28, verse 85, was revealed when Muhammad, then a solitary preacher with only a few followers, was compelled to leave Mecca. This verse foretells his triumphant return to Mecca, an event that history indeed confirms.

c) Following the Treaty of Hudaybiyah in 628 AD, Muslims believed they had entered into a disastrous agreement with the Meccans, one that would greatly harm them in the years to come. However, Quran 48:27 predicted the imminent Muslim takeover of Mecca, and just two years later, the Muslims indeed captured Mecca.

d) Quran 24:55 predicts that those who support Muhammad, the Messenger of God, will be made rulers of a massive empire as a divine reward. This prophecy was fulfilled as Muhammad's (PBUH) immediate followers, who initially lacked substantial military prowess, ended up as rulers of a truly vast empire historically known as the "Rashidun Caliphate," which emerged after defeating the two superpowers of that era, the Byzantine and Persian Empires. This empire encompassed territories which would include modern states such as Libya, Egypt, Turkey, Armenia, Azerbaijan, Jerusalem, Syria, Iraq, Jordan, Saudi Arabia, Yemen, Oman, the UAE, Iran, Afghanistan, Turkmenistan, and parts of Pakistan.

Question 23: Does the Quran Inaccurately Quote Earlier Religious Texts?

Another remarkable aspect of the Quran is that it corrects historical errors found in earlier scriptures. Even more astounding is the fact that there was absolutely no way anyone could have access to the information the Quran provides when correcting these historical errors. Let us consider two examples:

a) Haman, as described in the Book of Esther from the Bible (starting from Esther 3), was a minister to a Persian king. In contrast, the Quran in Surah 40:36 portrays Haman as a minister for Pharaoh, tasked with overseeing construction. For those who believe Muhammad (PBUH) copied from the Bible, this was deemed an error from Muhammad (PBUH).

It was impossible to determine whether Haman was with Pharaoh or the Babylonian king, as the Egyptian language had become extinct. No one could decipher it until the Rosetta Stone was discovered in 1799 AD. In his book, "Moses and Pharaoh in the Bible, Quran, and History," French researcher Maurice Bucaille noted that he uncovered "Haman" (represented in Egyptian Hieroglyphics as HMNH) was a title used under the Pharaohs of Egypt, signifying the official in charge of construction materials.

It is important to note that while it is a popular idea that Rameses I was the Pharaoh during the time of Moses (PBUH), there is no historical proof of this, and the Quran does not mention Rameses by name. Therefore, to be more accurate, we don't know for sure which exact Pharaoh the Quran is referring to in the story of Moses (PBUH).

b) The correct historical use of the title "Pharaoh": The Bible states that the Egyptian rulers who interacted with Joseph and Moses (PBUH) were called Pharaohs (Genesis 12:10-20 and Genesis 41:1-57).

We know that the title of Pharaoh was given to Egyptian kings much later, specifically in the New Kingdom era (from 1400 BC onwards).[65]

Although it is nearly impossible to provide a verifiable, exact date for the existence of the two prophets mentioned, there is a general consensus that Joseph (PBUH) lived in Egypt during its early kingdom period, before the mass migration of the Hebrews. Moses (PBUH), on the other hand, existed much later, at a time when Egypt had enslaved the Hebrews for many centuries. Therefore, it is highly probable that during Joseph's time, the Egyptian rulers of the early period were not referred to as Pharaohs. I find it extremely intriguing that, although the Bible refers to all Egyptian kings as Pharaohs, the Quran, in a remarkable display of historical accuracy, specifically calls the ruler of Egypt during the time of Moses (PBUH) "Pharaoh," as in Quran 40:26, but refers to the rulers during Joseph's (PBUH) era simply as "Ruler" or "King," as seen in Quran 12:54.

Question 24: If God Is the Sustainer, Then Why Are There Hunger, Drought, and Famines?

This answer is divided into three parts.

1) The Quran informs us that God tests creatures both through abundance and scarcity, thus some people are inevitably bound to have more than others.

2) This world operates in a cycle of life and death; therefore, animals, in particular, sometimes face death due to drought and famine.

3) On an individual level, one must make an effort to receive God's sustenance. This is God's law. For example, one must farm the land, open a shop, or perform certain labor; only then will sustenance be earned. God, being the Sustainer and Provider, does not imply that one can simply sit idly and expect God to rain down money or provisions. This principle applies to all humanity. God as the Sustainer means that He has provided sufficient resources on this earth to feed everyone. It is now humanity's responsibility to make an effort to earn this sustenance and, more importantly, ensure that it reaches everyone. Factors such as politics, poor economic policies, tremendous

food waste, the control and exploitation of resources, and border controls or restrictions on movement lead many people to suffer from starvation and hunger, despite the earth's capacity to feed significantly more than eight billion people.

Question 25: Why Is the World So Imperfect?

This world is imperfect and flawed by design, serving the purpose of testing people. The Quran repeatedly states that everyone is being tested, either through abundance, prosperity, and good times or through scarcity, loss, and hard times. Thus, it can accurately be stated that while this world is imperfect for living, it is perfectly designed for testing. According to the Quran, Paradise is the perfect world, created for eternal living.

Question 26: What are the Quran's Guidelines for Those Who Want to Preach God's Message.

The Quran provides detailed guidelines for those who wish to preach God's message. Quran 16:125 specifically demands particular manners and states:

> *Call people to the way of God but with wisdom and with kindness. If you are to debate, do it in the most amicable manner.*

The verse further stipulates that people should only preach God's message in the best way and prohibits them from passing judgment on others in matters of faith:

> *Only God alone knows who has strayed from His path and who is rightly guided.*

Even Muhammad (PBUH) was repeatedly told in the Qur'an that his duty was only to clearly deliver the message; proclaiming judgment is solely up to God. When a living Rasool of God is in the world, God proclaims judgment on matters of faith here on Earth. Now, because there will be no Rasool of God on Earth, all matters of faith will be judged by God on the Day of Judgment, and no one has any right to pass any judgment or punishment on anyone in this world on matters of faith.

Furthermore, the Quran makes it abundantly clear in various passages, such as Quran 14:4, that the primary role of a preacher is to convey the truth to the best of his abilities. However, it is not within the preacher's power to ensure that others are guided; rather, it is God who determines who receives guidance and who does not. God decides the extent of guidance granted to each individual based on various factors, including the sincerity with which a person follows his moral compass, the seriousness, sincerity, and persistence of the seeker, the honesty and truthfulness of the individual, and the person's ability to rise above all biases when analyzing facts.

Question 27: Is the Quran meant to Provide Scientific Explanations of Natural Phenomena?

When the Quran comments on the sun, moon, stars, and other natural phenomena, it is not attempting to elucidate the science behind these phenomena. Instead, it aims to appeal to what the 7th-century Arabs, its immediate audience, observed with their own eyes, thereby arousing their intellectual faculties to contemplate God and the afterlife. For example, in Quran 36:40, it addresses the 7th-century Arabs, urging them to observe how the sun does not overtake the moon and vice-versa, thereby encouraging reflection on existential questions. This passage is not intended to educate him or future readers of the Quran about astronomy or astrophysics.

Thus, the correct view of the Quran is that it is not a book of science, nor does it claim to be one. However, when there is information in the Quran with scientific implications—such as details about the multiverse or human origin—established science and the Quran do not contradict each other.

Question 28: Why Does the Quran Mention the Carnal Pleasures of Paradise for Men, and What Will Women Receive?

Quran 43:31, along with many other verses, clearly states that those in Paradise—both men and women—will receive whatever they wish for. It is inherently implied that one cannot wish for anything unjust or evil. Therefore, regardless of whether you are a man or a woman, you will receive everything you desire in Paradise.

The Quran specifically mentions the fulfillment of carnal desires for men, as they were the primary audience during its revelation, being central to the political and military efforts of Islam. These men were called upon to exercise extreme self-control while simultaneously being required to engage in war and perform other strenuous duties for Islam.

Islam does not view sexual desire as inherently evil; however, the expression of sexual desire is strictly limited to marriage in this worldly life to safeguard the family institution, as previously discussed. In Paradise, the institution of family will be an optional wish rather than a human necessity, hence there will be no restrictions on sexual desire.

Question 29: How Does the Quran Describe Paradise, and Are These Descriptions Literal or Symbolic?

The Quran fundamentally asserts that the true essence of the life to come—Paradise, Hell, the nature of God, Angels, and so forth—cannot be completely understood at present. Therefore, it employs parallels and analogies to offer humans a glimpse of what the future world might be like.

While making a principled statement that Paradise is a place of utmost contentment, pleasure, fulfillment, peace, and happiness, the Quran also provides specifics, stating that there will be rivers of milk and honey in Paradise and that people will wear silk and ornaments.

These specific details were conveyed with the immediate audience in mind, reflecting their conception of what luxury and abundance encompass.

The principles governing Paradise are eternal and timeless; for instance, one will receive whatever they wish for, and there will be perfect contentment and satisfaction. However, the particulars of Paradise explained in the Quran are laid out with the immediate audience in mind.

Question 30: Why Did God Choose Arabic to Deliver His Final Message?

Because the immediate recipients of God's message at the time spoke Arabic (Quran 12:2 & 41:3).

Question 31: Why is God invisible?

So people can have freedom of choice. This freedom of choice is at the core of the life test we are undergoing. The whole point of this test is to see whether we choose to be truthful and good or dishonest and wicked. It makes sense because if such an all-powerful phenomenon like God (along with angels) were visible and immediately held people accountable, then it would most definitely compromise human freedom to do anything we want. Consider this overly simplistic parable: if a traffic sergeant is standing right in front of the traffic light, no sane person would cross at the red light.

Moreover, how could anyone have the option of rejecting God and His message if they could directly see God? Therefore, to afford people the freedom of choice, God and His entire realm are not directly visible. However, there are signs within us and around us that proclaim their existence.

Question 32: Are Human Beings at the Center of Existence?

We humans often feel we are special, and this sense of self-importance is frequently reflected in many religious ideologies that place humankind at the forefront and center of existence.

This concept is also popular among many Muslims who mistakenly believe that the Quran refers to humans as "Ashraf ul Makhlookaat," which translates to the most honored and superior creation of God. However, this phrase is not mentioned anywhere in the Quran. Quran 17:70 states that although God has exalted humans above "many" of His creations, it does not imply that humans are exalted over all of God's creatures. Furthermore, the Quran mentions the existence of angels and jinns, who are physically much superior to humans. The entire narrative of God demanding angels and jinns to accept human governance on earth was to see which of these creatures would obey His order, despite being physically superior to humans. The main objection of Iblees—the Devil—was his refusal to bow down to humans, citing his physical superiority. The Quran, in Surah Jinn, explains that apart from humans, jinns also undergo their own moral tests. Therefore, according to the Quran, the scheme of existence is not human-centric at all.

In essence, although the Quran states that humans are more special than many of God's creatures, it presents a model of existence that is not human-centric.

Question 33: What Is Islam's Stance on Homosexuality and Transgenderism?

Before we delve into this discussion, it is essential to understand that this matter is a subject of intense debate among liberals and conservatives. There are knowledgeable and accomplished individuals on both sides of the spectrum regarding this issue, and all parties claim to have scientific research supporting their perspectives. If you are liberal on the matters of sexual orientation and gender identity, you can find research material that supports your point of view. Similarly, if you are conservative on these issues, you will also find research material that supports your stance.

Islam on Transgenderism:

Proponents of transgenderism argue that biological sex and gender identity are distinctly separate concepts. They assert that chromosomes, sexual organs, and other biological traits do not define gender; instead, they view gender as a state of mind and a social construct.

Islam makes no such distinctions—if you are a biological male, you are a male; if you are a biological female, you are a female. The Quran treats this as an understood matter and does not specifically address the issue of whether one can identify as a different gender than their biological sex. However, there are certain Hadiths that directly address this issue and prohibit men from imitating women and vice versa (Sahih of Bukhari, No: 5885; Sunan of Abu Dawood, No: 4098 and 4099).

However, there is a general consensus among Muslim scholars that individuals with a biological anomaly should be allowed to undergo gender-affirming surgery. Conversely, if there are no biological anomalies and the individual's experience of a different gender identity is purely psychological, then, from the perspective of Islam, it is treated as a psychological disorder.

Islam and Homosexuality:

When addressing homosexuality, the Quran explicitly states that it is a sin, particularly in the context of the nation of Lot, the Prophet of God. But why is it deemed sinful? The primary reason is that the Quran strictly prohibits all forms of sexual activity outside of the marriage between a biological male and a biological female. This prohibition serves to protect and strengthen the institution of the family. Although we discussed earlier why the God of the Quran is so intent on fiercely protecting the family institution, I will reiterate it here for context.

The union of a man and woman serves as a mechanism to bring new human beings into this world. From day one, these new humans require tremendous care, extending up to at least 15 years or more. A human being is not merely a physical entity but also encompasses psychological, emotional, moral, and spiritual dimensions. Thus, the extensive care and nurturing a newborn requires must address all these categories. A human needs physical, psychological, emotional, moral, and spiritual care to enhance their well-being in this life and, more importantly, in the hereafter. God has established the institution of the biological family unit, which consists of a biological male and a biological female united in marriage. According to the Quran, God desires a stable family unit that can provide for and nurture this new human in all the aforementioned areas effectively.

Another extremely crucial function of the family institution is to care for individuals as they reach old age. A stable family institution is the best mechanism for providing physical and emotional care to the elderly. While old age homes are a viable plan B for many, and some individuals in developed countries might prefer them as their plan A, it is evident—without needing to cite specific research—that old age homes cannot provide the same level of psychological and emotional fulfillment and care as a stable family institution can.

Therefore, to protect and strengthen the institution of the biological family, any sexual behavior outside the marriage between a biological male and a biological female is considered a sin.

Through my learnings of the Quran, I have learned that if you are a Muslim who identifies as bisexual or gender fluid, accepting God's plan and choosing heterosexuality, along with identifying with your biological sex, is seen as a personal decision, generally made without the need for external assistance.

However, if you are transgender or homosexual and feel that your inclinations are so inherent that you have no control over them regardless of your efforts, I do empathize with you, for it is indeed a significant test and trial. The God of the Quran expects you to manage your desires. If this expectation from God seems overly demanding, know that you are not alone; many heterosexual individuals also undergo strenuous exercises of self-control in matters of sexuality and intimacy. Consider the requirement of being sexually and emotionally exclusive to your spouse—for instance, it demands an immense amount of self-control in heterosexual marriages, particularly if the marriage lacks emotional or sexual fulfillment. Nevertheless, the fact remains—if you identify as a compulsive transsexual or homosexual, your challenges are unique, and society should be tolerant and provide all possible assistance to alleviate your suffering and address your concerns. If you fail to suppress these urges and commit sins in this category, the Quran expects you to conceal those sins and not flaunt them. However, also be aware that the Quran doesn't condemn you to eternal hell for these sins. Continue to strive for abstinence, seek forgiveness, and maintain other aspects of your life to the best of your ability regarding God's teachings. Persist in prayer, giving to charity, and strive to be a humble and good person.

As a Muslim, if I encounter a transgender person or a homosexual, even though I do not agree with their ideology, I still respect their right to make their own personal choices. I will treat them with the same respect as I would any other person. This approach extends to people I know who covertly or overtly engage in behaviors that Islam forbids. For instance, many of my acquaintances engage in sexual relations outside of marriage, gamble, or drink alcohol. Although I disagree with these choices because they contradict my moral and religious beliefs, I respect their right to make these decisions for themselves. Indeed, the God of the Quran has given people the choice to make their own decisions out of their free will.

However, certain actions, when performed publicly and defiantly, have worldly consequences in Islam. I would like to briefly address the worldly punishment for homosexuality in Islam. In Islam, all sexual activities, whether heterosexual or homosexual, that occur outside of a marriage between a male and a female are considered sins. If these sins are committed in secrecy, the issue remains solely between the individual and God. However, if these sins are openly and shamelessly committed, then four credible witnesses are required to register a case. Should the investigation confirm that the sin occurred, it then becomes a crime, punishable under Islamic law. This standard applies to all sexual activities outside of marriage, including both heterosexual and homosexual acts.

The Quran does not specify any worldly punishment for homosexuality. It can be inferred that the punishment for adultery in the Quran applies to both heterosexual and homosexual acts. Consequently, all jurists agree that homosexuality is both a sin and a crime, but they differ significantly in their prescribed punishments. These discrepancies have always existed in Islamic juristic tradition regarding the nature and severity of worldly punishments for this crime. Some Hadith reports suggest that certain companions of Muhammad (PBUH) believed the punishment for homosexual adultery should be more severe than that for heterosexual adultery. However, other Hadith reports led esteemed scholars like Imam Shafi and Imam Ahmed to conclude that the punishment for homosexual adultery should be the same as that for heterosexual adultery. Scholars like Abu Hanifa considered the punishment for homosexual adultery should be less severe than that for heterosexual adultery, recommending that the punishment should be left to the discretion of the judge (Ta'zeer) rather than dictated by divine law or "Hadd."

There are reports in Hadith literature indicating that Muhammad (PBUH) ordained the death penalty for homosexuality (Jami' of al-Tirmidhi, No: 1456; Sunan of Abu Dawood, No: 4462; Sunan of Ibn Majah, No: 2561). We must revert to our principle of understanding Hadith through the framework provided in the Quran. As discussed earlier, according to Quran 5:32, the death penalty can only be administered for murder or crimes categorized as Fasaad fil Ardh, meaning "wreaking havoc on earth." When adultery is committed persistently, openly, and defiantly despite repeated attempts to stop it, it qualifies as a crime under the category of Fasaad fil Ardh. The Hadith literature informs us that Muhammad (PBUH) issued the death penalty for heterosexual adultery when it fell into this category. Therefore, one can reasonably infer that if the attribution of this narration to Muhammad (PBUH) is accurate, then, just like heterosexual adultery, he is mandating the death penalty for homosexual adultery if the crimes are committed openly, defiantly, and persistently.

In summary, any heterosexual or homosexual behaviors or actions outside the confines of marriage between a man and a woman are considered major sins, carrying severe punishment on Judgment Day. If these behaviors and actions are conducted publicly, persistently, and defiantly, then the sin escalates to a crime, which carries worldly punishment.

Question 34: Why Does the Quran State That All Glory and Praise Belong to God?

There are many passages in the Quran that state phrases such as "All praise and glory belong to God."

The Arabic word often translated as "Praise" is "Hamd." This term encompasses more than simply praising someone; it implies offering one's gratitude in a holistic sense.

Thus, these verses convey a fundamental truth: since God is the creator and sustainer of everything, all gratitude fundamentally belongs to God.

In other places, where the Quran declares that all praise and glory belong to God, it expresses a fundamental truth about God. Let me explain.

When we view this matter from a human perspective, it seems odd if someone says, "All praise belongs to me." We feel this way because, as far as humans are concerned, being praiseworthy is a subjective matter. However, when we view this from the perspective of God, the phrase "All Glory & Praise Belong to God" is not a subjective statement but an expression of a fundamental and literal truth. Imagine if there truly is a God, then it is an absolute truth that all glory and praise indeed belong to God because God created everything!

Moreover, when we are not directly praising God but praising anything else, we are still praising God because He created it. Thus, it is a literal fact that all praise—both direct and indirect—belongs exclusively to God.

Question 35: Could God Have Created Everything Without Creating Hell? Is Hell Eternal?

Hell serves some crucial and unavoidable purposes.

For me, the concept of divine punishments made sense. It seemed logical that one would need to atone for their sins and crimes through some form of punishment in this world or the hereafter, and then be released once purged of their sins. One purpose of Hell is to serve as a place where those whose deeds merit punishment can atone before being admitted to Paradise. Thus, Hell had to be created by God as a form of temporary purgatory.

But what about the concept of permanent Hell? Let us briefly analyze it. If your crimes are so heinous that no amount of purging can justify your release, then eternal death may seem appropriate. However, the idea of eternal suffering as punishment troubled me—no matter the crime committed in this world, it remains finite. How can someone suffer infinitely and eternally for a finite crime? Perhaps I am mistaken. Maybe a criminal does deserve eternal misery if they, while being mentally sound, are guilty of heinous acts such as the torture, rape, and murder of a child, committed entirely out of lust.

Quran 92:15 clearly states that the severest punishment in Hell is reserved for the most evil and wretched individuals. The Quran also unequivocally declares that those doomed to eternal Hell will reside there forever. However, there is a passage in the Quran suggesting that after everyone has received their due punishment, Hell, along with all its inhabitants, might eventually be permanently eradicated and subjected to eternal death by God. After all, being nothing forever is a form of punishment in itself.

Quran 11:106-107 states

> *Those who are bound for misery - they will be in the fire where they shall be sighing and gasping staying there forever as long as the heavens and the earth (of Hell) will remain - unless your Lord wills anything else. Surely - your Lord can do anything He wills.*

So, these verses indicate that the most evil and wretched individuals, once left in Hell, will remain there for as long as Hell exists. Then, God mentions that if He wills otherwise, He has the power to act—meaning, if He decides to permanently eliminate Hell along with all its residents, He can indeed do so.

Now the same question arises about Paradise—can God eliminate Paradise if He wills? In the very next verse, God assures us that no, Paradise is eternal and permanent and shall never be eliminated.

Quran 11:108 continues the discussion from the preceding verses:

And as for those destined for joy, they will be in Paradise - staying there forever as long as the heavens and earth (of Paradise) will remain - unless your Lord wills anything else. But Paradise is an eternal and permanent gift of your Lord that will never end.

There is a slight chance that Hell might be eliminated permanently and all of its residents given permanent death. However, ideas like "Hell being a temporary purgatory" or the "possibility of the elimination of Hell and its permanent residents" should not cause a sigh of relief for anyone. This is because someone who ends up in Hell will have to endure it for God knows how many trillions upon trillions of years before they are given any relief..

Question 36: Who Is the Devil? Do We Commit Sin Because of the Devil?

Quran 12:53 clearly states that the tendency to commit evil resides within humans. The verse explains that a part of our soul persistently incites us to engage in wrongdoing. Ultimately, it is our decision whether to succumb to this aspect of ourselves or resist it.

The Quran clearly states that we have a formidable enemy in the race of Jinn. Jinn are sentient beings who are physically superior and more powerful than humans. According to Quran 7:27, they can see us from places where we are unable to see them—this could suggest that Jinn might be higher-dimensional beings.

The Jinn race is also undergoing its own test of free will and morality. Like us, they form communities and encompass both virtuous and malevolent individuals. However, one specific Jinn named Iblees, mentioned in Quran 18:50, along with his progeny, are declared adversaries of humankind. Their enmity towards humans stems from their expulsion by God for Iblees's refusal to submit to humans as commanded by God. Iblees justified his disobedience by claiming superiority over humans, having been created from what he perceived as a superior essence. It was this arrogance and discriminatory belief that led to his banishment (Quran 7:12 & 38:76). Following this expulsion; Iblees and his descendants vowed to lead as many humans as possible into sin, aiming to prevent them from entering God's paradise.

The only power that Iblees and his progeny possess is to instill thoughts into our minds, inciting us to commit wrongful acts. However, it is entirely up to us whether we listen to and obey these thoughts, or resist and reject them. Consequently, on the Day of Judgment, when people attempt to blame Iblees for their wrongdoing, he will respond:

> *I did not have any authority over you. I only invited you – it was your decision to accept my invitation. So do not blame me, blame yourself. I cannot save you now nor can you save me (Quran 14:22).*

Hence, the ability and tendency to do evil are within us, and it is our decision to do evil or to refrain from it. Satan and his progeny can only instill thoughts and ideas into our minds and try to exploit our weaknesses to incite us to do evil.

Question 37: Why Does God Need Everyone's Worship?

Quran 51:56 states that humans and jinn were created to worship God. However, this does not imply that humans and jinn are meant to constantly engage in rituals of worship. Rituals are merely one form of expressing worship.

Worship is a holistic term that encompasses meanings such as love, loyalty, devotion, gratitude, and obedience. Therefore, the Quran states that humans and jinn are created to live with the acknowledgment that they are crafted by God and that it is God who has provided them with everything. In return, basic morality requires that they be humble and grateful, rather than rebellious and arrogant toward God.

Question 38: What Kind of Guidelines Must I Follow as an Actor/Artist?

Starting in 2014, I began to consider that Islam might be the truth. I use the phrase "might be" because, although Islam answered many of my existential questions, there were still numerous inquiries left unanswered. During this period, Mr. Javed Ahmed Ghamidi played a crucial role in my quest for answers to these lingering questions. I cannot pinpoint the exact time, but it was around 2018-19 when I realized that all of my questions had been addressed, and I transitioned from believing that Islam "might be" the divine truth to being convinced that Islam "really is" the divine truth. This realization was life-altering.

In 2019, I made a video to announce to the public that I had concluded that Islam, scriptures, prophets, messengers, angels, and the Day of Judgment—all of this is true! I announced that I would be taking a very long hiatus from acting in order to learn more and preach about what I now believe is the divine truth from God.

In this video message, which remains uploaded on my YouTube channel, I specifically mentioned two things.

1) I clearly said that my hiatus from acting should not be interpreted in the manner that I have left showbiz because Islam prohibits Art and I made it amply clear that the interpretation of Islam I have come to agree with does not forbid any art form like Music, Painting, Sculpting, and Acting. Instead, it sets

certain moral limits set by God in which a Muslim can engage with all of these art forms.

2) I also said that I am not sure when or if I will come back to acting because now, as someone who is deeply concerned about being accountable to God on Judgment Day, I can only work in projects which are within the moral limits set by God and there are not many projects which are made completely within these divine moral limits especially when it comes to films. I also vowed that if I don't find projects which are within the moral boundaries of God, then I will abstain from working, as God has provided me with other means to live my life relatively comfortably.

However, despite my clarity and unambiguity on the points mentioned in the video message, newspapers and news channels the next day were filled with headlines stating, "Hamza Ali Abbasi quits showbiz for Islam." I believe this occurred because there is a deep-rooted belief in my society that Islam forbids all forms of art, and perhaps also because many people did not listen to the complete video message.

According to the interpretation of Islam that I believe to be true, championed by Mr. Javed Ahmed Ghamidi in contemporary times, men and women are permitted to study and work together, and engage in various art forms, provided they adhere to the moral boundaries established by God. The Quran elaborates extensively on these moral boundaries; however, I have selected Quran 7:33 to mention here because it delineates these moral boundaries clearly.

This verse prohibits the following:

1) All forms of intimate or sexual behavior must be strictly confined to marriage and conducted privately behind closed doors.

Hence, whether it's the lyrics of a song, dialogues in a film or drama, the clothing of the artists, or their interactions, anything even remotely sexual in nature is absolutely not allowed in Islam.

This means that as an actor, I cannot engage in any activities that require me to wear, do, or say anything that is even remotely sexual in nature. Additionally, I cannot touch any woman in any kind of intimate or sexual manner. Regarding women's clothing, in light of certain verses of Surah Nur which I will discuss later, they must not wear anything that is tight or reveals their body in any way from the neck to wrists down to the ankle. If a woman has to wear jewelry or other adornments, she must ensure that she covers them, except for what is on the face, hands, and feet. If she cannot cover the adornments, then the least she can do is to ensure that her adornments do not make her sensual areas prominent or draw attention to these areas. For example, she should not wear necklaces that accentuate or draw attention to the chest area.

2) Injustice is prohibited.

Whether it's the lyrics of a song or the storyline of a film, if anything within an art form justifies or glorifies injustice, then it is prohibited.

3) Unlawfully harming another person's life, property, or dignity is prohibited.

If any element of an art form promotes or glorifies the infliction of unlawful harm to a person's life, property, or dignity, then such art is prohibited. Violence itself is not prohibited; however, if violence is depicted in a way that glorifies or justifies unlawful and immoral behaviors and actions, then it is prohibited.

4) Associating partners with God is prohibited.

If any art form promotes or glorifies shirk—the practice of associating partners with God or worshiping multiple gods—then such art is prohibited.

5) Lying about God is prohibited.

If any art form is spreading false ideas about God, then such art form is prohibited.

Apart from these five prohibitions, the Quran also says in multiple places that if anything is done at the cost of any religious obligation, then that becomes an unlawful action. For example, trade is a completely lawful activity in Islam but if trade is done while neglecting a religious obligation, then the Quran in chapter 61 verse 11 has forsaken such trade. Same goes for any art form; if one engages with any art form while being negligent towards any religious duty, then it is a sin.

Another very important point is that as a Muslim, I cannot endorse the use of any substance that is prohibited by God - for example I cannot endorse consumption of alcohol.

Also, the prevalent interpretation of Islam in my society believes that Islam makes gender segregation a compulsion, all musical instruments are prohibited, painting or sculpting living things is prohibited, an ideal Muslim woman should not step out of the house, she should cover herself up head to toe, and not have her voice heard by anyone outside of the family! The interpretation I have come to agree with negates all of these ideas, and I shall explain these points in detail in a later section.

It is a constant battle trying to abide by these guidelines because many things God has prohibited have become very normal in present times in the media. Hence, whenever I feel I have knowingly or unknowingly been a part of something which might exceed the limits set by God, I remind myself of the Quranic verse that God will forgive minor sins. Quran 4:31:

> *If you avoid the major sins prohibited to you - I (God) will certainly forgive your minor sins and admit you into a place of honor.*

CHAPTER 7B

QUESTIONS AND ANSWERS BASED ON MY LEARNINGS FROM JAVED AHMED GHAMIDI

I want to reemphasize what I mentioned at the beginning of the book—I am not a scholarly student of Mr. Javed Ahmed Ghamidi. I am merely a layperson who has found some answers to my questions through Mr. Ghamidi's teachings. If I make any errors in my understanding or in my explanation of what I have learned and understood from Mr. Ghamidi, he bears no responsibility for these mistakes.

For those interested in exploring further details of the answers I share below, I recommend checking out Mr. Javed Ahmed Ghamidi's books and videos across various platforms online. Some notable works include his books Meezan, Muqamaat, Burhan, and Al-Islam, as well as his video lecture series "Response to 23 Questions…" and "Dallas Lectures," available on his primary YouTube channel, "Ghamidi Center of Islamic Learning."

Let us revisit the correct understanding of the sources of Islam that I learned from Mr. Javed Ahmed Ghamidi. Although we have discussed this in detail in an earlier section, it is important to briefly analyze this point again to refresh our understanding before we dive into the question-and-answer section.

Sources of Islam

The Quran explicitly states on multiple occasions that God conveyed His message and religion solely through His Messengers and divine scriptures. Since Muhammad (PBUH) is God's final Messenger, any belief or practice deemed part of God's religion must have clear evidence of Muhammad's (PBUH) approval. This means that for anything to be included in or excluded from the religion, there must be clear evidence that it was approved by Prophet Muhammad (PBUH).

Muhammad (PBUH) conveyed God's teachings through the Quran and Sunnah.

The Quran asserts that it should be the primary lens through which all other religious literature is understood. For something to be deemed halal (lawful) or haram (unlawful), the Quran must allow or prohibit it, either directly or in principle. If the Quran represents the theory, then the Sunnah embodies the practical aspect of this theory. Both the Quran and Sunnah have been transmitted collectively from the Prophet (PBUH) through generations up to the present day. All of Islam is contained within the Quran and Sunnah.

The key to understanding the Quran is to approach it by first grasping its correct introduction. The Quran is the preserved communication from God, demonstrating His divine judgment on Earth through Muhammad (PBUH), His last Rasool. It contains:

- Details of how all humans will face divine accountability on Judgment Day and how to attain success in that accountability.

- God's narration of events and His instructions to believers as events unfolded with Muhammad (PBUH) and his companions.
- God's commands on laws and guidance for humanity.
- The Quran is a record of the revelations God imparted to Prophet Muhammad (PBUH), directed towards Jews, Christians, and Pagans.
- God's account of how He fostered a nation through the descendants of Israel, how they propagated God's message worldwide, and why God concluded His covenant with them.
- God's commandments and how He raised a new nation to preach His message to the world through Muhammad (PBUH).
- In the Quran, God also tells us how He unleashed His judgment on earth before Muhammad (PBUH) through other Rasools.
- Instructions about punishments and rewards for those who oppose and support the Messenger

The Quran asserts that it is written in clear Arabic and has been clearly explained, making it easy to understand. Therefore, interpreting the Quran must adhere to the prevailing rules of language comprehension. For instance, when discerning the meanings of Quranic verses, one must consider the most commonly understood meanings of the words, the implications derived from the sentence structure, and the context.

Additionally, Quranic verses cannot be understood in isolation. Instead, they must be understood in conjunction with all other verses relating to a particular subject. For instance, when analyzing what the Quran says about a Muslim's relationship with non-Muslims, all verses on this topic must be considered to form a correct opinion.

As a layperson, the most effective method for analyzing the Quranic text was first to comprehend its proper introduction, as previously mentioned, and then to read a straightforward translation from beginning to end. Whenever I encountered something that I did not understand in the text, I marked it and consulted scholarly opinions on the internet or from books. If something still did not make sense, I endeavored to contact scholars and experts to discuss the matter with them. Additionally, while reading the translations, I made sure to distinguish between the translation and the additional explanations written in footnotes and parentheses, as those are usually the translators' own opinions or interpretations of the text.

Hadith literature consists of reports about the actions and sayings of Prophet Muhammad (PBUH), transmitted not through mass transmission like the Quran and Sunnah, but through individual reports. It is a historical record of Muhammad's (PBUH) life and must be understood through the lens of the Quran and Sunnah. This historical record contains explanations and applications of the religion as outlined in the Quran and Sunnah but does not introduce any new commandments of religion. All commandments of Islam are issued directly or in principle through the Quran and Sunnah only.

The history of the immediate companions of Muhammad (PBUH) is a significant resource for understanding their interpretations of Islam. However, these historical records have reached us via individual reports and must be scrutinized and understood within the framework of the Quran and Sunnah.

Let us now move on to the Question and Answer section.

Question 1: Is Muhammad (PBUH) The Last Messenger And Prophet Of God?

Yes—the Quran and Hadith clearly state that Muhammad (PBUH) is the last messenger and prophet of God, and no prophet or messenger shall come after him.

While earlier scriptures, such as the Old Testament, New Testament, and even Hindu scriptures, predicted the coming of the last Messiah and Prophet, whom Muslims believe to be Muhammad (PBUH), the

Quran does not predict the coming of any more prophets or messengers after Muhammad (PBUH) and in fact clearly and very unambiguously states in one verse that Prophethood has ended with Muhammad (PBUH).

Quran 33:40 addresses this matter very clearly and says:

Muhammad is not the father of any of your men, but is the Messenger of God and the seal of the Prophets. And God has 'perfect' knowledge of all things.

The word used for seal is "khaatam," which commonly means to put a seal on something or to conclude something. Therefore, Muhammad (PBUH) is very clearly proclaimed as the seal or conclusion of Prophethood.

The Quran proclaims that God's message and religion were completed with Muhammad (PBUH), negating the need for any additional Prophets or Messengers. Quran 5:3 states:

Today I have perfected your religion for you, and I have completed my blessing upon you, and I have approved Islam for your religion.

This concept is further reinforced by several authentic Hadiths in which Muhammad (PBUH) proclaimed that all forms of Prophethood and Messengerhood ended with him. Let us analyze some of them below.

1) Sahih of Bukhari, No: 3525; Sahih of Muslim, No: 2287
   Muhammad (PBUH) is reported to have said: "The example of me and the example of Prophets of earlier times is like the example of a most beautiful palace constructed by a man. The man left a blank space for the last brick in one of its corners. People went around it and were surprised to look at its matchless beauty and exclaimed: 'Why is a brick missing in the building?'

The Prophet (PBUH) said: 'I am that last brick - I am the last Prophet of God.'"

2) Sahih of Muslim, No: 523 Muhammad (PBUH) is reported to have said: "I have been given the honor of excellence over other Prophets in six matters: (1) I have been bestowed with the ability to communicate ideas comprehensively with a few words; (2) I have been supported by being given awe and might; (3) Spoils of war have been made lawful for me; (4) The whole earth has been made a mosque and a means of purification for me; (5) I have been sent as a Prophet for the whole of humanity; (6) the chain of Prophethood has come to an end with me."

3) Sahih of Musilm, No: 1842, 2404. Muhammad (PBUH) is reported to have said: "... there will be no Prophet after me."

4) Sahih of Bukhari, 3455, Sahih of Muslim, 1842 Muhammad (PBUH) is reported to have said: "Prophets themselves led Bani Israel. After the death of a Prophet, another Prophet took his place. But there shall be no Prophet after me."

5) Sahih of Bukhari, No: 6589. Muhammad (PBUH) is reported to have said: "Nothing remains of prophethood except for things which give glad tidings." They asked: "What are these?" He replied: "Good dreams."

Some claim that Quran 33:40 proclaims that only law-bearing prophets have ended, suggesting there is still room for prophets who will preach the same law as Muhammad (PBUH). However, the wording of the verse is so clear, and there is such overwhelming reinforcement from Hadith literature, that there is simply no room for this interpretation of the verse.

Question 2: Why Did All Forms Of Messengerhood And Prophethood Conclude With Muhammad (PBUH)?

Even for a layperson, studying the Quran will clarify that God aimed to achieve three objectives through Muhammad (PBUH). Since all three objectives were successfully met, Prophethood concluded with Muhammad (PBUH). Let us briefly discuss what these three objectives were and how they were accomplished.

1. Raising a new nation to practice and preach God's message to the world: God relieved the Israelites of their duty to proclaim His message and chose to establish a new nation among the descendants of Ishmael. This goal was realized when God raised an entire nation through Muhammad (PBUH), consisting of over a hundred thousand individuals who were comprehensively groomed and trained for their divine mission.

2. Provide humanity with the most compelling worldly evidence of Judgment Day: As discussed earlier, God unleashes a worldly demonstration of His judgment through His Rasools to their immediate addressees. The primary aim of this demonstration is to provide conclusive worldly proof of the divine judgment that awaits all humankind after death.

In the case of Muhammad (PBUH), this worldly demonstration of divine judgment occurred on a massive global scale at a time when history was being meticulously recorded, making it a historical fact. Whether one believes that Muhammad (PBUH) was divinely inspired or not, with the exception of some extreme conspiracy theorists, it is undeniable that the major events involving Muhammad (PBUH) and his immediate companions truly happened.

God's objective to provide and preserve conclusive evidence of divine judgment for humanity was achieved, as the events demonstrating divine judgment have been preserved in the established history of humanity.

3. Preserving Divine guidance for all future generations: The Quran 5:3 proclaims that divine guidance for humanity was completed with Muhammad (PBUH). Therefore, there is no need for new guidance. This divine guidance was perfectly preserved and transmitted as the "Quran" on a truly massive scale during Muhammad's (PBUH) lifetime. The "Sunnah" was also preserved and transmitted en masse to more than a hundred thousand immediate followers. Hence, the objective of completing and preserving divine guidance for all humanity to come was also achieved through Muhammad (PBUH).

Question 3: How Does Islam View Religious Authority and the Role of Muhammad (PBUH) in Guiding Believers?

God is not directly visible in this world, allowing for freedom of choice as part of a test, but the Quran mentions various instances where God indirectly guides people by instilling thoughts directly in their minds (8:24) or through angels who constantly bestow blessings on the righteous (Quran 41:30). However, the Quran also specifies that the individuals who are contacted directly by the Almighty for the purpose of guiding others are Prophets and Messengers.

Since Muhammad (PBUH) is the last Prophet and Messenger, he is the ultimate authority on what God truly desires. In other words, Muhammad is the final source of God's teachings. Anything deemed part of Islam, or excluded from it, must have clear evidence of being taught by Muhammad (PBUH).

Furthermore, everyone following Muhammad (PBUH), regardless of their knowledge or achievements, must acknowledge their fallibility as students of God's religion, capable of both correct and incorrect interpretations. No one after Muhammad (PBUH) can claim to be infallible in their teachings about Islam or assert themselves as an authority on Islam.

In this regard, there is a very important Hadith that must be shared, in which Muhammad (PBUH) strictly forbade any addition or innovation in Islam that is not proven through the Quran or Sunnah:

> *The truest word is the Book of God (Quran) and the best guidance is the guidance of Muhammad (PBUH). The most evil things in religion are those which are newly invented, for every newly invented matter is an innovation, every innovation is misguidance (Mishkat al Masabih No: 134).*

Question 4: What Are The Miracles In Islam?

People may experience divine miracles in their personal lives. However, a straightforward reading of the Quran reveals that the display of divine miracles to ordinary individuals was an exercise specifically reserved for Prophets and Messengers of God. This was done to capture the attention of individuals and evoke profound amazement, enabling the Messengers and Prophets to effectively deliver God's message. Since this role concluded with Muhammad (PBUH), there will no longer be miracles for human beings. Consequently, according to the Quran, anyone claiming to perform divine miracles is likely either lying or deluded.

In my personal opinion, after reading the Quran, anyone claiming to see angels or the souls of saints or to perform miracles after Muhammad (PBUH) is either lying, experiencing psychiatric issues, or being deceived by Jinns into believing that they are seeing angels and saints.

Question 5: What Is The Relevance Of The Events That Occurred After Muhammad (PBUH)?

As a Muslim, I believe that Prophet Muhammad (PBUH) conveyed God's religion to humanity through the Quran and Sunnah, which encompass all the moral dos and don'ts that I must follow to ensure my success in the divine accountability on the Day of Judgment. The details and application of these principles are further elaborated in the Hadith literature. Within this Hadith literature, there is a specific Hadith in which the entirety of religion is laid out in concise pointers; this specific Hadith is known as the Hadith of Gabriel. I limit my focus to this framework—I strictly adhere to the clear DOs and DON'Ts of Islam. As I am neither a student of history nor an academic, I do not engage in studying events that occurred after the passing of Muhammad (PBUH).

Events following the time of Muhammad (PBUH), which have led to significant divisions among Muslims, are irrelevant to my eternal salvation or damnation. For instance, according to the teachings of the Quran and Sunnah, no one will question me on the Day of Judgment about whom I believed should have succeeded Muhammad (PBUH) or which of the Prophet's companions (PBUH) I considered to be righteous or superior in rank to others.

Question 6: Is Muhammad (PBUH) Considered Superior To All Other Prophets?

A Naat is a poem recited in praise of Muhammad (PBUH). I grew up in Pakistan listening to a very popular Naat called "Shah e Medina," which means "Chief of Medina." It starts off with the following verse:

> *Oh Chief of Medina, oh guardian of Yathrib—all prophets*
> *are beggars at your doorstep*

The belief that Muhammad (PBUH) is superior to all other prophets is a prevalent notion among Muslims in the sub-continent. However, both the Quran and Hadith clearly and sternly discourage Muslims from making comparisons between prophets.

The Quran proclaims in Chapter 2, Verse 253, that God indeed raised some Prophets higher in rank than others. The verse further states, as examples, that God spoke directly to Moses (PBUH) and gave the clearest proofs to Jesus (PBUH), while also providing him with the constant support of the Holy Spirit, Gabriel.

However, Muslims are clearly instructed in Quran 2:136 that they should believe in all prophets of God as the bearers of the divine message and should not indulge in the practice of making distinctions between them.

> *Say, O believers, we believe in God and what has been revealed to us and what was revealed to Abraham, Ishmael, Isaac, Jacob, and his descendants (peace be upon them), and what was given to Moses, Jesus, and other prophets (peace be upon them) from their Lord. We make no distinction between any of them. And to God we all submit (Quran 2:136).*

Muhammad (PBUH) possesses several prestigious attributes as a Prophet. For instance, he reportedly stated in a Hadith that he has been distinguished in six matters in comparison to other Prophets..

As per Sahih of Muslim, No: 523:

> *Muhammad (PBUH) is reported to have said: I have been given the honor of excellence over other Prophets in six matters: (1) I have been bestowed with the ability to communicate ideas comprehensively with a few words; (2) I have been supported by being given awe and might; (3) Spoils of war have been made lawful for me; (4) The whole earth has been made a mosque and a means of purification for me; (5) I have been sent as a Prophet for the whole of humanity; (6) the chain of Prophethood has come to an end with me.*

While acknowledging that some prophets hold higher ranks than others, Muhammad (PBUH) passionately and repeatedly denied that his rank was the highest among the prophets.

Sahih Muslim records that a man approached Muhammad (PBUH) and addressed him as "Oh best of creation." Muhammad (PBUH) interrupted him and corrected him by saying, "That is Abraham – upon whom be peace" (No: 2369).

In the Sahih of Bukhari No: 3234 and Jami of Tirmidhi No: 3245,

Muhammad (PBUH) is reported to have said, "No one should say that I am better than Jonah, son of Mata," and "Whoever says that I am better than Jonah, son of Mata, has told a lie.

According to Sahih Muslim (No: 2373), Muhammad (PBUH) instructed his followers not to claim that he was superior to Moses (PBUH). He further explained that on the Day of Judgment, when he is resurrected, Moses (PBUH) will already be standing by the throne of God.

Moreover, Muhammad explicitly instructed his followers to abstain from comparing Prophets and considering one superior to others. He is reported to have said:

Do not indulge in comparisons of making one Prophet better than the other (Sahih of Bukhari, No: 228).

In essence, God exalted some prophets above others in various respects, yet Muslims are instructed not to make comparisons among them. Muhammad (PBUH) received numerous honors and distinctions as a prophet, but he never declared himself superior to other prophets. In fact, he expressed the opposite.

Question 7: Why Were All the Prophets in the Middle East?

I discussed this in detail while exploring Muhammad (PBUH) as a Rasool of God. The Quran proclaims that prophets were sent to every nation and society until the time of Abraham (PBUH) (Quran 10:47, 17:15, 28:59). After Abraham (PBUH), the role of prophethood was made exclusive to his descendants with the purpose of elevating nations to spread God's message (Quran 29:27, 3:33). The Quran states that some prophets are mentioned within its pages, but there are many whom only God knows about (Quran 25:38, 14:9). It also clarifies that the reason for narrating stories of specific prophets from the Middle East is that the Quran's immediate audience—the Arab pagans and the People of the Book—were already familiar with these prophets' stories (Quran 54:4).

Question 8: Why Did Muhammad (PBUH) Have Multiple Marriages?

Many critics of Islam object to the multiple marriages of Muhammad (PBUH), arguing that a person who claims to be as holy as a Prophet of God should not marry multiple women.

I find this objection incorrect for the following reasons:
1) According to the Quran, there is nothing unholy or morally wrong with being attracted to the opposite gender as long as everything intimate and sexual is confined within the limits of marriage.
2) The concept of men marrying multiple times was a very normal practice in Muhammad's (PBUH) era and culture; this practice continues to be a norm in many cultures and societies today. Even Muhammad's (PBUH) fiercest opponents among the Meccan idol-worshippers made no moral objections to this aspect of his life.
3) Despite polygamy being common, Muhammad (PBUH) married for the first time at the age of 25 and remained monogamous for 24 years until his wife Khadija passed away. Therefore, Muhammad (PBUH) spent his entire youth loyal to one woman, demonstrating that he was not a man driven by lust.

4) Since male polygamy was the norm in Muhammad's (PBUH) era and culture, where there was no limit on the number of times a man could marry, Muhammad (PBUH) married ten times after his first wife passed away. Given that Muhammad (PBUH) led a significant social, ideological, military, and political movement, most of these marriages aimed to fulfill the needs of his mission. It is also noteworthy that all the women Muhammad (PBUH) married were either divorcees or widows, with the exception of Aisha (RA).

If you wish to analyze the reasons behind each of Muhammad's (PBUH) marriages, please check out my podcast titled "Conversing Islam with Hamza Ali Abbasi - Episode 10," uploaded on the YouTube channel "Ghamidi Center of Islamic Learning." This podcast is available in Urdu with English subtitles.

Given the context I mentioned above, I personally do not find anything objectionable with Muhammad (PBUH) marrying multiple times. Yes, it would have been disturbing if he had mistreated any of his wives. However, there is absolutely no evidence to suggest that Muhammad (PBUH) did not treat his wives well. In fact, his wives were given the utmost respect by both Muhammad (PBUH) and his followers. Evidence from the Quran confirms that all his wives were treated very well by Muhammad (PBUH). Let me briefly discuss this evidence.

In Quran 33:28-34, God informs Muhammad's (PBUH) wives that, due to their role as his spouses, they will be subjected to special restrictions owing to the turbulent circumstances surrounding Islam's struggle. Before imposing these limitations, they are given the option to depart through divorce if they prefer not to adhere to these conditions. Should they choose to leave, they were to be provided with a gracious monetary compensation and allowed to go in a dignified manner. However, none of them left; instead, they voluntarily accepted these additional restrictions, despite having the option to leave amicably. This serves as compelling evidence that Muhammad (PBUH) did not mistreat his wives. After all, their willingness to accept such strict additional restrictions, knowing they could have safely exited, raises a significant question: How could they so readily obey, through the command of a God whose prophet their husband claimed to be if they were being oppressed or treated poorly?

Question 9: Does The Quran Justify Domestic Violence?

Quran 4:34 is often criticized as a verse that justifies domestic violence and grants husbands free rein to use physical force against their wives. This verse posed the most significant challenge for me within Islam, and it took years to find an answer that was both morally and rationally justified.

A detailed examination of this verse, along with its context, clearly indicates that the act of using physical force on a wife is generally considered a criminal act. However, it is permitted as an extreme measure in exceptionally rare situations as a final attempt to save the marriage. This comes with the stringent condition that the physical punishment must not leave any marks or injuries on the body.

Analysis of Quran 4:34:

As previously discussed in detail, the Quran regards the institution of marriage and family as the most important institution created by God to provide long-term physical, spiritual, emotional, and psychological care to both the young and the elderly.

The Quran goes to great lengths to protect the institution of family. For example, the strength of the family unit weakens in societies where sexual relations outside of marriage are normalized and not considered taboo. Consequently, Islam has criminalized all forms of sexual behavior and actions outside of marriage.

There is another crime lethal to every institution, including marriage, and that is "rebellion." Whether it concerns the state, military, bureaucracy, corporate world, or marital relationships, rebellion is not tolerated because even a minimal acceptance of it guarantees the destruction of the institution. This is why even the most liberal countries enact extremely severe punishments for acts of rebellion. For example, in Norway, known for having some of the most lenient laws among modern states, prison sentences for acts of rebellion can range from 6 to 21 years.[67]

Every institution requires a leader to guide it. Without a head, no institution can function effectively. The Quran designates husbands as the heads of the family. Let me explain.

Women and men are equal in the sight of God. However, when they enter into marriage, the Quran assigns more responsibility to the husband—particularly in financial matters. Due to this significant responsibility, the Quran designates the husband as the head of the family institution. This elevated rank of the husband means one thing: whenever there is a deadlock on a family-related decision, where both husband and wife cannot come to a common ground, the husband gets the final say.

The Quran has absolutely no issues with a woman earning money and choosing to contribute to the family. However, her contribution is optional, meaning she can keep all her earnings and does not carry the burden of financial responsibility for the family. On the other hand, the husband must fulfill the financial needs of the family as an obligation. Additionally, there are voices within Islam that suggest the office of the head of the family can transfer to the wife if she stipulates in the marriage contract that she will assume the financial responsibilities of the family. However, the Quran clarifies that the husband has more responsibility, and hence, he is granted more authority in decision-making as the head of the family institution.

The Quranic directive that assigns a husband a higher rank than his wife is not an act of gender discrimination. As previously mentioned, men and women are equal in the eyes of God. It is only within the confines of marriage that the roles and responsibilities designated to the positions of husband and wife differentiate their ranks.

It is worth mentioning that within the same institution of the family where the husband is given a rank higher than the wife, the mother is accorded a higher rank than the father with respect to the children (Sahih Muslim, No: 6181).

So, it is not about gender, but the rights and responsibilities of different relationships within the institution of marriage.

Now, let us examine the verse Quran 4:34. This verse addresses an extreme situation involving a wife guilty of "Nushuz," which signifies outright recalcitrance. The term implies that the wife is displaying such extreme and persistent rebellion, causing significant nuisance and threatening to disrupt the entire family unit

In such a situation, the husband is first advised to make a persistent effort to talk to her—this may need to be done over an extended period, possibly spanning several weeks or months. If the recalcitrance continues, the husband is advised to end all interaction with the wife to underscore the severity of the situation. It is important to note that both the husband and the wife are free to leave each other during this time. However, if the wife's rebellion persists and neither spouse has departed, then as a last resort to save the marriage, the husband is allowed to use physical force. Three things are to be noted here.

1) The use of physical force is permitted only as a corrective measure, akin to how a parent or teacher might lightly reprimand a misbehaving child. It should not leave any mark or injury on the body; otherwise, the act becomes a punishable criminal offense. These guidelines were issued by the Prophet Muhammad

(PBUH). According to a Hadith, he instructed that any physical reprimand on the wife should not leave any mark or injury on the body (Sunan Ibn Majah, No: 1851).

2) The allowance of physical force is an option, not a divine obligation; therefore, if societies believe that men are abusing this option, governments have the authority to create laws that remove this option from men entirely.

3) The husband may invoke his right to physical chastisement only if there is a realistic possibility that it might save the marriage. One might wonder whether the use of physical force by a husband towards a wife, who exhibits persistent and blatant misconduct, is more likely to worsen the situation and expedite the dissolution of the marriage rather than prevent it. However, the Quran is considered relevant for all times and cultures. There may be scenarios in certain cultural contexts, both historical and contemporary, where the use of physical force could potentially assist in correcting the wife's blatant misconduct and preserve the marriage.

If there is Nushuz on the part of the husband, God has provided guidelines for the woman in Quran 4:128-130. In these verses, God instructs the woman should try to resolve the matter, and if it cannot be settled through passive means and the husband persists with Nushuz, then the woman is advised to leave the husband. However, it is not suggested that the wife attempt physical disciplinary action on the husband, for the following reason:

God has decreed that both men and women are equal in His sight. However, in the context of marriage, where men and women assume the roles of husband and wife, the husband holds a higher rank than the wife for the reasons previously discussed. The Quran views marriage strictly as an institution and mandates that it be governed according to the norms and laws that apply to any other institution.

In this context, much like a senior-ranking Major in the army can reprimand a junior-ranking Captain but not vice versa, and just as a CEO can reprimand a Managing Director but not the other way around, so too in the institution of marriage is it typically seen that the husband can reprimand the wife, and not the other way around.

Now consider the alternate scenario—if the higher-ranking officer is misbehaving, although the junior-ranking officer cannot reprimand the senior-ranking officer, he is free to resign from the organization. Similarly, if the husband is guilty of Nushuz, then the wife has the right to leave the husband or resign from the marriage if the husband does not amend his behavior.

Muhammad (PBUH) understood very well that this allowance of using physical force provided it causes no scars or injuries, was meant to be an exceptionally rare measure in extraordinary situations. He likely also knew that many men would misuse this allowance to justify domestic violence. Therefore, Muhammad (PBUH) consistently preached against the beating of women. For example, it is reported that Muhammad (PBUH) said:

> Do not beat your women and do not be rude to them (Sunan of Abu Dawood, No: 2144).

Elsewhere, he is reported to have said:

> The best of you are those who are best to their women (Sunan Al Tirmidhi, No: 1162).

Before we go on to the next few questions, it is important to mention here that whenever I have talked to many of my fellow Muslims about the commandments of face veil, hijab, gender segregation, music, and arts in Islam, the popular answer always starts with an elaborate monologue about the benefits of face veil, hijab, gender segregation and the harms of music and arts. I always clarify at this moment that my primary inquiry is not about the potential social, moral, and cultural benefits or harms of these things. My primary inquiry is about knowing what the commandments of God are in these domains as far as their allowance or prohibition is concerned.

Question 10: Does Islam Prohibit Music And Other Art Forms?

Important Note: For detailed answers to this subject with references, please watch the video series titled "Response to 23 Questions - Singing and Music (Ghina aur Moseeqi) - Javed Ahmed Ghamidi" on the YouTube channel "Ghamidi Center of Islamic Learning."

Music And Other Art Forms Are Not Prohibited In The Quran

For something to be deemed as prohibited or Haraam in Islam, it must either be directly prohibited by the Quran or be prohibited in principle by the Quran. For instance, the Quran explicitly forbids all sexual activity outside of marriage. On the other hand, an example of prohibiting something in principle is the Quran's prohibition of intoxication. Therefore, according to this principle, anything that causes intoxication—whether in liquid, smokable, or injectable form—is prohibited in both large and small quantities. Another example is the Quran's principle against "Injustice"; thus, any specific activity that causes any kind of injustice to anyone is prohibited. In the case of music and other art forms, there is no place in the Quran that directly or in principle, prohibits music, musical instruments, or any other form of art..

Music And Other Art Forms Are Not Prohibited In Hadith Literature

As far as the Hadiths are concerned, there is no authentic Hadith where Muhammad (PBUH) proclaims a complete ban on musical instruments. In fact, there are multiple authentic Hadiths where Muhammad (PBUH) approves of singing and dancing. According to these Hadiths,

Muhammad (PBUH), his wives, and his companions listened to both male and female singers on various occasions. Moreover, there are numerous Hadiths where Muhammad (PBUH) encourages singing and music at weddings and festivals such as Eid. While Muhammad (PBUH) does caution his followers about the potential harms of music in many of these Hadiths, he does not outright prohibit it. Here are some examples:

- Muhammad (PBUH) and his wife Aisha (RA) listened to a female singer's song. At the end of the performance, Muhammad (PBUH) cautioned about the potential harms of music and singing by stating, "The devil has breathed his breath into this singer's nostrils" (Musnad of Ahmed, No: 15720).
- A female singer performed a song for Muhammad (PBUH) and his companions (Musnad of Ahmed, No: 2311).
- People are said to have sung and danced in rejoicing as Muhammad (PBUH) returned triumphant from war (Sunan Kubra, No: 4236).
- Muhammad (PBUH) asked his wife, Aisha (RA), as she was heading to a wedding, to ensure that a singer was arranged for the event (Sunan of Ibn Majah, No: 1900).
- Muhammad (PBUH) encouraged singing songs for Eid despite Abu Bakr's objection to musical instruments (Sahih Bukhari, No: 952).

The Misconception That Only The Use Of "Daff" Is Allowed

In the Hadith mentioned above, the singers are typically accompanied by the use of a Daff (hand drum) as a musical instrument. This has led many Muslim scholars to form the opinion that only the Daff is permitted while other musical instruments are not. For this perspective to be accurate, there must be a Quranic verse or Hadith explicitly stating that all musical instruments are prohibited, with Muhammad's (PBUH) approval of the Daff being a specific exemption to this rule. However, there is no passage in the Quran or Hadith that clearly declares all musical instruments as forbidden. Consequently, there is no basis to believe that all musical instruments are banned in Islam, with the sole exception being the Daff. Moreover, this notion is further challenged by an intriguing Hadith where Muhammad (PBUH) reflects on an instance from his youth, before receiving prophethood, where God prevented him from sinning by engaging him in listening to the music of the Daff and "other musical instruments" at a wedding. This anecdote suggests that musical instruments, other than the Daff, are not inherently sinful; otherwise, how could they be utilized by God as a means to prevent sin? Let us briefly analyze this particular Hadith.

In Sahih Ibn Hibban, (No: 6272), Muhammad (PBUH) explains to his friend that a long time before receiving Prophethood, during his younger days, he intended to commit a sin twice, yet God saved him. Muhammad (PBUH) explains that in two separate instances, he attempted to go to those gatherings where "young men of Mecca used to go." Muhammad (PBUH) could be referring to those kinds of gatherings that involved adult entertainment like intoxicants, gambling, and women. Muhammad (PBUH) elaborates in this Hadith that while on his way, both times he got distracted by music and singing at a wedding taking place in a house. He kept enjoying that music and singing until he dozed off and did not make it to the gatherings he was going to, and that is how God saved him from sinning. He specifically mentions that at these weddings there was singing with "drums" (Daff in Arabic) and "other musical instruments" (Mazaameer in Arabic).

In a nutshell, musical instruments, singing, and other art forms are not directly or fundamentally prohibited in the Quran or Hadith. In fact, there are numerous hadiths where Muhammad (PBUH) permits singing and the use of the Daff, among other musical instruments.

There are certain passages in the Quran and Hadith that some segments of the Muslim community interpret as directives prohibiting musical instruments and all forms of art. However, upon closer inspection, these passages are instructions to avoid the unlawful and immoral usage of musical instruments and other forms of art, rather than imposing a total ban on them. Let us briefly analyze these Quranic verses and Hadith.

A - Analysis of verses from the Quran presented to establish that Islam prohibits music and singing:

In the Quran, there are primarily three passages that are often cited as evidence that God has forbidden music. However, upon closer examination, these verses actually prohibit the misuse of music and other art forms, rather than imposing a comprehensive ban on them.

1) Quran 31:6 states,

> *There are some who use distraction and amusement for the sole purpose of turning people away from God's path ... and to make a mockery of it. They will suffer a humiliating punishment*

The term "Lahv" refers to anything that distracts or amuses people, such as poetry, sports, music, dancing, or any other activity that can occupy individuals. Those who argue that Islam prohibits music claim that "Lahv" in this context specifically denotes music. However, this interpretation is flawed because the word "Lahv" appears in various other places in the Quran, including Surah Anaam verse 32, Ankabut verse 64, Anbiya verse 17, and Araaf verse 51. In each instance, "Lahv" is used to signify distraction and amusement, not necessarily music or singing. Although music can be a form of distraction, the Quran does not explicitly use the word "Lahv" to refer only to music but employs it more broadly to indicate anything that might divert people from religious obligations. Esteemed scholars such as Tabari, Zamakshari, and even Maududi—someone who deems music as prohibited in Islam—all translated Lahv as things that amuse and distract people, not specifically as music.

However, these verses were revealed when the pagan leaders of Mecca deployed singers and dancers to distract people from listening to Muhammad's (PBUH) preaching of the Quran. Even if we agree that this particular verse implies singing and dancing, it is clearly addressing the misuse of these arts, rather than proclaiming a complete ban on them. The verse suggests that any art form used to distract people from religious obligations is an unlawful use of art. In fact, the Quran proclaims that any activity, otherwise lawful, becomes unlawful if it interferes with religious duties. Take trade, for example, which is a perfectly lawful activity according to Islam. Quran 62:11 states that if trade distracts a person from their religious obligations, then that trade activity becomes sinful.

So, in short, these verses do not specifically address music or singing, but instead refer to any activity that serves as a distraction or a source of amusement. However, if one interprets the word "Lahv" to mean music and singing, even then, the verse does not declare an outright ban on art. Rather, it suggests that music, singing, or art becomes problematic if people engage in these activities to the extent that they neglect their religious obligations.

2) Quran 17:64: This verse communicates that the devil is granted the freedom to incite people through his voice. The verse states:

> *And incite whoever you can of them with your voice, mobilize against them all your cavalry and infantry - manipulate them in their wealth and children and make them promises. But Satan promises them nothing but delusion.*

The Arabic word for "voice" is derived from "Sawt," which literally means "voice."

For those who consider music prohibited in Islam, they argue that the "devil's voice," as mentioned in the verse, refers to music and singing. However, this is not true because, firstly, even a beginner-level student of Arabic can easily discern that the word used in the verse, the construction, and the context of the sentence all make it clear that Satan's voice here refers to his whispers, which invite people to evil. Secondly, renowned Islamic scholars such as Tabari, Zamakhshari, Shah Abdul Qadir, and Maududi did not translate this word as singing or music.

3) Quran 53:59-61: These verses address individuals who belittle and mock the verses of the Quran while they continue to engage deeply in amusements. Many believers assert that music and singing are prohibited in Islam, interpreting the Arabic word "Saamidoon" used in this verse for "amusement" as specifically implying music and singing. However, no distinguished translator has explicitly defined this word as denoting music and singing. In its literal sense, "Samidoon" could refer to any entertaining activity, including sports.

Secondly, if, for the sake of argument, one accepts that the Quran implies music and singing by the term "amusement" in this verse, it still emphasizes that engaging in music and singing while being heedless of the Quran and mocking it is prohibited. Therefore, the Quran reiterates that any activity, whether trade or art, pursued while neglecting one's religious duties is haram. These verses do not suggest an all-out prohibition on music and art.

B - Analysis of some Hadith presented to establish that Islam prohibits music and singing:

There are several narrations that are cited as evidence that all kinds of musical instruments are prohibited. Let's examine them briefly.

Hadith #1: In Bukhari 5590, Muhammad (PBUH) is reported to have said, "There will come people in my nation who will make lawful for themselves sexual intercourse, silk, intoxicants, and musical instruments."

This Hadith does not prohibit all forms of sexual intercourse, silk, and musical instruments, but only those types that are deemed unlawful in Islam. Let me explain:

This Hadith states that people will consider four things lawful which are otherwise unlawful in Islam. Let's examine whether these four items are entirely prohibited in Islam or only conditionally prohibited.

1) **Intoxicants:** All forms of intoxicants are strictly prohibited in the Quran, as evidenced by Quran 5:90. Thus, the Hadith states that people will openly consume various types of intoxicants.

2) **Sexual Intercourse**: Not all kinds of sexual intercourse are prohibited in Islam, as sexual relations between a husband and wife are lawful. Therefore, the Hadith does not suggest that all forms of sexual intercourse are prohibited and that people will declare them permissible on their own. Instead, the Hadith indicates that people will regard types of sexual intercourse prohibited in Islam—such as intercourse outside of marriage—as permissible..

3) **Silk**: Silk is prohibited for men but entirely lawful for women. Therefore, the Hadith does not suggest that all kinds of silk are prohibited in Islam and that people will make it permissible for themselves. Rather, the Hadith implies that men will openly wear silk, which is unlawful in Islam.

4) **Musical Instruments:** We discussed above that, as per the Quran and Hadith, musical instruments are not entirely prohibited, but their unlawful usage is prohibited. Hence, this Hadith is stating that people will freely enjoy the kind of songs and music which contains things prohibited in Islam.

Hadith #2: In another Hadith, recorded in the Musnad of Ahmed (No: 4535), Muhammad (PBUH), while traveling on a camel, hears someone playing a flute. He puts his fingers in his ears and asks his companion to continue listening to the flute and to let him know when the sound fades away. Those who claim that Islam prohibits musical instruments argue that since Muhammad (PBUH) put his fingers into his ears upon hearing a flute, this action serves as evidence that musical instruments are prohibited.

The question arises: If the flute was a prohibited musical instrument and it was considered a sin to listen to it, why did Muhammad (PBUH) ask his companion to continue listening? Why didn't he instruct him to block his ears, and suggest that they both unblock their ears after traveling a bit further to avoid the sin of listening to a prohibited instrument? Did Muhammad (PBUH) request the flute player to stop, or did he announce in Medina that the flute was a prohibited instrument? The answer is no!

Since Hadiths typically lack contextual information, it's largely speculative to determine why Muhammad (PBUH) was disturbed by the flute. A more plausible hypothesis is that Muhammad (PBUH), known for reciting the Quran and engaging in other acts of worship during his journeys, might have found the flute distracting, which could explain why he blocked his ears.

Hadith #3, 4, and 5: In other Hadiths (Musnad of Ahmed, No: 8783; Musnad of Ahmed, No: 7566; and Sunan Kubra, No: 9483), Muhammad (PBUH) appears to express disdain for bells, particularly those hung under the necks of cattle, and he also mentions that angels are repelled by bells. This has been used as evidence to suggest that musical instruments are prohibited. Firstly, a bell is not considered a proper musical instrument. Secondly, these Hadiths, like the one mentioned above, seem to reflect instances where Muhammad's (PBUH) focus was disturbed and his worship interrupted, rather than a proclamation banning all musical instruments.

Prohibition Of Making Paintings And Sculptures Of Living Things

The correct approach to Islam and art is that Islam does not completely prohibit art; rather, it prohibits forms of art that include elements forbidden in Islam. This understanding should be applied to Hadiths that appear to ban painting or sculpting living things. These Hadiths are primarily found in Bukhari, Nos. 5951, 5957, 5954, and in Muslim Nos. 2109c/2110a.

When viewed within the complete framework of the Quran—especially through the lens of Quran 7:33—it becomes clear that image-making of living things was condemned by Muhammad (PBUH) because, in 7th century Arabia, painting and sculpting were primarily conducted for the purpose of idol worship. There is absolutely no prohibition against these art forms if they are not intended for idol worship and if they do not contain anything prohibited in Islam.

Moral Limitations On Music, Singing, And All Other Art Forms

At this point, a question arises: if Islam permits all forms of art but with certain moral conditions, what exactly are those conditions?

Even though the entire Quran is filled with these moral dos and don'ts, I will share a very special place in the Quran where these moral guidelines are explained concisely—it is Chapter 7, verse 33. In this verse, the following things are prohibited:

1) *Any kind of sexual behavior or action outside of marriage:* Whether it is the lyrics of a song, dialogues in a film or drama, the clothing of artists, and interactions between artists—if it is remotely sexual or physically intimate in nature, it is absolutely not allowed in Islam.

2) Injustice is prohibited: Whether it is in the lyrics of a song or the storyline of a film, if any element of an art form justifies or glorifies injustice, it is prohibited.

3) Unlawfully harming anyone's life, property, or dignity is prohibited: If any aspect of an art form promotes or glorifies the infliction of unlawful damage to anyone's life, property, or dignity, then such art is prohibited.

4) Associating partners with God is prohibited: If any art form promotes or glorifies Shirk—the practice of associating partners with God or worshiping multiple gods—then such art is prohibited.

5) Lying about God is prohibited: Any art form that spreads false ideas about God is therefore prohibited.

Apart from the five prohibitions previously discussed, if any art form is pursued or enjoyed at the expense of a religious obligation, it becomes an unlawful action, even if the art form falls within the aforementioned five limitations.

So, in a nutshell, neither the Quran nor the Hadith explicitly ban music or any other art form; they only prohibit their wrongful use. All art forms are permissible in Islam as long as they do not encompass anything forbidden by Islam.

Question 11: Does Islam Prescribe A Dress Code For Women, And Does It Mandate Covering Their Heads Or Faces?

The answer to this question can be divided into three parts:

1. Dress code for women in Surah Nur: The Quran, in these specific verses, outlines principles concerning women's attire. It does not make it obligatory for women to cover their faces and head.

2. Verses from Surah Ahzab: Certain verses are drawn from Surah Ahzab to justify the face veil and social restrictions imposed on women. However, when viewed in context, these verses specifically address instructions meant solely for the Prophet's (PBUH) wives and delineate temporary measures for ordinary Muslim women under specific circumstances. These directives were issued against the backdrop of a particularly turbulent phase in Islam's development, during which the Prophet's (PBUH) household faced a vicious slander campaign and Muslim women experienced harassment and molestation in the streets of Medina. Thus, I aim to demonstrate that one set of verses from Surah Ahzab provides instructions exclusively for the Prophet's wives and are not intended for ordinary Muslim women, while the other set of verses prescribes a temporary measure for Muslim women in an extraordinary situation, not meant to serve as an eternal policy for all women at all times.

Let's discuss these two points one by one.

1. Dress code for women in Surah Nur: The dress code for women is discussed in Quran 24:30-31, while discussing how men and women should behave in their interactions, the Quran in Surah Nur issues specific moral instructions for both genders with the aim of purifying their interactions from any moral impurities. In this context, both men and women are instructed to look at each other with the utmost respect, encapsulated in the term "Lower your gaze," and they must refrain from any kind of sexual behavior or action, underscored by the command to "Guard your private parts."

"Guard your private parts" is a broad term that encompasses the following two things:

A) No sexual, sensual, or intimate contact of any kind is permissible without marriage.

B) Clothing that draws attention to private parts should not be worn. Therefore, it is necessary to adequately cover private parts and their surrounding areas. For both men and women, the pelvic area is considered private; additionally, for women, the chest is also regarded as a private part. As such, women are obligated to cover both the chest and its surrounding areas, as well as the pelvis and its surrounding areas.

The analysis above indicates that women should cover themselves from neck to ankle with attire that is neither tight nor transparent—this is the basic minimum requirement. If women choose to further cover their heads or even their faces to garner additional goodwill from God, that decision is commendable. However, as far as God's obligatory commandments are concerned, they are as previously stated.

There is an additional directive for women concerning the wearing of jewelry or adornments around the chest area that might accentuate or draw attention to their chests. They are required to cover their bosoms with a garment and conceal other adornments from the public, except for those worn on the hands, feet, and face. In Quran 24:60, it is noted that older women are given the relaxation that allows them to remove their outer garments in public, provided that there is no deliberate intention to display their beauty and adornment.

The term used in the Quran 24:31 for a covering garment is "Bi'khumurihinna," which is often translated by some as "head covering." Consequently, this verse is frequently cited to support the argument that since God directs Muslim women to cover their bosoms with their head coverings, these coverings were already in use among Muslim women and should be recognized as an ordained duty by God. This interpretation leads many Muslims to believe that it is a divine obligation for women to have their heads covered at all times, which is not accurate.

This case rests on weak footing because, firstly, even though the Quran, from 24:30 onwards, discusses the specific subject of how men and women should conduct themselves if they intermingle, it does not issue a clear instruction that women must cover their heads or faces at all times. There is not a single verse that directly states, "Oh believing women, you must ensure that you cover your heads (or your faces) at all times when interacting with others."

Secondly, the Quran uses the Arabic phrase "Bi' khumurihinna" when instructing women to cover the adornment or jewelry on their chests. There is no unambiguous linguistic or historical evidence indicating that the term "Bi' khumurihinna" refers exclusively to a head covering. This term generally means anything that covers, not specifically a head covering. In the specific context of this verse, it could denote any form of covering—an outer garment, a shawl, or even a head covering. However, it does not imply a specific type of cover. Thus, a more reasonable interpretation of the verse suggests that if a woman is wearing adornments—particularly in the chest area—she should cover these with a shawl or veil. [68]

So, in a nutshell, regarding women's clothing, the Quran stipulates that if a woman is not wearing adornments, then she should be appropriately covered from neck to ankle, clothing should not be tight or transparent in the slightest. That is the basic and absolutely compulsory obligation. If any woman chooses to go further by covering her head or face, that is commendable, but the compulsory requirement I just mentioned is based on Quran 24:30-31. If a woman is wearing adornments that draw attention to her private areas, particularly the bosom, she must cover such adornments in public, except for those on her hands, feet, and face.

2. Verses from Surah Ahzab: Let's divide this section into two subcategories.

A) Instructions meant exclusively for the Prophet's (PBUH) wives.

B) Instructions for ordinary Muslim women as a temporary measure in an extraordinary situation.

I will explain these points briefly.

A) Instructions meant exclusively for the Prophet's wives: There are specific verses in Surah Ahzab—primarily 33:32-33 and 33:53—that were revealed at a time when the struggle for Islam was at its peak. During this period, Muhammad's (PBUH) opponents initiated a full-scale slander campaign against his household, specifically targeting his wives. Moreover, certain hypocrites were harassing Muslim women in Medina.

Keeping the entire context in mind, in the verses mentioned in Surah Ahzab, specific additional restrictions were placed on the wives of Muhammad (PBUH), emphasizing that these extra restrictions did not apply to ordinary Muslim women. Before imposing these additional restrictions, God asked them if they were unwilling to accept these extra burdens—they could amicably separate from Muhammad (PBUH) without any bitterness and be like ordinary Muslim women. However, the wives of the Prophet chose to accept these extra restrictions. These restrictions include:

- They need to confine themselves to the house and must not step out without being accompanied by a male family member.
- If they need to speak with a man who is not an immediate family member, they must do so from behind a veil and use a stern tone.
- They cannot remarry after Muhammad's (PBUH) passing.
- If someone is invited as a guest to eat at the Prophet's (PBUH) house, they should arrive when the food is ready and leave immediately after finishing their meal. Guests are discouraged from staying seated for extended periods of time.

Many scholars of Islam have deemed that the extra restrictions issued specifically for Muhammad's (PBUH) wives should be taken as ideal values for all Muslim women. This view is flawed because the Quran specifically cautions that these extra restrictions are meant only for Muhammad's (PBUH) wives in the context of an extraordinarily unique situation.

Many scholars within Islam maintain the viewpoint that the restrictions mentioned are specific to the Prophet's (PBUH) wives and are not intended for ordinary Muslim women. This view is supported by early Islamic thinkers like Imam Ahmed, Abu Dawood, Ibn e Qutaiba, Qazi Ayaz, Ibn e Battal, and Hisham ibn al-Kalbi. Likewise, contemporary scholars such as Muhammad Abduh, Muhammad Rashid Rida, Mohammad Sayas, and Abdul Haleem also uphold this perspective.

The Quran clarifies that these additional measures are specified not for ordinary Muslim women but rather for the wives of Muhammad (PBUH). Contemporary Islamic scholar Dr. Amir Gazdar shows in his book "Ahkaam al Hijab wal Ikhtalaat" that there is absolutely no evidence suggesting that ordinary Muslim women during the time of Muhammad (PBUH) considered these verses as ideal values for themselves, nor is there any evidence indicating that these instructions were imposed upon them.

As we discussed before, the content of Hadith is more comprehensible when it is interpreted in light of the Quran, rather than the other way around. There is a narration in Hadith literature where Muhammad's (PBUH) wives avoid appearing in front of a blind companion of the Prophet (PBUH). Although this is considered a weak (Zaeef) narration, such Hadiths—where the Prophet's (PBUH) wives take extreme measures to remain out of public view—are often cited as evidence that Muslim women should not be visible to anyone except their immediate family, despite the Quran not issuing such a command. However, when these narrations are viewed through the lens of Surah Ahzab, it becomes clear that these incidents were not demonstrations of ideal values for all Muslim women to follow. In fact, these were efforts by Muhammad's (PBUH) wives to adhere to specific extra restrictions, which were exclusive to them and not applicable to ordinary Muslim women.

B) Instructions for ordinary Muslim women as a temporary measure in an extraordinary situation: A second citation in Surah Ahzab used to justify the face veil and hijab as divine obligations is verse 33:59. Here, Muslim women are instructed to cover themselves with a garment when heading out. Some Muslim circles suggest that this implies covering everything except the hands, feet, and eyes. However, when this verse is read in context—from verses 58 to 62—it becomes evident that this instruction was issued as a temporary measure in an emergency situation, primarily to establish identity rather than as a moral directive for achieving purity. Let me elaborate.

The verses describe a scenario where Muslim women in Medina were being harassed and abused by some hypocrites. Before taking action against the perpetrators, the Muslim women were advised to cover themselves with a long garment. This was to distinguish them clearly as Muslim women, ensuring there was no ambiguity or excuse for anyone to claim they mistook them for someone else. Even if after these extreme measures the harassers do not stop, then Muhammad (PBUH) is instructed to capture them and execute them without mercy.

Hence, the only lesson to be taken from these verses is that if a similar situation arises in present times, then a similar temporary measure can be taken. However, the fact remains that these verses are about an emergency measure in an emergency situation and not an eternal command for Muslim women to cover themselves head to toe at all times.

For detailed answers on this particular subject with references, please watch the video series titled "Response to 23 Questions - Veil

(Parda) - Javed Ahmed Ghamidi" on the YouTube platform "Ghamidi Center of Islamic Learning."

Question 12: Does Islam Mandate Gender Segregation?

It is completely logical to state that in order to avoid any potential sexual misconduct, men and women should not be secluded together. The Prophet (PBUH) firmly prohibited men and women from meeting in seclusion. According to a Hadith, he said:

> Behold! A man is not alone with a woman but the third of them is the devil (Jami of Tirmidhi 2165).

However, when it comes to public gatherings—such as a dinner event for friends, a wedding, or men and women working or studying together in offices and universities—what does the Quran instruct in these scenarios?

One prevalent concept in Islam is gender segregation—the belief that men and women should be kept separate in public congregational areas. To my surprise, I found that the Quran actually states otherwise.

Firstly, men and women are not required to be segregated in the two holiest mosques of Islam in Mecca and Medina. Additionally, there is no gender segregation during the holy pilgrimages of Hajj and Umrah. Secondly, the Quran directly addresses the issue of gender segregation and states in 24:61 that when Muslims visit the homes of their family and friends for a feast, it is up to them to choose whether to eat separately or together. This verse indicates that men and women are permitted to mingle at both family events and gatherings of friends. Thus, it appears that the God of the Quran has not ordained gender segregation; rather, He has left this decision to the discretion of the Muslims, provided they adhere to the moral guidelines regarding gender interactions as set forth in Quran 24:30-31.

Question 13: Does Islam Prohibit Men and Women from Shaking Hands?

It is a matter of personal choice and cultural norms, and Islam does not issue specific commandments about refraining from shaking hands with the opposite gender.

In this regard, two popular Hadiths are presented. In one, Muhammad (PBUH) is reported to have said:

> *An iron nail being driven into one's head is better than him touching a woman who is not lawful for him (Tabrani - al Mujam al Kabir, No: 16910).*

When Hadith is understood through the Quran, and from the directives issued in Surah Nur regarding etiquettes in situations where men and women must interact, it becomes evident that the Hadith is addressing the act of touching a woman in an inappropriate manner with wrongful intentions. Briefly touching a woman's palm for a handshake as a cultural norm, or, for instance, a doctor checking a woman's pulse for medical purposes, are not included in the meaning of this Hadith.

At this point, some of my Muslim friends often argue that if there isn't a general prohibition on all forms of touch, then hugging and kissing the cheeks of the opposite sex as greetings should be acceptable. My response is that outside of marriage, all forms of sensual contact are forbidden in Islam. Therefore, any touch that is sensual in nature or could lead to sensual arousal should be avoided as a precaution.

Another hadith presented is Bukhari (No: 2564), where it is mentioned that Muhammad (PBUH) never held a woman's hand while taking an oath of allegiance from her. This should not be interpreted as a directive against handshakes. Since the hand needs to be held for a prolonged time during the oath of allegiance, it appears that Muhammad (PBUH) adopted this precautionary measure to avoid scandal, rather than issuing a directive against handshakes.

Another argument presented is that there are no recorded instances of men shaking women's hands during the time of Muhammad (PBUH). My response is that perhaps it simply wasn't the custom of that culture. If the norm within a culture is to shake hands or fist bump as a form of greeting, Islam appears to have no objections to it.

A word of caution, though—Islam strictly forbids all kinds of intimate and sexual behaviors and actions except with one's spouse. Hence, if someone believes that shaking hands with the opposite gender might arouse intimate or sexual feelings, then such a person must abstain from it.

Question 14: Does Islam require Muslim Men to Have Long Beards?

Important Note: For detailed answers on this subject with references, please watch the video series titled "Response to 23 Questions - Beard (Darhi) - Javed Ahmed Ghamidi" on the YouTube channel "Ghamidi Center of Islamic Learning."

There is no passage in the Quran that specifically mandates Muslim men to keep a beard as a religious obligation.

If someone wishes to maintain a long beard out of love for Muhammad (PBUH) because he had a beard, that's wonderful. However, the question is whether Islam makes it an obligation upon Muslim men to grow long beards.

The beard is termed the Sunnah of the Pophet solely because Muhammad (PBUH) himself had a beard. As we discussed before, Sunnah is the aspect of religion comprising actions that Muhammad (PBUH) sanctioned as part of Islam. Just because Muhammad (PBUH) wore something, rode a camel, or ate a specific type of food does not automatically make it a Sunnah or a part of the religion. For an action to be considered Sunnah, Muhammad (PBUH) must have sanctioned it and widely transmitted it as part of the religion.

Certain Hadiths are often interpreted to imply that Muhammad (PBUH) mandated long beards for Muslim men. In these narrations, Muhammad (PBUH) directs his followers to differentiate their facial hair from that of the polytheists and the People of the Book by growing their beards long and trimming their mustaches (Sahih Muslim, Nos. 603 and 625; Sahih Bukhari, No. 5893).

Since this Hadith does not provide the context of why Muhammad (PBUH) made his statement, we must analyze the matter in light of the Quran. When Hadith is viewed from the perspective of the Quran, as it should be, the context becomes clear. Let me explain briefly.

The monks, among people of the book—Christians and Jews—even up until today, do not trim their beards or mustaches. Their long mustaches usually cover the entire lip area, which is visibly against the norms of physical cleanliness, especially when eating. In contrast, polytheists, particularly their leaders, used to trim their beards short and keep long mustaches with tips bent upwards as a sign of pride. This practice is still prevalent in many cultures today, especially in South Asia. The Quran commands Muslims to pursue physical cleanliness and to abstain from all forms of arrogance. Therefore, when these Hadiths are interpreted in the context of the Quran, it becomes clear that Muhammad (PBUH) provided these guidelines to promote physical cleanliness and eliminate any signs of arrogance in one's appearance.

The correct perspective on this matter is that maintaining a long beard is not considered Sunnah; rather, trimming the mustache is the Sunnah. Islam does not mandate that Muslims maintain any specific style of facial hair. However, if a Muslim man chooses to grow long facial hair, keeping the mustache short aligns with the Sunnah of the

Prophet. The rationale behind this practice is to promote cleanliness and avoid any displays of arrogance.

Simply put, Islam does not require the adherence to a long beard. You are free to shave your face or maintain any length of beard you desire. However, if you choose to keep a long beard, Islam obligates you to keep your mustache short.

Question 15: What are Some Misconceptions about Muhammad's (PBUH) First Revelation and the Cave of Hira?

Important Note: For detailed answers to this subject with references, please watch the video series titled "Response to 23 Questions - Pehli Wahi ka Waqia, Ghar e Hira," by Javed Ahmed Ghamidi, available on the YouTube channel "Ghamidi Center of Islamic Learning."

The popular story about Muhammad's (PBUH) first revelation states that before receiving the revelation:
- Muhammad (PBUH) used to visit the Cave of Hira in pursuit of enlightenment and to contemplate existential matters.
- He was in great turmoil after receiving the revelation, unsure of what had happened to him, and often contemplated suicide because of the ordeal until Gabriel intervened.

This entire story is based on a narration from a single chain of narrators found in Bukhari No: 6982. In this narration, Ibn Shahab Zuhri reports from Urwa bin Zubair, who was the nephew of Muhammad's (PBUH) wife, Aisha (RA). According to Zubair, he heard this narration from Aisha (RA).

There are numerous issues with the narration of Ibn e Shahab Zuhri. Let us briefly discuss these problems.

1) Ibn e Shahab Zuhri is known to report hearsay: For instance, the entire episode of Muhammad (PBUH) attempting suicide is recounted by Zuhri as information that reached him without a continuous chain of narrators.

2) Quran says that Muhammad (PBUH) never pursued enlightenment or religious knowledge: According to the narrative, Muhammad (PBUH) practiced "Tahannus" in the cave of Hira, which many interpret as meditation and seeking answers to the larger questions of life. However, Quran 28:86 and Quran 10:16 clearly indicate that Muhammad (PBUH) was not seeking religious knowledge or enlightenment and was not known to preach about these matters.

Then the question arises— if Muhammad (PBUH) was not making efforts to attain divine knowledge or enlightenment through meditation, then what kind of worship does this "Tahannus" mentioned in the narration refer to? What was Muhammad (PBUH) doing in the cave of Hira during his visits? I will soon explain what Tahannus actually means.

3) Experience of the first revelation of Moses (PBUH) and Muhammad (PBUH) cannot be so opposingly different: In the Quran, verse 73:15, Muhammad (PBUH) is recognized as a Prophet akin to Moses (PBUH). The incident of Moses's (PBUH) first revelation is described in the Quran in verses 20:9-36 and 27:7-12. In these passages, God reassures Moses (PBUH) by telling him that messengers should not fear in the presence of God, and Moses (PBUH) is clearly informed about what is happening to him and what his mission entails.

On the other hand, when Muhammad (PBUH) was contacted for the first time, he had no idea what was happening and was terrified to the core. If Muhammad (PBUH) is a Messenger like Moses (PBUH), why then was the first contact so clear and calm for Moses (PBUH), yet so confusing and terrifying for Muhammad (PBUH)? Why does God reveal all the details of his role and mission to Moses (PBUH), assuring him that Messengers should not fear in God's presence, yet

Muhammad (PBUH) is left feeling absolutely terrified and confused, with no understanding of what is happening?

4) Ibn e Hisham does not take the popular narration of Ibn e Shahab Zuhri in his biography: Ibn Hisham is one of the earliest biographers of Muhammad (PBUH), and he based his work on an earlier biography written by Ibn Ishaq. When Ibn Hisham's book reaches the point of Muhammad's first revelation, he only includes Zuhri's narration up to the point where Zuhri states that Muhammad (PBUH) started to see true dreams before the first revelation and began to prefer isolation. After this, Ibn Hisham introduces a different narration from another chain of narrators to explain the incident of the first revelation of Muhammad (PBUH). This alternative narration makes more sense than Zuhri's, as it is free from the discrepancies mentioned in the above three points. In his biography, in the chapter titled "How was Muhammad (PBUH) given Prophethood," Ibn Hisham quotes a narration from Wahab ibn Kaisaan who heard it from Abdullah bin Zubair, the nephew of Aisha (RA), who in turn heard it from Ubaid bin Umair bin Qatada al Laisi.

Let us now briefly analyze the narration by Wahab ibn ul Kaisaan utilized by Ibn e Hisham and examine how it is more logical.

Analysis of narration of Wahab ibn e Kaisaan and why it is free from all discrepancies present in Zuhri's narration: Hisham writes that Muhammad (PBUH) would retreat to the cave of Hira for Tahannuf—a correction of the word Tahannus mentioned in Zuhri's narration. Hisham clarifies that this was Aitikaaf during the month of Ramadan, a ritual involving fasting and worship. Muhammad (PBUH) participated in this worship as a follower of Deen e Hanif, a tradition of beliefs and practices of Abraham (PBUH) that was prevalent in Arabia. Muhammad (PBUH) often took his wife and children to the mountains with him, and at the end of this ritual worship, they would feed the poor.

This narrative continues, describing that in the year of revelation, Muhammad (PBUH) began to experience prophetic dreams. During this significant year, while practicing Itikaf in the Cave of Hira, he had a dream in which a figure appeared, presenting him with a book wrapped in silk cloth. This figure instructed him to recite a few verses from the book, which would later become the first five verses of Surah Alaq. Upon awakening, Muhammad (PBUH) was uncertain of the dream's meaning, yet he vividly remembered the verses. He then stepped out of the cave and saw the same figure from his dream appearing on the horizon. This figure clearly stated that Muhammad (PBUH) had been appointed the Messenger of God and introduced himself as the angel Gabriel, leaving him with no sense of fear or uncertainty.

The narration further explains that Muhammad (PBUH) continued to gaze at Gabriel until a group of men, who had been sent by Khadija (RA) from her camp at the base of the mountain, called out to him. Muhammad (PBUH) recounted the incident to Khadija (RA). There is no mention of any panic or turmoil in this exchange. Khadija (RA) then left to share the details of this encounter with her cousin, Warqah bin Naufal, who was a Christian scholar. Meanwhile, Muhammad (PBUH) returned to the Cave of Hira to complete his Aitikaaf. After finishing his Aitikaaf, he went to the Kaaba to perform the ritual Tawaaf. It was during this Tawaaf that he encountered Warqah, who reassured him that he had indeed been chosen as the Messenger of God.

In the sequence of events narrated by Wahab ibn ul Kaisaan, there is neither fear nor confusion and certainly no instances of suicide attempts. Furthermore, Muhammad (PBUH) did not partake in enigmatic quests for enlightenment in the Cave of Hira. Instead, he engaged in ritual fasting and worship in isolation (Aitikaaf), following the tradition of Deen e Hanif—a set of beliefs and practices of Abraham (PBUH) adhered to by many in Arabia at that time. This version of events appears more credible and lacks the discrepancies present in the narration by Ibn e Shahab Zuhri.

Question 16: What Was The Age Of Aisha (RA) When She Married Muhammad (PBUH)?

Note: For more information on this topic, please refer to the chapter titled "Syeda Aisha (RA) Ki Umar" in Javed Ahmed Ghamidi's book "Mizan."

It is a commonly held belief that Aisha (RA) was six years old when she married Muhammad (PBUH) and that the marriage was consummated when she was nine. This view is supported by narrations found in Hadith literature, such as Sahih al-Bukhari (No: 5134, and 70). However, there are also authentic hadiths within the same literature that clearly contradict the notion that Aisha (RA) was between six to nine years old at the time of her marriage to Muhammad (PBUH). Let's examine some of these examples.

Child marriage goes against the clear injunctions of the Quran: Quran 4:6 states that those responsible for the wealth of orphans should evaluate and assess the orphans until they reach the age of marriage. If they are found to be mature and sound in judgment, then their wealth should be handed over to them.

Thus, Quran 4:6 clearly equates the age of marriage to an age where a person is mature enough to make sound judgments about their life and finances. This unequivocally negates the concept of child marriage.

Now, let us examine the Hadith literature which firmly establishes that Aisha (RA) was not 6 years old when she married Muhammad (PBUH).

Analysis of Hadith Literature which negates the idea that Aisha (R.A) was 6 to 9 when she married Muhammad (PBUH):

1) After Khadija (R.A) passed away, Muhammad (PBUH) was left all alone to take care of the household and children along with the pressure of performing duties as a Prophet of God. Khaula bint e Hakim, who was a close companion of Muhammad (PBUH), suggested that he should remarry so someone can take care of the household and the children. For this purpose, she suggested two names—one of Sauda bint e Zamah (R.A), who was an elderly widow, and the other name was of Aisha (R.A). This narration puts a huge question mark on Aisha (R.A) being only 6 when married to Muhammad (PBUH) and 9 when the marriage was consummated. Muhammad's (PBUH) own daughter Fatima (R.A) is said to be around 5 to 10 years old at the time of the marriage proposal to Aisha (R.A). How can Khaula suggest a 6-year-old to take care of Muhammad's (PBUH) children and the household?[69]

2) As per early biographers of Muhammad (PBUH) like Ibn e Ishaq and Ibn e Hisham, Aisha (R.A) was one of the earliest people who accepted Islam. Ibn e Ishaq is quoted to have said that Aisha (R.A) converted to Islam when only 18 people had accepted Islam, and Ibn e Hisham says that Aisha (R.A) accepted Islam at the same time as people like Abu Ubayda Jarrah (R.A). Abu Ubayda Jarrah and other early converts converted to Islam around 611-612 AD, while the Prophet (PBUH) married Aisha (R.A) in 620 AD. The question arises here: if Aisha (R.A) was 6 years old at the time of marriage to Muhammad (PBUH), then technically she wasn't even born in 612 AD. Even if she was born with an error margin of 1 or 2 years, she would be an infant in no position to accept the message of Islam. This doesn't make sense.[70] [71]

3) According to tradition of al-Bukhari, Chapter "The Compilation of Quran" – (No: 4876 and 4993), Aisha (R.A) says that she was a "*Jaariyah*" when Quran 54:46 was revealed. Jaariyah in classical Arabic means a young girl around adolescence or older.[72] Quran 54:46 was revealed in 617 AD, five years before Muhammad's (PBUH) migration to Medina in 622 AD. If Aisha was 6 years old when marrying Muhammad in 620 AD, that means she was a 3-year-old baby when 54:46 was revealed and she was in no way a *Jaariyah*!

4) Another set of Hadiths is presented to support the claim that Aisha (RA) was a child when she married Muhammad (PBUH). These traditions include the Sunan of ibn e Majah, No: 1982, Sahih of Muslim, No: 117, Sahih of Muslim, No: 83, and Sahih of Bukhari, No: 157. In these narrations, Aisha (RA) mentions she played with dolls in the presence of Muhammad (PBUH). At first glance, one might assume that Aisha (RA) must have been a child since typically only children play with dolls. However, another authentic hadith challenges the assumption that Aisha (RA) was a child during this time, suggesting instead that her enjoyment of making and playing with dolls extended into her mid to late teens. Allow me to explain briefly. Those who assert that Aisha (RA) was six years old when she married Muhammad (PBUH) refer to the year 620 AD as the year of the marriage. A credible narration in Abi Dawood recounts that Muhammad (PBUH) discovered Aisha's (RA) dolls in a closet after his return from either the Battle of Tabuk or Khaybar. He noticed the dolls behind a curtain and asked, "What are these?" Aisha (RA) responded, "These are my dolls." Muhammad (PBUH) then asked about another item, to which Aisha (RA) explained that it was a horse with two wings (Sunan of Abu Dawood, Nos: 4932, 160, and 4914). The narrative recounts that the incident where Muhammad

(PBUH) first discovered Aisha's (RA) dolls occurred either after the Battle of Tabuk or the Battle of Khyber. The Battle of Tabuk took place in 630 AD; therefore, if Aisha was 6 years old when she married Muhammad (PBUH), she would have been 16 at that time. Conversely, if this event transpired after the Battle of Khyber in 628 AD, Aisha (RA) would have been 14 years old. Thus, assuming Aisha (RA) was 6 years old at the time of her marriage to Muhammad (PBUH) in 620 AD, she was between 14 to 16 years old when Muhammad (PBUH) first encountered her dolls. Her mention of playing with dolls in Muhammad's (PBUH) presence should not be regarded simply as a recollection of her childhood, but rather as a reference to events occurring in her mid to late teens. It is plausible that Aisha (RA) continued her affection for creating dolls and other artifacts and engaging with them into her late teens. Similar interests persist among many young people today, who often continue their enjoyment of dolls and action figures into their late teens and beyond.

Estimating the Correct Age of Aisha (RA) When She Married Muhammad (PBUH): At this Juncture, The Question arises what was the actual age of Aisha (RA) when she married Muhammad (PBUH)? Within the Hadith literature, there is clear evidence that Aisha (RA) was 15 or 16 years old at the time of her marriage to Muhammad (PBUH) and approximately 18 or 19 when the marriage was consummated. Allow me to explain briefly.

We know that Aisha (RA) was ten years younger than her sister Asma (RA). Asma (RA) is said to have been born 27 years before Muhammad's (PBUH) migration to Medina in 622 AD. This places Asma's (RA) birth around 595 AD, and consequently, Aisha (RA) was born around 605 AD. This information establishes Aisha's (RA) age as approximately 15 or 16 when she was married to Muhammad (PBUH) in 620 AD and 18 or 19 when her marriage was consummated in 623 AD.[73]

Additionally, Asma (RA) is commonly known to have died in 692 AD at the age of 97 to 98. This means that Asma (RA) was 25 to 26 years old in 620 AD. Hence, if Aisha (RA) was 10 years younger than Asma (RA), then Aisha was 15 to 16 years old in 620 AD when she married Muhammad (PBUH).

Hadith literature is a complicated science: This field of knowledge is vast, containing narrations that some scholars deem authentic while others consider weak. It is possible to find material supporting whichever stance one prefers in these matters. Ibn Kathir serves as a significant example of the flexible use of Hadith literature. On one hand, he accepts Hadiths that establish Asma (RA) as being 10 years older than Aisha (RA), which would imply that Aisha (RA) was 16 when she married Muhammad (PBUH) in 620 AD. However, Ibn Kathir also accepts those Hadiths that claim Aisha (RA) was 6 years old at the time of her marriage and agrees with the notion that she was 6. –74 This illustrates the complex nature of Hadith literature. The Hadith literature that is used to support the idea that Aisha (RA) was 6 years old when she married Muhammad (PBUH), this same Hadith literature also contains ample material to support the claim that she was 16 years old at the time of her marriage to Muhammad (PBUH) and 19 when the marriage was consummated. This is why it is extremely important to interpret Hadith through the lens of the Quran and not the other way around.

Possible causes of the mix-up of Aisha's age: Then the question arises: what could be the possible cause of the existence of narrations in Hadith literature that state Aisha (RA) was 6 years old at the time of marriage to Muhammad (PBUH) when the same Hadith literature contains much information that thoroughly negates this idea? It probably has something to do with how Arabs pronounce their numbers.

In Arabic, 6 is pronounced "Sittah" and 16 as "Sittatah 'Asharah." Similarly, 9 is pronounced "Tis'ah" and 19 as "tis'ahta 'Asharah." A parallel in English numbers would be saying 16 as "Six-Ten" and 19 as "Nine-Ten." It is possible that either Aisha (RA) or later hadith transmitters took the decade part as something everyone already knew and didn't record it. For example, if it is already understood that a person is talking about the 1900s and he mentions that such-and-such event happened in 83, you automatically know the person means that the event happened in 1983, not 83 BC or 83 AD. Thus, it is conceivable that either Aisha (RA) or later transmitters were simply highlighting the exact year of the marriage while assuming that the term "Ashara" or decade part is already known.

Question 17: What Is The Story Of The Creation Of Humankind According To The Quran, And Did The Children Of Adam And Eve (Peace Be Upon Them) Commit Incest To Expand The Human Population?

The Quran discusses various aspects of human creation. In one verse, it asserts that humans are created from water, while in another, it claims that we are molded from clay. Because the Quran states that humans are made from clay, ancient scholars often conceived that God sculpted the first human as a statue and breathed life into it.

There are some weak narrations attributed to Muhammad (PBUH) that are used to support this idea. However, when studied with an open mind, it appears that the Quran presents a very different story about the emergence of modern humans, a story that seems to be supported by what we know about our origins.

Analysis of Quran 32:7-9 to Understand Human Origins:

The Quran mentions human origins in various passages, but specifically in Quran 32:7-9, which outlines the stages of human development in a sequence.

"God started the process of creation of humankind from clay. Then He made humankind's descendants from a meager fluid - then He fashioned and perfected them and after that He had a spirit from the Divine breathed into it. He granted you hearing, sight and intellect" (Quran 32:7-9).

Along with the previously mentioned verse, Quran 21:30 asserts that all living things were created from water, while Quran 25:54 states that humans were created from water. When viewed in conjunction with the other two verses mentioned above, Quran 32:7-9 helps divide the story of human creation into three stages.

Stage 1 - Earliest ancestors of humans came out directly from the earth's crust: The process of human creation began in muddy pools of water, with the primordial human-animal forms emerging from the earth, akin to an organism emerging from an egg buried in the ground. According to Quranic verses, one can infer that the first ancestors of humans—initially just in animal form, devoid of a soul—came directly from the earth. This process appears to mirror what transpires in a mother's womb, taking place within the earth's crust, leading to the creation of primordial animal forms of humans and possibly other species as well.

It is neither magical nor incomprehensible. Consider this: we consume the same raw materials found in nature, such as amino acids, iron, and calcium. Remarkably, there exists a factory within the female body that transforms these basic ingredients into living organisms. The Quran suggests that this same process occurred within the earth, transforming the basic ingredients of life found in mud and water into living organisms.

Does the idea of primordial animal forms emerging from the earth sound ridiculous to you? It shouldn't, because this concept has historical precedence. Take, for instance, the "Cambrian Explosion," a remarkable event documented in the fossil records. This occurred approximately 500 million years ago, marking a period when most of the major animal groups abruptly made their appearance in the fossil record. I am not suggesting that primordial human forms emerged during the Cambrian Explosion. Rather, I aim to illustrate that events such as the Cambrian Explosion support the possibility—scientifically speaking—that the Quranic depiction of the primordial biological ancestors of humans emerging from the earth near muddy pools of water might not be as far-fetched as it seems.

Stage 2 - Humans' animal form went through biological evolution possibly over many generations: The Quran states that once the animal-like human ancestors emerged from the earth, their progeny was produced through the usual means of sexual reproduction. Then, as Quran 32:9 suggests, the descendants of this human-animal form underwent a process of gradual development, possibly spanning many generations, until they reached perfection.

It can be inferred that the Quran supports interspecies evolution by stating that primordial forms of animal species emerged directly from the earth. Subsequently, they reproduced through biological means and underwent a process of gradual development over time. Indeed, evidence exists of primitive humanoid creatures such as Ramapithecus, Australopithecus, and Homo erectus. Moreover, the fossil record indicates that biologically modern Homo sapiens evolved as a result of gradual development from these earlier primitive versions.

It is a consensus among scientists that the earliest known human ancestor, the most ancient known primitive biological humanoid creature, existed 4.2 million years ago. --75 Till about 300,000 years ago, primitive humanoids had evolved into archaic Homo sapiens—the direct ancestors of modern Homo sapiens—and about 160,000 years ago, the first group of biologically modern Homo sapiens appeared.

So, the Quran does not support Darwinian evolution from a single cell; however, it does seem to endorse the concept of interspecies evolution, positing that the primordial ancestors of these species emerged directly from the earth.

Stage 3 - Once biological evolution was complete - the soul was transferred to humans: Finally, Quran 32:9 states that once humans reached the stage of biological completion, they were endowed with the soul, after which they became individuals distinguished by pronounced intellect, aesthetics, and morality. This notion is also supported by what we understand about our reality—let me briefly explain.

Once the human species evolved into modern Homo sapiens around 160,000 years ago, there was a notable shift in behavior. There are two predominant theories regarding the emergence of modern human behavior. The first suggests that this behavioral modernity developed gradually over a long period. The second posits that there was a sudden shift around 50,000 years ago. In either scenario, it is widely agreed that after humans reached biological modernity, they soon exhibited signs of behavioral modernity. This included practices such as burying their dead, creating art, adorning themselves with ornaments, and constructing temples for worship. –76 Hence, it seems plausible that humans achieved biological modernity, and subsequently, a transfer of the soul could have sparked these behavioral changes as well..

Did the children of Adam and Eve (PBUT) commit incest to expand the human population? No, because according to the Quran, Adam and Eve (PBUT) were not the only humans in a world devoid of others. In the narrative presented by the Quran, biologically modern humans existed but were akin to animal forms, lacking souls. God selected two individuals from these humans and bestowed upon them the divine essence known as the human soul. It can be inferred that the offspring of Adam and Eve (PBUT) also received this divine essence. As the children of Adam and Eve (PBUT) reproduced with other members of their species who did not possess the soul, they transmitted this divine essence to their descendants. Over many thousands of years, this resulted in the entire human population possessing it.

To further summarize, the Quran states that humankind's initial biological forms originated from the earth. This is reminiscent of events such as the Cambrian explosion, which shows in our biological history periods where complex life forms appear to suddenly emerge. Additionally, the Quran explains that these primitive human forms reproduced sexually and underwent extensive biological evolution over numerous generations—a claim that seems to be supported by the fossil record. Ultimately, the Quran describes how, once the human biological form was fully developed, God selected two individuals and imbued them with souls. This assertion aligns with evidence from our history when biologically modern humans began to exhibit behavioral modernity.

A brief note about the Quran's idea of the brain vs. soul and why it seems true: The Quran supports the concept of the duality of the human body and soul. It states that the body and brain are creations of this world, while the soul—the "Me" that experiences everything—is not of this earthly realm and belongs to a higher dimension. The notion that the brain and soul are distinct is underscored by observations of the brain's separate areas where environmental inputs are processed. However, there appears to be no specific location in the brain where these inputs converge into a singular unified experience that is Me!

It seems that the soul impacts the brain and vice versa, as the mind can influence the material brain, with mere thoughts capable of altering the brain's physical structure. We also know that the material brain can change mind, as damage to certain parts of the brain can alter our personalities and views. We have discussed this in detail in the section addressing the mind versus brain debate..

Question 18: Were Adam And Eve (PBUT) In Heaven Before Coming To Earth?

The Quran does not state anywhere that Adam and Eve (PBUT) were born in heaven and then banished to Earth. Instead, it mentions that they were in Jannah, which translates to "garden" in English. Since Jannah is also a term used in Islam for Paradise, alongside other terms like Bahisht and Firdaus, it is commonly understood that Adam and Eve's presence in Jannah indicates that they were created in Paradise and subsequently banished to Earth.

There are many reasons to infer from the Quran that Adam and Eve (PBUT) were created here on Earth.

Reason 1: The Quran states in 2:30 that God proclaimed His plan to create humans on Earth as successors to Him, indicating that God intended for humans to be created on this planet. Additionally, numerous verses in the Quran support this, stating humans were created from water and mud. For example, Quran 32:7-9 further elaborates on this concept.

Reason 2: Secondly, Quran 14:48 states that the world of the hereafter, including Paradise and Hell, has yet to be formed. The verse explains that when the time comes to unleash judgment on humankind, this world and the entire universe will transform into a new world where people will be judged and recompensed for their deeds. Thus, the world of the hereafter, including Paradise, is yet to materialize.

These verses clearly imply that Adam and Eve (PBUT) were created here on Earth. The word "Jannah" used in verses like 2:35, relating to Adam and Eve (PBUT), refers simply to a garden or a forest abundant in food, water, and shelter, not the heavenly Paradise.

Another reason why many believe that Adam and Eve (PBUT) were in Paradise in heaven stems from interpretations of verses like

2:36, where Adam and Eve (PBUT) are told to "Ihbitu" or "go down" from the garden they were in. This term "Ihbitu" does not imply that Adam and Eve (PBUT) were instructed to descend from heaven to earth; rather, this word is also found elsewhere in the Quran, such as in 2:61, to simply mean travel in or out from. Thus, considering the entire context mentioned above, Adam and Eve (PBUT) in 2:36 are being told to leave the garden rather than descend from heaven to earth.

It should be noted that the Quran confirms the existence of a place called "Jannat ul Mawa" in 53:15. Additionally, another verse in the Quran, 32:19, suggests that it is either a material or a spiritual world, serving as a welcoming place for the truly righteous souls—a place where they are kept and given a certain type of life before the final resurrection on the Day of Judgment.

Question 19: What Was The Forbidden Tree That Adam And Eve (PBUT) Ate From, And Why Was This Tree Forbidden?

It is evident from Quran 7:20-22 that Adam and Eve (PBUT) were prevented from engaging in sexual relations. This passage states that Satan offered them a suggestion to reveal their hidden shame. Further, the verse states that after eating from the tree, they became aware of their sexuality—their private parts—and began to cover themselves with leaves. Despite being husband and wife, this restriction was imposed on them as a test to illustrate the consequences of disobeying God.

Question 20: Why Are Men Allowed Four Marriages, And Why Are Women Not Allowed Multiple Marriages?

God created Eve for Adam (Peace Be Upon Them) and not four, clearly indicating that the ideal relationship in God's view is one husband and one wife. Moreover, in Quran 4:3, where the permission for four marriages is mentioned, the God of the Quran discourages polygamy and actually promotes monogamy. Let me explain briefly.

Quran 4:3 states:

> *Give the orphans their wealth with utmost honesty and do not exchange your possessions for their wealth nor cheat them by mixing their wealth with your own, for this would indeed be a great sin. If you fear you will not be able to take proper care of the orphans, marry women of your choice, one, two, three, or four, but do justice between them. And if you fear you shall fail to do justice with them, then marry only one ... this is better for you as you are less likely to commit injustice this way.*

Conditional allowance of polygamy to men: First, it was a norm for men to marry multiple women 1400 years ago in almost all cultures, including the Arabs. It is still a norm in many societies today. Therefore, it is not the Quran that initiated the practice of polygamy; it was already very prevalent in almost all human societies. The appropriate perspective is that the Quran did not prohibit the already existing practice of men marrying multiple times but instead placed a limit on it to a maximum of four.

Secondly, Quran 4:3 acknowledges the difficulty of doing justice between multiple wives and thus recommends that men marry only one. It is evident that even in situations where there is a genuine need for men to marry multiple times, the God of the Quran strongly advises them to marry only one.

So, the Quran permits men to marry more than once but also imposes a condition that they must treat their wives justly—this includes both financial and emotional justice. There are situations where it might be justified for a man to marry more than once. For example, if a woman cannot bear children and the man desires offspring, or if the woman suffers from a disease that prevents her from fulfilling the physical needs of her husband. In such cases, it appears morally justified and closer to fairness for the man to marry again without the consent of the first wife.

Another scenario might involve a man who does not encounter any of the previously mentioned need-based challenges but wishes to marry multiple times simply because he desires multiple women. In this case, justice requires that each woman be informed beforehand about his intentions to marry multiple times, and each woman must consent to this arrangement before marrying such a person. If the woman is not informed beforehand in this specific situation, it constitutes a gross and blatant act of emotional injustice. It is important to note that any form of injustice—whether financial or emotional—is strictly prohibited in Islam.

Furthermore, Islam grants women the right to stipulate in the marriage contract that the husband will not take another wife. If he violates this condition, the marriage will be considered annulled.

It is a fact that some men have exploited this verse to cater to their own lusts. It is crucial that measures are taken to ensure that men have justified reasons for marrying more than once. States can enact laws to regulate the permission of polygamy and require a man to justify his reasons in court if he wishes to marry more than once. Women cannot have multiple husbands: Islam views marriage as an institution—in fact, it sees marriage as the most important institution—and an institution can only have one head. Islam designates the man as the head of the family institution since he is given more responsibility - especially the financial responsibility.

Women are not allowed to practice polyandry for the following reasons: A country can only have one head, such as a Prime Minister or President, yet it may have many ministers. Similarly, a company can have only one CEO, yet many managing directors. In the same way, a family in Islam can have one head, who is the husband, and potentially multiple wives, but not vice versa. No institution can thrive with multiple heads; therefore, since Islam views marriage and family as an institution and designates the man as the head of this institution, it does not allow a woman to marry multiple men. However, the God of the Quran has insisted that the ideal family should consist of one husband and one wife, exemplified by Adam (PBUH) having one wife, and Quran 4:3 also insists that men should marry only one woman; otherwise, they risk committing injustice.

Thus, if a woman is in a justified situation where she needs to marry another man, the only solution is for her to leave her husband to marry this other man..

Question 21: Why Are All Forms Of Sexual Behavior Strictly Prohibited Outside The Marriage Between A Man And A Woman, And Why Are They Considered Major Sins And Serious Crimes?

Human beings are not merely physical creatures; we are psychological, emotional, and spiritual beings as well. When a baby is born, this completely helpless newborn requires constant long-term care and nurturing in all these aspects, potentially extending over a decade. The Abrahamic God has ordained that the family unit, comprising a man and a woman—a father and a mother—is the institution created by God Himself. This institution is not only for bringing new human beings into the world but, more importantly, for providing the essential long-term physical, emotional, psychological, and spiritual care a child needs until reaching maturity. Similarly, as humans reach old age, they too require physical and emotional support, and a stable family is the ideal institution to provide this care. Even the best old age homes cannot compare to the emotional fulfillment a stable family can offer. For this reason, the Quran goes to great lengths to protect the institution of marriage and the family.

The entire ritual of marriage is designed to provide a solid foundation for the relationship by encouraging both the man and the woman to invest deeply in the institution. In the presence of their family and society, they publicly proclaim their full responsibility for each other. Both parties promise, with God as their witness, to remain honest and faithful in the union they are entering.

There are many elements necessary for a strong marriage, such as mutual respect and a bond of trust. However, I believe that sexual fidelity is arguably the most crucial aspect of a stable and enduring marriage. It is often considered the foundation upon which a marriage stands. To protect the institution of family, the God of the Quran has decreed that all kinds of sexual behaviors and actions must be strictly confined to marriage. Any sexual behavior or action outside of marriage is viewed as a punishable offense in Islam and a major sin that threatens one's salvation on Judgment Day. Therefore, whether one is married or unmarried, straight or homosexual, engaging in sexual behavior with anyone outside of a heterosexual marriage is strictly prohibited and regarded as a major sin and a severe crime, carrying serious worldly consequences if discovered. Many verses in the Quran, such as Quran 7:33, categorize sexual relations outside of marriage as a major sin. Persisting on this sin risks eternal damnation because it directly compromises the societal institution, created by God Himself, intended for the well-being of children and the elderly.

It makes sense for a newborn to receive such complex, long-term, dedicated care, and for the well-being of the elderly, no other institution can replace a stable family. Indeed, a stable family provides the optimal infrastructure for the physical, emotional, psychological, and spiritual nourishment of a child from infancy to adulthood. It makes sense to restrict all types of sexual behavior and actions within the confines of marriage to strengthen the family institution. It is indeed true that in any society where sexual and intimate behavior outside of marriage is normalized, the institution of family is likely to suffer.

It is a well-known fact that unstable families and broken homes have a devastating impact on children. There is a plethora of research available indicating that children from such families have extremely deep-rooted and long-term negative effects on their personalities.

A brief note about sexual fidelity in marriage and chemicals in our body: There is a chemical rationale for strictly limiting all sexual and intimate behavior to the confines of marriage to strengthen this institution. Dopamine and serotonin, substances in the body that elicit feelings of pleasure and happiness, are released during various activities such as exercise, completing tasks, and eating. A major source of these chemical releases is sexual and emotional gratification.

Concerning sexual, physical, and emotional intimacy, if these substances are released exclusively during interactions with one's spouse, it can significantly strengthen the marital relationship. Conversely, releasing these chemicals through other means—such as viewing pornography, sexually admiring others, or engaging in physical intimacy outside the marriage—can dilute the special bond with one's spouse. Engaging in such behaviors, which also trigger dopamine and serotonin, may soon make the relationship with the spouse seem less appealing, overshadowed by the intense rewards from these other sources.

Hence, among other reasons, even the nature of chemicals in our bodies demands that we strictly limit all kinds of sexual behaviors and actions toward our spouse. This strengthens the marital bond and increases the likelihood of creating a stable family institution.

Question 22: Why Is The Husband Given A Rank Higher Than The Wife? Does That Mean Men Are Superior To Women In Islam?

Men are absolutely not superior to women in Islam. Quran 33:73 indicates that both men and women are equal in the sight of God, and Quran 49:13 clearly states that humankind was created from a male and a female, with the most noble in the sight of God being the one who is the most righteous and God-conscious. In Islam, it is neither gender, ethnicity, bloodline, race, nor color that determines superiority but righteousness and God-consciousness. Women and men are equal in the eyes of the God of the Quran; however, within the institution of marriage, husbands are given a rank higher than their wives for the following reasons.

Just like the institution of the state or any other organization, Islam views marriage as a pivotal institution, thereby establishing specific rights and responsibilities for its members. God commands that both men and women should physically and emotionally devote themselves solely and sincerely to their spouses. If the wife earns an income, it is her own wealth, and she is not obligated to contribute it to the family's upkeep. However, the husband bears the responsibility for the financial maintenance of the family. Therefore, if the family's rightful expenses are not met, the husband is solely blamed and held accountable. Due to this greater degree of responsibility, the husband is accorded a higher rank in the family's decision-making process. In the event of a deadlock on issues, the husband is granted the deciding vote.

It is important to note that Islam allocates a larger share of inheritance to men, guided by the principle that men have been given the responsibility for the financial upkeep of the family.

This is not gender discrimination, as previously mentioned because men and women are considered equal in the eyes of God. It is only when entering into the contract of marriage that the roles and responsibilities assigned to the offices of husband and wife establish a hierarchy. The husband is burdened with heavier responsibilities; therefore, he holds a higher rank in family decision-making. Similarly, within the same family institution, the mother is given a higher rank than the father concerning the children (Sahih of Muslim, No: 6181). Thus, it is not about gender but rather the rights and responsibilities within the marriage institution.

It does make sense—whether it is a state, a corporate company, or, in this case, a family—whoever holds the higher responsibility should also wield greater influence in the decision-making process. It also makes sense to put financial responsibility on the man because, firstly, men are not bound by the physical requirements of pregnancy and breastfeeding children. Secondly, both in humanity's past and present, apart from very few exceptions in modern times, earning a living has mostly been an extremely physically strenuous task for which men have been deemed more suited. Additionally, the protection of the family or country from external threats was and still is seen as a man's job since militaries are comprised mostly of men, and, before the age of guns, protecting the family or tribe was a very physically demanding task intended for men.

Hence, it seems reasonable that, exceptions aside, the Quran establishes a general principle of placing more responsibility on the husband and, consequently, assigns him a higher rank in family decision-making.

A question arises: if a woman assumes the financial responsibility of the family, can she become the head of the family institution? I believe she can. If a woman officially takes on the full financial responsibility of the family and the man relinquishes it to her, then she can indeed be the head of the family institution.

Question 23: Does The Quran Provide A Political System?

Yes, Islam prescribes certain punishments and authorizes Muslim governments to collect Zakat tax. In addition to this, Islam establishes broad principles for political and governance systems, but it does not prescribe a specific system. Let me explain.

If by "political system" one means a detailed framework describing how representatives are elected to office, the responsibilities they will carry, the mechanism of power transfer, and the nature of relationships among the executive, judicial, and legislative branches, along with the powers held by the ruler, then no! None of these specifics are detailed in the Quran. In this sense, the Quran does not outline in detail a political system.

However, the Quran establishes certain principles upon which societies should base their systems and conduct. These principles are broad directives, and it appears that the God of the Quran has left the specifics to the intellect of the people. For instance, Quran 42:38 directs that Muslims should decide their collective matters through mutual consultation. This implies that individuals responsible for making decisions on public affairs should be chosen through public consultation, and the transfer of power should also occur through this process. However, no specific method of public consultation is prescribed, leaving Muslims to use their intellect to choose an appropriate form. For example, they might opt for a Presidential system, a Parliamentary system, or develop any other system that meets the unique needs of each society and culture.

Other broad principles for a Muslim society to follow include universal values such as ensuring justice, promoting good values, prohibiting evil, caring for the less fortunate, and safeguarding religious freedoms and protection from persecution.

Along with specific principles on which Muslims are expected to base their political system, Islam also mandates particular punishments for certain crimes. We will discuss the details of these punishments in the next section.

Hence, Islam does not ordain any specific political system but establishes certain broad principles on which Muslims must base their system, and prescribes specific punishments for certain crimes.

Question 24: Is Islam Opposed to Democracy?

No! Quran 42:38 instructs Muslims to decide their collective matters by mutual consultation. As discussed above, the Quran entrusts Muslims to use their intellect to determine the specific methods of involving people in the decision-making processes of the Muslim collective. Options may include a Presidential System, a Parliamentary System, or the development of another mechanism.

Question 25: Amar Bil Maroof Wa Nahi Anil Munkar - Can Governments Force Islam On Me?

This verse of the Quran is highly popular and often used as a justification for governments to enforce head or face coverings on women and beards on men. The phrase "Amar bil Maroof wa nahi anil Munkar" translates to "Call people to what is good and forbid them from what is evil."

This instruction is primarily commanded to Muslims in three places in the Quran: 3:104, 3:110, and 9:71.

There are three main concepts to understand in this regard:
1. The word used for "call people to" is "Amr," which means "to order someone to do something." It has also been used in the Quran to mean "to invite someone to do something," for example, in Quran 2:169. Therefore, the verse implies that if you are in a place of authority, such as the police, then you can

forcefully forbid people from doing something wrong. If you are a common person, then your jurisdiction is only to advise and admonish people.

2. The words used in this verse for good and evil are "Maroof" and "Munkar". The meanings of these words imply things that are universally recognized as good and things that are universally recognized as evil, from both the perspective of Islam and universal human morality. Thus, these words do not suggest that governments have unrestricted authority to impose their interpretation of Islam on others in all matters. In fact, the verse indicates that governments can promote what is commonly known as good in society, such as honesty, cleanliness, and kindness, and can forcefully prevent actions that are universally recognized as detrimental, such as theft, dishonesty, fraud, robbery, unlawful violence, and injustice..

3. If a government wants to force something on others from the perspective of Islam, then it has to have a clear sanction from the Quran, meaning that the Quran has to give a clear authorization to a government to force that particular thing on others. For example, the Quran gives a clear sanction to Governments to enforce the collection of Zakat tax from people, to stop people from committing open adultery, and to punish them if they do so, etc.

In this context, if the Quran does not authorize the enforcement of a specific injunction of Islam by a government, then it should not be enforced. For example, decisions about women covering their heads and faces, or men being obligated to grow beards, are not granted enforcement rights by any government according to the Quran. Therefore, everyone is free to follow the interpretation they agree with without governmental imposition.

Personally speaking, in the interpretation of Islam that I agree with, currently led by Mr. Javed Ahmed Ghamidi, men are not obligated to have a beard, and women are not obligated to cover their heads or faces (it is considered an optional good deed), and God has not ordained gender segregation at public events. The Quran does not sanction any government to enforce their interpretation of Islam on individuals in such matters.

Question 26: What Are Different Islamic Punishments?

The Quran prescribes worldly punishments for certain crimes for three main reasons:

1. To establish the severity of certain sins and crimes.
2. To create deterrence in society regarding these crimes and sins.
3. These punishments are embodiments of divine wrath inflicted on a person who commits such serious crimes even after accepting the existence of God and making a covenant of righteousness with God by accepting Islam.

The Quran mandates that the Muslim community enforce divinely ordained punishments for certain crimes. These severe penalties apply only to Muslims and pertain to specific offenses. However, Muslims have the discretion to assign lesser punishments if they deem the offender deserving of leniency.

Quran 5:32 states that the death penalty can only be imposed for two offenses: murder and crimes of "Fasaad fil Ardh." The term Fasaad fil Ardh, meaning wreaking havoc on Earth, encompasses all crimes that harm another person's wealth, life, and dignity, including rape, armed robbery, terrorism, and kidnapping.

The Quran specifies particular punishments for the following crimes:

1. Sexual intercourse outside marriage: Consensual sexual intercourse without marriage is termed "Zina" in Arabic and is considered an extremely serious crime and sin. The Quran strives to prohibit all sexual activity outside of marriage; thus, Quran 24:2 prescribes the punishment of 100 lashes if this crime is proven. It is important to note that a case can only be registered against someone if there are four credible witnesses who have seen the act occurring. After the case is registered, a proper investigation must be conducted to prove the crime beyond doubt before any punishment can be executed. For rape cases, which fall under the category of Fasaad fil Ardh, four witnesses are not required to register the case.

The Quran does not differentiate based on the marital status of the individual committing zina when it comes to punishment. This means that the perpetrator, whether married or unmarried, will receive lashes. This punishment is administered after a thorough investigation once the case is registered and in the presence of four credible witnesses who have directly observed the act.

Because Muhammad (PBUH) administered the death penalty to certain individuals seemingly for the crime of Zina, a misconception has developed that the death penalty is mandatory for married individuals who commit this act. However, upon closer examination of these instances, it becomes evident that Muhammad (PBUH) issued the death penalty not simply because the perpetrators were married, nor solely for the crime of Zina, but for crimes like rape and persistent, open, and defiant sexual misconduct, categorized as Fasaad fil Ardh.[78]

2. Qazaf: It refers to false testimony in general, and specifically, it pertains to falsely accusing someone of engaging in sexual intercourse outside of marriage. This act is considered a punishable crime, and the accuser is subject to lashing.

3. Theft: According to the Quran, theft is a punishable crime, and if there are no grounds for leniency, the ultimate worldly punishment prescribed is the amputation of the thief's hand. However, if the offender merits consideration for leniency, a lesser punishment may be administered..

4. Murder: The ultimate earthly punishment for murder is the death penalty, granted the criminal does not deserve any leniency.

5. Hiraaba or Fasaad fil Ardh: As discussed previously, we outlined the types of crimes that fall under this category. The ultimate worldly penalty for these crimes is the death penalty unless the perpetrator is deemed deserving of leniency.

The Quran mentions no punishment for apostasy and blasphemy, so if Muslims wish to legislate on this matter, it is their prerogative. However, they must adhere to the Quranic injunction that the death penalty can only and solely be imposed for murder or Fasaad fil Ardh.

Question 27: Does Islam Mandate The Death Penalty As Punishment For Blasphemy?

For references and a detailed analysis of the content in this section, please refer to Javed Ahmed Ghamidi's book "Maqamaat," specifically the chapter titled "Punishment for Blasphemy."

The Quran is extremely clear that the death penalty can be applied to only two crimes: murder and Fasad fil-Ardh. As discussed above, Fasad fil-Ardh encompasses all crimes that create chaos in society and cause harm to people's lives, property, and reputation, such as rape, armed robbery, rebellion, kidnapping, and acts of terrorism.

Those who advocate for the death penalty claim that the act of blasphemy falls under the category of "Muhaarba," meaning "Waging War on God and His Rasool," as well as under the category of "Fasaad fil Ardh." This is because mocking, insulting, and abusing Muhammad

(PBUH) constitutes the act of fighting God's Rasool and causing unjust damage to someone's respect. The argument is logically true, however, the terms Muhaarba (waging war) and Fasaad fil Ardh (creating havoc on land) suggest that the criminal must be persistent and unapologetic in their insulting and abusive behavior despite all attempts by society and authorities to resolve the matter passively. Only under these circumstances would such a crime fall under the severe categories of Muhaarba or Fasaad fil Ardh.

Proponents of the death penalty point to specific incidents in which the Prophet (PBUH) issued the death penalty to certain individuals. However, upon closer examination, it becomes apparent that these individuals were not punished exclusively for insulting Muhammad (PBUH), but also for other crimes. For example, Abu Rafay was a notorious enemy of Islam who incited people and led them to attack Medina during the Battle of the Trench. Kaab bin Ashraf was responsible for inciting Meccans against Muslims and Muhammad (PBUH), urging them to attack Medina after the Battle of Badr, and he initiated numerous slander campaigns against prominent Muslim women. According to some accounts, he even secretly plotted to assassinate Muhammad (PBUH), despite having a peace agreement with the Muslims. Abdullah bin Khattal murdered his own slave and fled Medina to avoid punishment. All of these individuals committed additional crimes besides insulting Muhammad (PBUH). Furthermore, according to the Quran's law concerning the Rasool, which was discussed earlier, all these individuals were also guilty of unjustly rejecting a living Rasool of God. For pagans, the divine punishment for this crime was the death penalty. Therefore, it is evident that no one was sentenced to death solely for insulting Muhammad (PBUH), but rather for multiple crimes.

Two Hadiths are presented in this regard wherein Omar (RA) beheaded a person for mocking Muhammad (PBUH), and Muhammad (PBUH) is reported to have said, "Kill those who insult the Prophets of God." These narrations are deemed weak by most Hadith experts and cannot be presented as arguments to support the death penalty for blasphemy.

A narration from Abdullah bin Abbas (RA), a companion of Muhammad (PBUH), is presented in this context to suggest that God ordained the death penalty for blasphemy. He states:

Any Muslim who insults or mocks Muhammad (PBUH) or any other Prophet of God becomes guilty of rejecting the Messenger of God. This constitutes apostasy, and the individual will be asked to repent. If they repent, they will be spared; if they do not, they will be executed. If a non-Muslim engages in these actions, they break the peace agreement between us and will also be subject to execution.[79]

When we view this issue through the lens of God's law as it relates to Prophets, which we discussed earlier in detail, it becomes clear that Ibn Abbas (RA) was specifically referring to the immediate recipients of the Prophet's messages. In the context of God's specific laws pertaining to Prophets, those among a Prophet's immediate recipients who reject and persecute him are subject to worldly punishment. In the case of Muhammad (PBUH), the pagans were sentenced to death, while the People of the Book were subjected to life under subjugation. Therefore, anyone among Muhammad's (PBUH) immediate recipients who rejected him after initially accepting his message became subject to the same punishments reserved for dissenters, and those who breached the peace treaty with Muslims were also subjected to punishment in accordance with God's laws with Rasools.

Hence, Islam ordains no punishment for the sole act of blasphemy. However, Muslims can legislate to punish this crime under Muhaarba and Fasaad fil Ardh, but these categories apply only when the perpetrator of abuse and insults is acting openly, publicly, and persistently, and is unwilling to cease the insults, apologize, or mend their ways despite all peaceful attempts.

Question 28: When Can Muslims Fight Others?

The Quran authorizes Muslims to engage in armed conflict for mainly three reasons. Let us briefly analyze these reasons.

1) In Quran 5:9, it is expressed that God commands Muslims to engage in combat with pagans until they embrace Islam, while Quran 9:29 states that God instructs Muslims to confront Jews and Christians until they either convert to Islam or agree to pay a tax that signifies submission and humility. We have already discussed in detail that the order to fight and inflict divine punishments on Pagans, Jews, and Christians was exclusive to the immediate addressees of a Rasool, as per the Quranic law of God, when a Rasool is present in the world. Muhammad (PBUH) is the last Rasool, which means there will be no more worldly demonstrations of God's judgment—no more divine punishments in this world for the immediate addressees of a Rasool. Therefore, Muslims after Muhammad (PBUH) cannot fight non-Muslims solely based on their beliefs.

2) In the Quran, verses 2:190-191, warfare is permitted strictly for self-defense.

3) In Quran 4:75 and Quran 22:39-40, war is allowed against clear and open oppression and persecution. The first reason was exclusive to Muhammad (PBUH) and his immediate audience. Reasons two and three relate to all Muslims; according to these reasons, Muslims can only take up arms either in self-defense or against clear and open oppression, injustice, and persecution. However, this must also occur under a lawful leader or ruler, as stated in the Quran:

Obey God, His Messenger and obey those in position of authority over you. (Quran 4:59)

If people deem that those in authority over them are not doing their job correctly and feel the need to change them, they must resort to peaceful struggle to change the rulers under the guideline of 42:38, which states that Muslims must decide their collective matters by mutual consultation.

I understand that extreme exceptions might exist where it might be justified to take up arms against rulers but as far as the norm is concerned, the above mentioned is the will of God as per Quran.

Question 29: Is Slavery Allowed in Islam?

No! Let me explain.

Prohibition of bringing in new slaves after warfare: In Islam, a free person cannot be made a slave. The only other method to acquire slaves was through warfare. If there was a conflict for any reason, the victors would enslave the prisoners of war. Quran 47:4 directs that prisoners of war must either be freed for ransom or out of goodwill. This verse effectively closed the door to acquiring new slaves.

Thus, Muslims cannot enslave a free person, nor can they create new slaves through warfare.

What about the existing slaves? At the time of Muhammad (PBUH), countless slaves were present in nearly every household—men, women, both young and old, along with children. The question arose: what should be done with these existing slaves? Allow me to briefly explain the Quran's remedy for this issue.

Quran's plan of managing existing slaves and encouragement of their freedom with economic independence: The Quran did not mandate an immediate end to all slavery because, in a less developed world, such a sweeping prohibition could have led to a humanitarian disaster, leaving hundreds of thousands of men, women, and children of all ages destitute, with their only prospects for survival being begging or prostitution. Therefore, for the existing slaves, the Quran maintains the status quo while issuing extensive directives to improve their conditions and promote their freedom through economic independence.

Quran 24:33 mandates that formal agreements be made with slaves, providing them the option of freedom if they demonstrate the ability to sustain themselves economically. God commands Muslims to share a portion of their wealth with slaves to help them attain economic independence.

The Quran deems the act of freeing slaves so great in its righteousness that it is prescribed as a means for Muslims to have their sins forgiven (Quran 4:92, 58:3). The Quran also states that one purpose of Zakat, or compulsory charity, is to free slaves (Quran 9:60).

Quran 4:36 instructs Muslims to treat their slaves with kindness and goodness. It was customary for men to have sexual relationships with their female slaves. The Quran acknowledges this practice and, in Quran 24:32, it encourages Muslims, both men and women, to marry their slaves if feasible.

Muhammad (PBUH) further elucidated Quranic guidelines by detailing the rights of slaves, as he relayed the following instructions to his companions:

> ... feed them with the same food you eat and clothe them with the same clothes you wear. Do not assign them a task they cannot do; if you do so, then help them (Sahih of Bukhari, No: 30; Sahih of Muslim, No: 1661).

Although slavery was extensively practiced in the Muslim world after Muhammad (PBUH), the truth is that the God of the Quran closed the door to acquiring new slaves and mandated the management of existing slaves to gradually phase out this practice without causing a humanitarian crisis.

Question 30: Why Did Muhammad (PBUH) Not Marry Maria al-Qibtiya, and How Did He (PBUH) Treat Her According to Islamic Teachings?

Muhammad (PBUH) was gifted a slave girl named Maria al-Qibtiya by the Governor of Alexandria in 628-629 AD. Around the same time, Muhammad (PBUH) married his last wife, Maymoona (RA). This period was also marked by Muhammad's (PBUH) wives voluntarily accepting extra restrictions upon themselves in response to slander campaigns by Muhammad's (PBUH) enemies. Pleased with their devotion, God commanded Muhammad in the Quran 33:52 that he could not marry any more women, nor could he divorce any of his wives. It is perhaps for this reason, Muhammad (PBUH) did not marry Mariya Qibtiya (RA) but treated her in accordance with the Quran's commandments regarding the management of existing slaves.

Regarding the question of why Muhammad (PBUH) did not return the gift to the Governor or grant freedom to Maria (RA) and allow her to marry someone else, we remain uncertain. It is possible that Maria (RA) herself did not desire such an arrangement, preferring the prestige associated with her relationship with the Messenger of God, one of the most powerful men in the world. What is certain is that Muhammad (PBUH) treated her well in accordance with the teachings of the Quran. She bore him a son, Ibrahim, who tragically died in infancy. Maria (RA) was accorded the same respect as Muhammad's (PBUH) wives and was honored with the title "Mother of all Believers."

Question 31: Is A Woman's Testimony Worth Half That Of A Man's?

There is a prevalent notion within Islam that in a court of law, a woman's testimony is considered half as credible as a man's.

The verse used to justify this is Quran 2:282. In this rather lengthy passage, God commands Muslims that when someone issues a loan to another, they should document the details in a binding contract and have two men from among them bear witness to this agreement. If two men are not available, then one man and two women should serve as witnesses. The Quran provides a rationale for the inclusion of two women, stating that if one woman hesitates or forgets, the other can support her. This precaution, ordained by God, specifically addresses loan contracts within a predominantly male-oriented culture where it was uncommon for women to travel with business caravans or participate in financial dealings. The Quran does not discuss the bearing of testimony against a crime in court. Mustafa Khattab, a renowned scholar of the Quran, explains:

> *Generally speaking, there is a difference between witnessing and giving testimony before a judge. Verse 2:282 talks about witnessing a debt contract, not giving testimony. To fully understand the context of this verse, we need to keep in mind that 1500 years ago women did not normally participate in business transactions or travel with trading caravans and, therefore, not every woman had the expertise to witness a debt contract. Even if two women were available at the time of signing the contract, perhaps the primary witness might not be able to recall the details of the contract or appear before a judge because of compelling circumstances such as pregnancy or delivery. In any of these cases, the second woman will be a back-up. Some scholars maintain that one woman can be sufficient as a witness so long as she is reliable. As for giving testimony, a ruling can be made based on available testimony, regardless of the number or gender of the witnesses. For example, the beginning of Ramadan is usually confirmed by the sighting of the new moon, regardless of the gender of the person who sights the moon. Also, the highest form of witness in Islam is for someone to testify they heard a narration (or hadith) from the Prophet (PBUH). An*

authentic hadith is accepted by all Muslims regardless of the gender of the narrator. Moreover, if a husband accuses his wife of adultery and he has no witnesses, each spouse must testify five times that they are telling the truth and the other side is lying. Both testimonies are equal (see 24:6-10).[80]

An important note: There are some Hadiths quoted to establish that the Prophet (PBUH) said that women are deficient in their intellect and their religion.

Upon closer inspection of these Hadiths, it becomes evident that Muhammad (PBUH) is not suggesting that women have lesser intellect or religious value compared to men. In fact, Muhammad (PBUH) indicates that God has placed a lesser burden on women's intellect regarding worldly matters and a lesser burden on them in terms of religious obligations. For instance, in worldly matters, God has not assigned women the financial responsibility of the family. Similarly, as far as religious matters are concerned, women generally have fewer obligations; they are not required to attend mosques for Friday prayers, they are not expected to participate in wars, and they are exempt from obligatory prayers and fasting during menstruation, yet they still receive the rewards for these deeds.

For more details and references about what I have just mentioned, you can watch my podcast titled "Conversing Islam with Hamza Ali Abbasi - Episode 11," available on the YouTube channel "Ghamidi Center of Islamic Learning." In this episode, I discuss in detail the above-mentioned misconceptions concerning women.

Question 32: What Were the Circumstances Surrounding the Incident of Banu Quraiza, and How Can Claims of an Unjustifiable Atrocity by Muhammad (PBUH) be Adressed?

For all the details and references related to the discussion below, please watch "Response to 23 Questions - Part 83 - Itmam e Hujjat - Javed Ahmed Ghamidi" on the YouTube channel "Ghamidi Center of Islamic Learning."

The incident of the killing of the men of Banu Quraiza is an event heavily discussed among critics of Islam, perceived as an unjustifiable atrocity against Jews by Muhammad (PBUH). Let us briefly explore what this event was, the circumstances leading up to it, and whether Muhammad's (PBUH) actions can be considered justified.

Medina was primarily home to three Jewish tribes: Banu Qainuqah, Banu Nadeer, and Banu Quraiza. When Muhammad (PBUH) became the ruler of Medina, he entered into a peace contract with these tribes. This agreement stipulated that they would mutually defend the city and establish a relationship based on sincerity and goodwill towards one another, and mutual trust.[81]

The first to violate this agreement was the Banu Qainuqah. Following the Battle of Badr, their hostility towards Muslims intensified. There were skirmishes, during which a Muslim woman was stripped naked in the market of Banu Qainuqah, and both a Jew and a Muslim were killed amidst the violence. Muhammad (PBUH) approached the Banu Qainuqah to remind them of their treaty obligations, but the tribe responded with threats of further violence. The leader of the tribe, Kaab bin Ashraf was executed by Muslims. His crimes included traveling to Mecca to incite Meccan pagans against the Muslims in Medina and secretly plotting to assassinate Muhammad (PBUH), all while being bound by a peace treaty and mutual defense agreement with the Muslims. The rest of the Banu Qainuqah were dealt with leniently and exiled from Medina.

The second tribe, Banu Nadeer, violated their pact with the Muslims by not defending Medina during the Battle of Uhud. Additionally, they secretly attempted to assassinate Muhammad (PBUH) by planning to drop a heavy stone from above while he was seated beneath a cliff. Given these breaches, Muhammad (PBUH) issued a ten-day ultimatum for them to leave Medina. When they ignored the ultimatum, Muslims laid siege to the tribe until their surrender. Despite these actions, the Muslims showed leniency; they allowed the tribe to depart from the city but prohibited them from taking their weapons.

This repeated leniency proved disastrous because, after the exile, Banu Nadeer played a crucial role in amassing a huge army against Muslims, besieging the town of Medina with 10,000 heavily equipped soldiers and resulting in the Battle of the Trench in 627 AD. This battle threatened the entire existence of Islam, as the total population of Muslims in Medina barely numbered a few thousand.

At this critical juncture, the treachery of the third Jewish tribe, Banu Quraiza, emerged. During the battle, while Medina was defended by Muslims, the tribe engaged in secret negotiations with the invading army. After the battle concluded, Banu Quraiza was not treated with the same leniency that had previously been extended to Banu Qaynuqah and Banu Nadeer. There were concerns that if the tribe of Quraiza were exiled, their men might join the ranks of the enemy and gather a larger force to attack Medina. Consequently, all the men of the fighting age were executed.

What about the women and children, though? It is understandable how tricky the question must have been regarding how to deal with hundreds of women and children who despise you for killing their adult males. What should be done with them? Quran 47:4 had earlier issued a command concerning POWs after the Battle of Badr that they must either be freed for a ransom or released out of goodwill—but who would take them? According to W. Montgomery Watt and Daniel C. Peterson, evidence suggests that members of other Jewish tribes, possibly the Banu Nadir, paid the ransom for these POWs and secured their release.[82]

Montgomery also acknowledges that Muhammad's (PBUH) actions with the Jews of Medina were a response to critical situations, not attempts to cleanse Medina of Jews simply because of their faith. He writes:

> *The continuing presence of at least a few Jews in Medina is an argument against the view sometimes put forward by European scholars that in the second year after the Hijrah Muhammad adopted a policy of clearing all Jews out of Medina just because they are Jews, and that he carried out this policy with ever increasing severity. It was not Muhammad's way to have policies of this kind. He has a balanced view of fundamentals of the contemporary situation and of his long term aims, and in the light of this he molded his day-to-day plans in accordance with the changing factors of the current events. The occasions of his attacks on the first 2 Jewish clans were no more than occasions; but there were also deep underlying reasons. The Jews in general by their verbal criticisms of the Quranic revelation were trying to undermine the foundation of Islamic community and they were also giving political support to Muhammad's enemies and to opponents such as the Hypocrites. In so far as the Jews abandoned these forms of hostile activity Muhammad allowed them to live in Medina unmolested.[83]*

The series of events involving Banu Quraiza has many versions with varying details. Some scholars, including Barakat Ahmed and Walid N. Arafat, even deny that a large-scale execution occurred.

History is a very tricky thing. An event in history can have multiple conflicting reports about why and how it happened, with no way to conclusively confirm one version over the other. Consider the tragic event of 9/11. A vast majority believe that Al Qaeda was responsible, but a significant number of people, particularly within the Muslim community, think it was orchestrated by the Jews or the CIA to create justification for attacking Muslim countries. This is why one must stick to the universally acknowledged parts of history when forming an opinion, without delving into the nitty-gritty details which can be vastly different and often conflicting.

What we know about the event involving Banu Quraiza is that a significant number of their men of fighting age were ordered to be executed. It is also somewhat certain that two Jewish tribes preceding Quraiza were exiled from Medina. If the accounts presented by Muslim historians about the prior treachery of Qaynuqa and Nadeer are accurate, and if it is true that they amassed an army to attack Medina after being exiled, then I believe that in the violent struggle for survival in 7th-century tribal Arabia, Muhammad's (PBUH) actions regarding Quraiza were justified. The leniency previously shown to the two tribes, who were guilty of blatant treachery, resulted in disastrous consequences, threatening the very existence of Islam and Muslims. Had leniency been shown again and the tribe of Quraiza merely exiled, there was a very real fear that their men of fighting age would join the ranks of Banu Nadeer and the pagans of Arabia and launch an even greater attack on Medina. It appears that the leniency toward Qaynuqa and Nadeer might have encouraged treachery from Quraiza's side, and this act of mass execution was intended to send a message of severe consequences to serve as a deterrent for anyone considering similar treacherous plans in the future.

Question 33: Do Quranic Verses Instruct Muslims to Avoid Befriending non-Muslims, and How Should These Verses Be Understood in Context?

Some verses in the Quran appear to support the notion that Muslims should not befriend non-Muslims. However, when viewed in context, these verses specifically address certain groups of non-Muslims who were contemporaries of Muhammad (PBUH) and do not dictate a perpetual stance towards all non-Muslims.

Take Quran 5:51 for example, which says:

> *O believers! Take neither Jews nor Christians as guardians – some of them are guardians of each other. Whoever does so will be counted as one of them. Surely Allah does not guide the wrongdoing people.*

When viewed in context with the subsequent verse, the Quran does not advocate a permanent policy towards all non-Muslims but specifically addresses a select group of non-Muslims who were in direct conflict with the followers of Muhammad (PBUH) at the time. It cautions Muslims that within their ranks, there are hypocrites who fear defeat and desire alliances with these hostile non-Muslims. The Quran further states that these hypocrites will regret their actions when God grants victory to the Muslims. This context is explained in Quran 5:51-52.

> *O believers! Take neither Jews nor Christians as guardians – some of them are guardians of each other. Whoever does so will be counted as one of them. Surely Allah does not guide the wrong doing people. You see those with sickness in their hearts racing for their friendship with them, saying ˹in justification˺, "We fear a turn of fortune will strike us." But perhaps Allah will bring about ˹your˺ victory or another*

favor by His command, and they will regret what they have hidden in their hearts.

This matter is further clarified in 60:8-9:

God does not forbid you from dealing kindly and justly with those 'non-Muslims' who have neither fought nor driven you out of your homes. Surely God loves those who are just. God only forbids you from befriending those who have fought you for 'your' faith, driven you out of your homes, or supported 'others' in doing so. And whoever takes them as friends, then it is they who are the 'true' wrongdoers.

We have already discussed in detail Quran verses 9:5 and 9:29. These verses instruct Muslims to fight, kill, and subjugate non-Muslims unless they convert to Islam. According to God's law, when a Rasool was present in the world, this was a divine punishment ordained for those who rejected him for unjustified reasons, fought against him, and persecuted him. These verses specifically address Muhammad's (PBUH) contemporaries and do not dictate a permanent policy for Muslims towards non-Muslims.

According to the Quran, all humans are descendants of Adam and Eve (PBUT), and in this way, all are family. Non-Muslims are not targets to conquer and rule but fellow humans to love, co-exist with, and deliver God's message to with utmost respect and goodwill..

Question 34: Was the Miraaj a Physical Journey?

If there really is an all-powerful God, can this deity enable a man to ride a winged horse and journey into higher dimensions? Absolutely, God can do that. It is commonly believed that Muhammad (PBUH) physically ascended to the heavens on a winged horse during the journey of Miraaj. However, a closer examination of the Quran and Hadith reveals that the experiences attributed to Muhammad (PBUH) in the context of Miraaj were not physical. They were, in fact, four distinct instances of true prophetic dreams and visions of literal events, which later Hadith transmitters conflated into a single instance of Miraaj and described as a physical, literal event. Let me briefly discuss these four instances.

The first instance is mentioned in Surah Isra, verse 1, which states: "Blessed is your Lord who took His servant (Muhammad) by night from the sacred mosque to the farthest mosque whose surroundings I have blessed, so that I may show him some of my signs. Indeed, I am all-hearing and all-seeing." Verse 60 of the same Surah confirms that this was a 'Roya,' which in Arabic means a dream. A prophet's dream is not like an ordinary person's dream—it contains truth, sometimes shown literally and sometimes depicted through analogy or symbolism.

In my opinion, the most apt interpretation of this dream, provided by Javed Ahmed Ghamidi, suggests that by showing Muhammad (PBUH) the mosque in Mecca and the mosque in Jerusalem, he was metaphorically shown that Muhammad (PBUH) and his immediate followers would take possession of both of these landmarks of divine importance.

Many argue that the Arabic word 'Roya' in this verse does not refer to a dream or a vision but to physically seeing something in person. This argument is flawed because the word 'Roya' has been used many times in the Quran to mean a dream or a vision—for example, in Surah As Saffat verse 105, Surah Yusuf verses 43, 5, and 100, and Surah Fatah verse 27. In Hadith literature, the word 'Roya' has been mentioned numerous times, and each time it has been used to signify a dream or vision.

The second instance involves Muhammad (PBUH) ascending to heaven and meeting various prophets. From Bukhari 7517, it is evident that this was a prophetic dream of Muhammad (PBUH) while he was asleep in the mosque in Mecca. This narration, attributed to Muhammad's companion Anas bin Malik (RA), describes how Gabriel, along with two other angels, came to Muhammad (PBUH), washed his heart and body parts, and then escorted him to heaven. There, Muhammad (PBUH) met all the prophets and God Himself. During this visitation, Muhammad (PBUH) saw many things in heaven and received the instructions for the five daily prayers. The narration explicitly mentions that Muhammad (PBUH) was asleep in the mosque, indicating that this instance was a dream and not a physical journey.

The third and fourth instances are from Surah Najm 53:1-18, where God assures Muhammad's (PBUH) opponents that he is not delusional. Indeed, Muhammad (PBUH) did see Angel Gabriel twice in his real form, literally with his own eyes. These instances from Surah Najm represent real visions seen through the eyes, unlike the prophetic dreams described in the first and second instances.

All these are four distinct instances, which some historians and hadith transmitters later merged into one narrative of the popular event known as Miraaj.

Question 35: Does The Quran Refer To Muslims As A Nation?

No, the Quran does not define Muslims as a nation. Although many Muslims might wish to live under a single united country—and rightly so, as I too desire for Muslims to unite and form a single powerful nation—God in the Quran does not impose a religious obligation on Muslims to strive to live under a single ruler or state. Instead, the Quran describes Muslims as a 'Fraternity' or 'Brotherhood' in Quran 49:10. Islam is not a national ideology but a universal message for all humanity; anyone can embrace Islam and become part of the Muslim fraternity.

Question 36: Can Someone Who Identifies As A Muslim Be Declared A Non-Muslim Or A Kafir?

For a detailed response, please refer to the playlist titled "Response to 23 Questions - Excommunication From Islam (Takfeer) - Javed Ahmed Ghamidi," available on the YouTube channel Ghamidi Center of Islamic Learning.

The Quran uses the term 'Kafir,' which simply means "Rejector," for those who have rejected Islam. It also applies to those who, knowing the truth in their hearts, reject it for wrongful reasons. We have explored this concept in detail in Chapter 5.

However, what about individuals who claim they do not reject Islam and identify themselves as Muslims, yet hold beliefs that clearly violate Islamic teachings? What if they justify their erroneous beliefs using the Quran, Sunnah, and Hadith, and insist they are Muslims? Is there an official mechanism in the Quran that authorizes Muslim scholars to excommunicate such individuals from Islam and label them as Kafirs or Rejectors? The answer is no. Let me explain.

There are various groups and sects within Islam that identify themselves as Muslims but hold views vastly different from each other—views that opposing sects consider completely against the basic teachings of Islam. For example:

One group believes that the leader of the Muslims is appointed directly by God. Another group contends that Muslims are directed by God to choose their leader through mutual consultation. A third group holds that God has appointed the souls of Prophets and Saints to manage the affairs of existence and make decisions on God's behalf. Conversely, other groups passionately reject these beliefs, stating that God has made no such hierarchy and has explicitly stated in various Quranic verses that no one shares in His authority. Additionally, one group claims that Prophethood ended with Muhammad (PBUH) in such a way that future prophets will not bring any new divine law and will be subservient to the law given through Muhammad (PBUH), while other groups assert that all forms of Prophethood ended with Muhammad (PBUH). Frequently, members within each group label others as Kafir, thereby attempting to excommunicate them from Islam. The question arises: has God ordained a mechanism through which someone can be excommunicated from Islam? The answer is No.

Only God and His last Prophet and Messenger, Muhammad (PBUH), had the authority to declare who is or isn't a true Muslim. God possesses this authority because only He knows what is in a person's heart, and Muhammad (PBUH) had this authority because he was in direct communication with God.

After Muhammad (PBUH), if someone who identifies as a Muslim believes in something clearly against basic Islamic teachings, it is impossible to determine whether this person is genuinely mistaken or deliberately embracing a falsehood for wrongful reasons. Therefore, others only have the jurisdiction to point out the flaw in such a person's belief but have no authority to expel this person from Islam.

Let me elaborate on what I am discussing through personal examples:

There are groups of Muslims who believe that saints and prophets have a share in God's authority and manage the affairs of creation on His behalf. They pray to these saints and venerate them as they should venerate God alone. In my view, their belief directly contradicts the Quranic idea that God does not share His authority with anyone. Can I brand Muslims who hold this belief as Kafir? No!

There are groups of Muslims who embrace the concept of "Haqeeqat-e-Muhammadi," which suggests that Muhammad (PBUH) was essentially the essence of God manifested in human form. Others subscribe to the idea of "Wahdat-ul-Wajood," which posits that the entire universe and everything within it are parts of God manifested materially. For me, such beliefs completely contradict the Quran's teachings on the oneness and uniqueness of God, but can I brand such Muslims as Kafir? No!

Some Muslims believe that various saints and holy personalities are directly designated by God to guide people and that God communicates with them for this purpose. This notion is in complete contradiction to the Quran's concept that God only guides people through direct contact with Prophets and Messengers. But has God given me the authority to brand Muslims with such beliefs as Kafir? No!

There are groups of Muslims who believe that the cessation of Prophethood with Muhammad (PBUH) means there will be no more law-bearing Prophets, though non-law-bearing Prophets who are bound to follow the law and religion brought by Muhammad (PBUH) can still appear. This belief directly opposes the Quran's explicit teaching, supported by numerous Hadiths, that all forms of Prophethood have ended with Muhammad (PBUH). Do I have the right to brand followers of this concept as Kafir? No!

The Quran and Hadith strictly warns against the idea of excommunicating people from the fold of Islam and branding them as Kafir. Quran states in various places that only God knows who is truly guided and who is misguided, such as in Quran 16:125: "Only God alone knows who has strayed from the right path and who is truly guided."

Hence the Quran insists that humans should restrict themselves to only educating each other on Islam and should not become judges on matters of faith to proclaim who is truly a Muslim and who isn't.

Quran 49:11 commands Muslims not to call others by offensive nicknames, which prominent commentators like Tabari, Ikrima, and Mujahid interpret as including calling someone a Kafir who identifies as a Muslim.

Numerous Hadiths prohibit the practice of declaring fellow Muslims as non-believers. For example:

1) The Prophet (PBUH) is reported to have said that "Whoever calls a Muslim a Kafir - it is like he has killed him and whoever declares someone as cursed (destined for hellfire) has also killed him" (Jami Maa'mar bin Rashid, No: 19710).

2) Muhammad (PBUH) is reported to have said that, "Whoever calls a Muslim a kafir then one of them definitely becomes a kafir. If the one who is accused of being a kafir turns out to be kafir on judgment day, then the one who branded him shall be spared and if the one who is accused of being a kafir does not turn out to be a kafir, then the one who branded him shall become kafir" (Sahih of Muslim, No: 60).

As per the Quran and Hadith, it is clear that judgment on matters of belief will be handed down by God on the Day of Judgment. As far as this world is concerned, people have to be labeled according to how they label themselves. Only those people can be called non-Muslims or disbelievers who call themselves disbelievers. Those who call themselves Muslims cannot be branded as non-Muslims, even if some of their beliefs seem flawed. If a group of Muslims has flawed beliefs, then other Muslims can only try to educate them on their flawed belief but cannot become judges in matters of belief and declare them Non-Muslims or Kafirs.

Question 37: Was Noah's (PBUH) Flood A Global Event And Was He Instructed To Get A Pair Of All Animal Species On Board?

While there is compelling evidence suggesting there might have been a global flood in the past, the Quran clearly indicates that the flood during Noah's (PBUH) time was not a global event. Noah (PBUH) was a Rasool of God, and as discussed earlier, God's worldly punishment typically targets those who directly reject the message of a Rasool.

Therefore, Noah's (PBUH) flood was a punishment specifically for the rejectors among his immediate addressees, indicating that it was a regional, not global, flood.

Accordingly, the directive given to Noah (PBUH) to bring animals on board the ark should not be interpreted literally as encompassing all animal species worldwide. Rather, it was an instruction to gather all animals necessary to sustain Noah (PBUH) and his fellow passengers. To illustrate, consider a scenario where you are preparing to leave for the airport for a vacation; when you tell a friend to ensure all necessary clothes are packed, you mean all the clothes needed for the trip, not every article of clothing in the world.

Question 38: Were We Asked Before Being Thrown Into This Test Of Life? If Yes, Then Why Do We Not Remember Making This Choice?

There are two verses from the Quran to consider in this matter.

1) *Quran 7:172:* This verse says that the souls of all human beings were created at once before coming into this world and they were made to testify that God is their creator.
2) *Quran 33:72:* This verse affirms that humankind made a choice to go through this test.

These verses imply that our presence in this life was a choice we made to be in this test. This raises questions, such as why we don't remember these pre-worldly events and the exact nature of our existence before entering this world.

Scholars like Mr. Javed Ahmed Ghamidi state that the memories of these events have been omitted from our conscious minds for the purpose of this test. This makes sense because if we clearly remembered what God is and our decision to come here to be tested, then a crucial element of the worldly test would be compromised. This element is the freedom of choice—to accept and be mindful of God or to reject Him and be negligent. How can anyone reject something they have clearly seen themselves? Therefore, in this existence, while there are signs of God within us and all around us, the literal memories of these events have been erased for the purpose of the test.

God or reject God and be negligent toward Him. How can anyone reject something they remember clearly and literally seeing themselves?

Hence, in this existence, there are signs of God within us and all around us, but the literal memories of these events have been wiped out for the purpose of the test.

My personal belief on this matter: I would like to offer a personal inference on this matter, which is a belief shared by Dr. Rehan Ahmed Yusufi, who is a friend of mine and also an Islamic scholar. He is also known by his popular pen name, Abu Yahya. Since the Quran states that all human souls were created simultaneously before entering this world, and it also states that we chose to undergo the test of this world, it can be rightly inferred that we also chose the specifics of the test we wish to face. This suggests that before entering this world, we decided on the exact nature of all the good and bad circumstances we would encounter.

My personal observation on this matter which explains the existence of mentally disabled people and death of children: If we ourselves chose to be tested and face divine accountability, it can be reasonably inferred that some souls opted for a safer path. They wished to enter paradise but avoided the risk of facing divine accountability on Judgment Day. These souls may enter the world either as mentally disabled individuals or as children who die before reaching adulthood. Because they are not fully capable of being accountable for their moral decisions, they will not face divine accountability on Judgment Day. Nevertheless, they will still attain the status of basic citizens of Paradise. In this divine scheme, they serve as a test for the people around them, and some may endure worldly suffering in this role.

Question 39: Why Is It Crucial For A Person To Act Upon What They Sincerely Believe To Be The Truth, Even If That Belief Is Mistaken?

We have already discussed this point, but due to its crucial importance, I feel it needs to be briefly mentioned again in this section.

The God of the Quran wants people to sincerely act upon what they genuinely believe is the truth, even if they are mistaken in their belief. The sincerity of belief and action is of utmost importance to God.

This principle is made clear in Quran 2:187. Let me explain briefly.

In this verse, while commenting on a few companions of the Prophet (PBUH), the Quran says that they mistakenly believed that God had prohibited intercourse between spouses for the entire month of Ramadan, even during the night after breaking the fast. Despite this belief, these companions had intercourse with their spouses at night after breaking their fasts. The Quran clarifies that those companions were mistaken in believing that a husband and wife are not allowed to have intercourse during the nights of Ramadan after breaking their fasts. However, God also addresses those companions who, despite their flawed belief, sincerely thought they were committing a wrongful deed by having intercourse with their wives under the mistaken belief that it was prohibited. The principle is that if you genuinely believe God has prohibited something, then you shouldn't do it, even if you are mistaken in believing so. Here is the literal translation of the verse:

> It is lawful for you to have sexual relations with your wives during the night of the fast. They are your garment, and you are theirs. God knows that you used to betray yourselves and He mercifully relented and pardoned you. You can intimately associate with your wives and benefit from the enjoyment

God had made lawful for you and eat and drink at night until you can distinguish the white streak of dawn against the blackness of the night; then (give up all that and) complete your fasting until night sets in. But do not associate intimately with your wives during the period when you are on retreat in the mosques (I'tikaf). These are the bounds set by God; do not, then, even draw near them. This is how God makes His signs clear to humankind so that they may stay away from sin (Quran 2:187).

Maulana Maududi writes while commenting on this verse in his Tafseer Tafheem-ul-Quran:

Although there was no categorical ordinance in the early days prohibiting sexual intercourse between husband and wife during the nights of Ramadan, people generally assumed that this was not permissible. Despite the feeling that their action was either not permitted or was at least disapproved of, they did at times approach their wives. Such a betrayal of conscience can encourage a sinful disposition. God, therefore, first reproaches them for their lack of integrity, for this is what was objectionable. As for the act itself, God makes it clear that it is quite permissible. Henceforth they might engage in sexual intercourse as a perfectly lawful act unencumbered by feelings of guilt.

The above-mentioned instance makes it clear that the Quran wants people to act upon what they sincerely believe to be divine truth, even if they are mistaken in their belief. However, we must remind ourselves here that the Quran also expects people to always be ready to lend a sincere and serious ear to anything about God and religion that seems to make sufficient sense and judge matters on merit by rising above all biases when analyzing any information about God and religion. We must also remind ourselves that on the Day of Judgment, genuine and sincere mistakes will be forgiven, but deliberate negligence and failure to accept the truth for wrongful reasons will not be tolerated.

CONCLUSION

The nature of my own self and the reality around me often compelled me to question: Where did everything come from, and what is everything all about? Many questions persistently plagued my mind—such as whether there is an objective purpose behind existence or none at all. I kept brushing aside these questions to focus on more immediate concerns and pursuits in life. Things were going great! However, the idea of divine accountability increasingly troubled me.

I kept hearing about post-mortem divine accountability, divine rewards, and punishments—every single day. Whether on TV, social media, in newspapers, or from friends and family, these ideas confronted me in one way or another, and they increasingly worried me. What if there is some truth to these ideas? What if God does exist? More importantly, what if there truly is divine accountability, where I will be judged based on my conduct in this life, and that judgment will determine a permanent outcome for me, good or bad?

These are serious prospects. The more I heard, the more I felt the need to investigate these ideas seriously, to come to a reasonable conclusion and lead my life accordingly. If there is no God and no divine accountability, then I have nothing to worry about and should make immediate worldly benefits and pleasures my only pursuit. However, if the other possibility—that there is, in fact, a God and divine accountability—seems more plausible, then success in that divine accountability should be my primary concern. Again, I knew that in this domain, obtaining conclusive answers is difficult, but I needed to come to a reasonable conclusion because, considering how serious the matter is, leading a life without addressing this issue felt like criminal negligence.

Initially, swayed by the passionate speeches of proponents of new atheism, I concluded that there is no God, and no God means no divine accountability. Gradually, however, rational considerations began to trouble me from a rational perspective. In a reality devoid of God, I am still compelled to believe in some kind of primordial substance as the first cause of everything. It is thought-provoking that this primordial substance somehow contains all the necessary ingredients to unfold over time as self-aware consciousnesses like you and me. We possess intellect, a sense of morality, and an appreciation for aesthetics. We can comprehend both beauty and grotesqueness. Moreover, this fundamental reality unfolds into the world we live in, a world rich and diverse enough to cater to all aspects of our consciousness and senses, providing beauty, music, and a rich variety of tastes, colors, and everything else we need and desire.

Furthermore, the most remarkable aspect of the reality around us is that it is so magnificently intelligible and useful to us. It provides us with all kinds of materials and tools to accomplish whatever we choose to pursue—from the Stone Age to the Industrial Age, from our dreams of flight, to the Information and Space Ages. We have been able to understand reality so brilliantly and fulfill whatever we plan from the resources that the reality around us provides.

How can inanimate matter give rise to all of this purely through mindless processes and coincidence?

One significant reason for my initial lean toward atheism was my belief that concepts like God, the soul, and the afterlife were purely religious ideas, conclusively disproven by non-religious minds in science, medicine, and other disciplines. I thought that believing in such ideas meant going against science and the established truths of the "real world." But I was proven wrong when I stumbled upon research, theories, and findings by non-religious individuals advocating for the possibility of a mind behind the creation of everything—what sounded like "God" to me—and the notion that I could have an existence separate from my material brain—akin to a "soul"—and that I might continue to exist post-bodily death, resembling an "afterlife." While I acknowledge that such theories are not proven facts, I was intrigued by the fact that non-religious individuals, including some who identify as agnostics or atheists, advocate for the plausibility of such ideas. This shattered my belief that concepts like God, the soul, and the afterlife were merely religious fables which have been unanimously and conclusively discredited by the non-religious world.

Furthermore, discoveries like DNA, which contains coded instructions for producing life and organisms, suggest the possibility of intelligence behind everything. Additionally, esteemed scientific voices claim to have made theoretical discoveries indicating that coded information might be embedded in the very fabric of reality. The only known source of instructions in code format today is the human mind. Thus, the most rational inference is that if instructions in code format exist that enable the most basic processes of nature, then they likely originated from a mind as well. Just because we do not know where that mind came from or what it truly is should not lead us to negate the most apparent explanation.

It became increasingly difficult for me to maintain the belief that everything is the result of undirected, mindless processes. The idea that some intelligence might be behind everything seemed more fitting as an explanation. Yet, despite all signs pointing to an intelligent creator, could it still be possible that everything is a result of a fantastic, mindless process beyond our comprehension? Yes, in the realm of inferences, anything is possible! I emphasize the word "inference" because both atheists and theists make inferences. An atheist cannot claim to have objectively negated all possibilities of God, and a theist cannot present a tangible being like God that we can see and converse with directly. Both present a set of facts and arguments and try to prove their points through inference. Yet, my increasing inclination toward theism grew even stronger, as human history is filled with claims that this intelligence has made contact with us countless times to guide us.

With my previous belief shattered—that the non-religious intelligentsia had conclusively negated religious ideas like God, the soul, and the afterlife—I became open to exploring religions. My aim was to investigate their arguments regarding the existence and identity of the creator intelligence and, more importantly, to assess the truth behind the possibility of divine accountability after death.

I discovered that religions can be broadly categorized into two types. First, there are mystic religions, where individuals claim to attain enlightenment and discover ultimate truths about reality through rational thinking, meditation, and acquiring knowledge and wisdom. I also include philosophy in this category. Second, there are revealed religions, where individuals claim to have been directly contacted by a higher intelligence who revealed information about us and our reality. I found revealed religions to be my primary focus of investigation because their fundamental premise is that the intelligence that created everything has revealed truths about our purpose and the afterlife.

I allowed common sense to guide me, believing that if there is divine truth in the world, it should be easily accessible to a layperson like me who is not a scholar or aspiring to be one. Hence, I decided to focus on the most popular tradition of revealed religions—the Abrahamic tradition, which has more than 4 billion followers worldwide, accounting for over half of the global population.

Within the spectrum of Abrahamic faiths, I chose to explore the Quran for several reasons:

1) Unlike scriptures like the Vedas and the Old and New Testaments, whose origins cannot be definitively established, it is reasonable to conclude that the Quran is indeed the same document handed down by Muhammad (PBUH) to his followers as the word of God.

2) The Quran is preserved in its original language.

3) The events surrounding the revelation of the Quran are well-documented in history. Even if one does not believe that Muhammad (PBUH) was a Messenger of God, it is difficult to deny—unless one is an extreme conspiracy theorist—that there was indeed a person in Arabia with the claims made in the Quran, who conquered the Arabian peninsula and whose immediate followers ended up conquering almost half of the civilized world.

The claim that the Quran is the direct word of God, its availability in its original language, and the historical verifiability of both the document and the events surrounding its origins made it the most suitable starting point for my inquiry into revealed religions.

The basic teachings of the Quran resonated with me, thanks to the brilliant work of mainstream scholars who have made Islam understandable for laypersons like me. However, I encountered many logical and moral issues within Islam that remained unresolved for a long time. It was then that I came across Mr. Javed Ahmed Ghamidi, whose insights not only resolved these issues but also introduced me to the Quranic concept of what a Rasool (Messenger) of God truly is. This became the single most powerful proof of divine accountability and the most convincing reason for me to take the Quran very seriously.

Understanding the concept of Rasool is essential for grasping the true and factual introduction of the Quran. Once I analyzed the Quran with this accurate context in mind, it unveiled a treasure trove of insights that addressed all of my existential questions. Allow me to share that introduction with you.

According to the Quran, human beings have basic guidance embedded within them, details of which are supplemented by direct divine contact. We are undergoing a test in this world to demonstrate how we exercise our free will, meaning we have complete freedom of choice regarding moral decisions. When people forgot or distorted this guidance, God sent His Prophets (Nabis) to all nations to guide them back to the truth. Rejecting or accepting a Prophet's message carried no worldly consequences.

However, when people persisted in denying divine guidance and accountability after death, God demonstrated His divine ac- countability here on earth multiple times throughout human history as the ultimate proof of post-mortem divine accountability. This divine court of law is established on earth through a Rasool. A Rasool is a Prophet who is directly contacted by God, but what elevates the Prophet (Nabi) to the rank of Rasool is the additional responsibility of executing God's judgment here on Earth.

In this life, while those who embrace His message are rewarded in the here and now. Through the Rasool, God makes the truth clear to his immediate audience: those who reject the Rasool are punished in this life, while those who embrace His message are rewarded in the here and now.

In essence, a Rasool serves as the divine court of judgment for his immediate audience. The Quran is the preserved communication of

God—the record of how God unleashed divine accountability on earth through His last Rasool, Muhammad (PBUH). It provides detailed accounts of how earlier nations were judged through their Rasools and outlines the exact step-by-step plan for divine judgment to unfold for the immediate audience of Muhammad (PBUH). History has witnessed events unfolding precisely as laid out by the Quran, occurring on a global scale for all humanity to witness.

Several factors further enhance the credibility of the Quran and Islam:

1) The Quran coherently aligns with earlier scriptures. The narratives of the Old and New Testaments correspond with the Quran's depiction of Rasools of God, such as Noah, Abraham, Lot, Moses, Jesus, and Muhammad (Peace be upon them all). The events related to these personalities were not random acts of divine wrath but, as per the Quran, were highly coordinated instances of God unleashing earthly demonstrations of His divine judgment for two purposes: First, to provide the most compelling proof of Judgment Day and second, to raise nations to practice and preach God's message to the world.

2) Muhammad (PBUH) had no military or political background, yet the Quran issues flawless military and political strategies that led to complete victories—Muhammad (PBUH) took no credit for these, insisting he was merely following God's orders.

3) Despite lacking formal education in religious studies or preaching, yet the Quran engages in profound inter-religious debates that are intellectually sound and factually grounded.

4) Although illiterate and with no background in poetry, Muhammad (PBUH) produced a linguistic and poetic masterpiece in the Quran over 23 years. It is astounding that many verses were revealed and recited in response to immediate events.

5) Shakespeare and Allama Iqbal didn't become brilliant poets overnight. Leaders like George Washington, Jinnah, and Gandhi didn't emerge as great figures in an instant, nor did military geniuses like Alexander the Great and Genghis Khan suddenly appear as paragons of strategy. Each of these individuals underwent a gradual evolution in their respective fields of brilliance. In contrast, Muhammad (PBUH) appears to have had no such evolution. Before the age of 40, he showed no interest in seeking knowledge or engaging in discussions about politics, philosophy, military affairs, religion, or poetry. Then, seemingly out of nowhere, he began producing the Quran—a masterpiece that encompasses all these subjects. This raises significant questions about the origins of the Quran, suggesting it could not have been a product of Muhammad's (PBUH) own intellect. Moreover, there is no evidence to suggest that he had a team of experts in these diverse fields crafting the Quran for him, often in response to specific circumstances. Together, these points present a compelling case that Muhammad (PBUH) may indeed be speaking the truth about having been contacted by a higher intelligence.

6) The Quran contains accurate predictions about future events, from the Muslim takeover of Mecca, prophecy about the immediate companions of Muhammad (PBUH) ruling over a great empire, to the miraculous prophecy of Byzantine victory over Persia, all of which were fulfilled as predicted.

7) There are predictions in other scriptures that seem to align perfectly with the personality and life of Muhammad (PBUH).

I find it truly miraculous that a book given 1,500 years ago by an illiterate desert dweller can address the existential inquiries of a 21st-century person like me in such a compelling manner.

These combined factors led me to conclude that Islam is the divine truth, and I surrendered to it. The name "Islam" itself signifies surrender to truth and to God. However, I remain open to being corrected, and I will maintain this openness for as long as I live.

Regarding the existence of God, personal experience is also a potent reason for many to believe in God. Billions of people across various religions and ideologies report instances of feeling the Divine presence in their lives. While I do not present personal experience as evidence of God due to its subjectivity, I affirm that I have felt the presence of God in my life. I find that the more conscious and mindful one is of God's guidelines and the more one engages in voluntary acts of worship, the more one feels God's presence.

At the beginning of this chapter, I shared my reasons for writing this book. I will conclude with one last reason: discovering the God of the Quran means discovering my Creator. I found that my only true relationship I will ever have is with my Creator; all others are secondary. My family, friends, and even my self-identity would be different if I had been born elsewhere. My only true relationship is with the One who created me out of nothing before my conception in my mother's womb. I wish to make my Creator happy and proud of me. Along with other good deeds, sharing His message with others is something that truly earns merit with Him, which is why I strive to share what I believe is God's message. Whether I reach many or just a few doesn't matter; God appreciates the simple act of sharing His message, and I hope and pray to keep my intentions sincere.

I want to emphasize that I am not a scholar or an academic; I am just a layperson who persistently asked existential questions and eventually found satisfying answers. Whether you agree or disagree with me, I am grateful for your time and attention. However, I urge you to explore the Quran with its proper introduction, as I have mentioned throughout this book. The Quran claims to be the easiest book to attain guidance, with a simple message: There is a God who will hold everyone accountable after worldly death. Everyone will be questioned about their actions in this world. Success in that accountability depends on the purity and goodness of your character, how seriously you approached matters concerning God, and how sincere your quest for answers was. It also depends on how many of your beliefs were based on merit rather than bias, the good deeds you performed, and the righteousness of your intentions behind those deeds. Sincere mistakes will be forgiven, but deliberate and persistent wrongdoing will be severely punished.

> *Be mindful of the day when you shall all return to your Creator - then all human beings shall be fully held accountable for whatever good or bad they have done, and no one shall be treated unjustly - (Quran 2:281).*

Thank You!

NOTES

Chapter 3

1 "Are We Wired to Believe in a Higher Power?," *BBC Teach*, accessed April 17, 2024, https://www.bbc.co.uk/teach/are-we-wired-to-believe-in-a-higher-power/z74xkmn.

2 See: Flew, Antony, and Roy Abraham Varghese. *There is a God: How the World's Most Notorious Atheist Changed His Mind.* HarperOne, 2007.

3 Brooks, Michael. "Is the Universe Conscious? It Seems Impossible Until You Do the Maths." *New Scientist 29* (2020): 40-44.

4 Gareth Cook, "Does Consciousness Pervade the Universe?," *Scientific American,* accessed March 1, 2024, https://www.scientificamerican.com/article/does-consciousness-pervade-the-universe/.

5 John Horgan, "Can Integrated Information Theory Explain Consciousness?," *Scientific American,* accessed March 15, 2024, https://www.scientificamerican.com/blog/cross-check/can-integrated-information-theory-explainconsciousness/

6 See: "The Third Way of Evolution," accessed March 15, 2024, https://www.thethirdwayofevolution.com/.

7 Bill Gates, *The Road Ahead* (New York: Penguin Group, 1995), 188.

8 American Museum of Natural History, "2016 Isaac Asimov Memorial Debate: Is the Universe a Simulation?," accessed April 8, 2016, https://www.youtube.com/watch?v=wgSZA3NPpBs.

9 Leonard Susskind, *My Battle with Stephen Hawking to Make the World Safe for Quantum Mechanics* (Little Brown and Company, 2008).

10 Hoover Institution, "By Design: Behe, Lennox, and Meyer on the Evidence for a Creator," accessed February 29, 2024, https://www.youtube.com/watch?v=rXexaVsvhCM.

11 Wilder Penfield, *Mystery of the Mind: A Critical Study of Consciousness and the Human Brain, Princeton University Press eBooks,* accessed April 1, 2024, https://doi.org/10.1515/9781400868735.

12 *Neurosurgeon Wilder Penfield on Free Will,* accessed May 27, 2024, https://evolutionnews.org/2018/07/neurosurgeon-wilder-penfield-on-free-will/

13 Jeffrey M. Schwartz and Sharon Begley, *The Mind and the Brain* (Springer Science & Business Media, 2009), 338.

14 NYU Langone Health, "Recalled Experiences Surrounding Death: More Than Hallucinations?," accessed April 2, 2024, https://www.prnewswire.com/news-releases/recalled-experiences-surrounding-death-more-than-hallucinations-301519733.html.

15 Sam Parnia et al., "AWARE-AWAreness during REsuscitation-a Prospective Study," Resuscitation 85, no. 12 (December 2014): 1799–1805, https://doi.org/10.1016/j.resuscitation.2014.09.004.

16 "Is Life After Death Possible? - Sam Parnia," *Closer To Truth* (blog), accessed April 2, 2024, https://closertotruth.com/video/parsa-003/.

Chapter 4

17) Javed Ahmed Ghamidi, "Heaven Only for Muslims and Hell for All Non Muslims?," Ghamidi Center of Islamic Learning, Uploaded November 19, 2015, accessed April 1, 2024, https://www.youtube.com/watch?v=XS9DyjzNR8o.

Section 4A

18) Javed Ahmed Ghamidi, Meezan (Lahore: Al-Mawrid, 2015), 63.

19) Ghamidi, Meezan, 64.

Section 4C

20) Abu Muhammad al-Husayn b. Masood Al-Baghawi, *Sharh al-sunna* (Beirut: al-Maktab al-Islami, 1983), 4:526.

21) Badr al-Din Muhammad b. Abd Allah al-Zarkashi, al-Burhan fi uloom al-Quran (Cairo: Maktaba Dār al-Turāth, nd.) 1:227.

22) For details on the difference of opinion between Umar and Ubayee bin Kaab (RTA) see: Sahih of Bukhari, No: 4481, 5005.

Chapter 5

23 "Are We Wired to Believe in a Higher Power?," BBC Teach, accessed April 4, 2024, https://www.bbc.co.uk/teach/are-we-wired-to-believe-in-a-higher-power/z74xkmn.

24 "Zoroastrianism," study.com, accessed April 4, 2024, https://study.com/academy/lesson/zoroastrianism-definition-beliefs-history.html.

25 "Indian Religion - Fort Raleigh National Historic Site (U.S. National Park Service)," accessed April 10, 2024, https://www.nps.gov/fora/learn/education/indian-religion.html

26 "Anishinaabe," in Wikipedia, accessed March 15, 2024, https://en.wikipedia.org/w/index.php?title=Anishinaabe&oldid=1213911119

27 "Nanabozho," in Wikipedia, March 15, 2024, https://en.wikipedia.org/w/index.php?title=Nanabozho&oldid=1213850139.

28 Cierra Tolentino, "Chinese Mythology: History, Culture, Myths, and Heroes,"accessed April 2, 2024, https://historycooperative.org/chinese-mythology/.

29 Onukwube Anedo and Anedo Ngozi, "Ghosts in Chinese and Igbo Religion,"Journal of African Studies & Development, Vol. 13, pp. 1 – 14.

30 Scott Linklater, "What Is Aboriginal Dreamtime?," accessed April 5, 2024, https://www.aboriginal-art-australia.com/aboriginal-art-library/aboriginal-dreamtime/.

31 Arthur Cotterell, "Bamapana," in A Dictionary of World Mythology (Oxford University Press, 2003), https://www.oxfordreference.com/display/10.1093/acref/9780192177476.001.0001/acref-9780192177476-e-487.

32 Robert a Armour, Gods and Myths of Ancient Egypt (American Univ in Cairo Press, 2001), 99-100.

33 Ibid., 135.

34 "African Religions | Traditional Beliefs & Practices | Britannica," March 19, 2024, https://www.britannica.com/topic/African-religions.

35 Ibid.

36 "Valhalla | Definition, Myth, & Meaning | Britannica," accessed April 5, 2024, https://www.britannica.com/topic/Valhalla-Norse-mythology.

37 "Niflheim | Frost Giants, Helheim & Yggdrasil | Britannica," accessed April 5, 2024, https://www.britannica.com/topic/Niflheim.

38 "Loki | Mythology, Powers, & Facts | Britannica," March 25, 2024, https://www.britannica.com/topic/Loki.

39 "Elysium | Paradise, Afterlife, Immortality | Britannica," accessed March 28, 2024, https://www.britannica.com/topic/Elysium-Greek-mythology.

40 "Hell - Greek, Roman, Mythology | Britannica," accessed April 10, 2024, https://www.britannica.com/topic/hell/Greece-and-Rome.

41 "Prometheus | God, Description, Meaning, & Myth | Britannica," accessed March 27, 2024, https://www.britannica.com/topic/Prometheus-Greek-god.

42 "DOLUS (Dolos) - Greek God or Spirit of Trickery & Guile," accessed April 10, 2024, https://www.theoi.com/Daimon/Dolos.html.

43 Javed Ahmad Ghamidi, "Response to 23 Questions - Itmam e Hujjat," Ghamidi Center of Islamic Learning, December 25, 2022, YouTube videos, https: https://www.youtube.com/playlist?list=PLvDnnnkYLWQeKq8ny1IDf2bgZRTihI28a)

44 Abdullah al Andalusi, "What Is a Kafir? The Confusion in English Regarding the Quranic Use of the Word 'Kafir,'" (blog), May 5, 2016, https://abdullahalandalusi.com/2016/05/05/the-quranic-use-of-the-word-kafir/.

45 "A Flood of Myths and Stories | Blog | Independent Lens," accessed April 11, 2024, https://www.pbs.org/independentlens/blog/a-flood-of-myths-andstories/.

46 "A Flood of Myths and Stories | Blog | Independent Lens."

47 Ibid.

48 Ibid.

49 Ibid.

50 "Floods - Myth Encyclopedia - Greek, God, Story, Legend, Names, Ancient, Snake, World, Chinese, Roman," accessed April 11, 2024, http://www.mythencyclopedia.com/Fi-Go/Floods.html#ixzz8IwvcMIZ5

51 "The Flood of Noah and the Flood of Gilgamesh | The Institute for Creation Research," accessed April 11, 2024, https://www.icr.org/article/noah-flood-gilgamesh/.

52 Joshua J. Mark, "Book of the Heavenly Cow," World History Encyclopedia, accessed April 11, 2024, https://www.worldhistory.org/Book of the Heavenly Cow/

53 "Flood Myths," Indigenous Peoples Literature (blog), June 29, 2022, accessed March 21, 2024, https://indigenouspeoplenet. wordpress.com/2022/06/29/flood-myths/

54 "Flood Myths - Africa," accessed April 11, 2024, https://www. meta-religion.com/World Religions/Ancient religions/Flood myths/flood myths africa.html

55 The Exodus Decoded, directed by Simcha Jacobovici, (2006, Canada, Associated Producers), Documentary.

56 Carole Hillenbrand, "Muhammad and the Rise of Islam," in The New Cambridge Medieval History, vol. 1, 4 vols. (Cambridge: Cambridge University Press, 2005), 340. My Discovery of God, Islam & Judgment Day 333

57 Andrew Louth, "The Byzantine Empire in the Seventh Century," in The New Cambridge Medieval History, vol 1, 4 vols. (Cambridge: Cambridge University Press, 2005), 298.

58 Barnaby Rogerson, "The Caliph: Part 1: Foundation," Al-Jazeera English, accessed April 5, 2024, https://youtu.be/P3O9d-7PsI48.

59 This detail on Ibn e Hisham's view is based on the following discussion by Javed Ahmad Ghamidi: Javed Ahmad Ghamidi, "Response to 23 Questions - Part 43 - Pehli Wahi ka Waqia, Ghar e Hira," Ghamidi Center of Islamic Learning, Uploaded March 4, 2021, accessed April 30, 2024, https://www.youtube. com/watch?v=Z9h-o0AOS2g&list=PLvDnnnkYLWQca1Aw-pk-FmXIwjolLVsZkhr

60 Amin Ahsan Islahi, Tadabbur-e-Qur'an, vol. 1, 9 vols. (Lahore: Faran Foundation, 1985), 25-26.

61 "Shambhala - New World Encyclopedia," accessed April 11, 2024, https://www.newworldencyclopedia.org/entry/Shambhala.

Chapter 6

62 "Humans 'predisposed' to Believe in Gods and the Afterlife,"-ScienceDaily, accessed April 11, 2024, https://www.sciencedaily.com/releases/2011/07/110714103828.html

63 For details see Quran 3:179, Sahih of Muslim, No: 5113 as quoted by Javed Ghamidi in "(86) Response to 23 Questions - Itmam e Hujjat - Javed AhmadGhamidi - YouTube," accessed May 1, 2024, https://www.youtube.com/playlist?list=PLvDnnnkYLWQeKq8ny1IDf2bgZRTihI28a.

Chapter 7A

64 "Hajj as a Symbolic Expression of Sacrifice | Javed Ahmad Ghamidi (With English Subtitles) - YouTube," accessed May 25, 2024, https://www.youtube.com/watch?v=JLiBWbCiSCw; Explaining Purpose of Animal Sacrifice to Non-Muslims | Javed Ahmad Ghamidi, 2019, https://www.youtube.com/watch?v=MHQ7g1cizLQ.

65 "Pharaoh," in World History Encyclopedia, May 22, 2024, https://www.worldhistory.org/pharaoh/#:~:text=The%20Pharaoh%20in%20ancient%20Egypt,and%20means%20%60Great%20House'.

66 "The Punishment For Homosexuality - Islam Question & Answer," accessed May 25, 2024, https://islamqa.info/amp/en/answers/38622.

Chapter 7B

67 "The Penal Code - Chapter 17. Protection of Norway's Autonomy and Other Fundamental National Interests - Lovdata," accessed May 27, 2024, https://lovdata.no/dokument/NLE/lov/2005-05-20-28/KAPITTEL2-2#%C2%A7116.

68 For a detailed discussion on the meaning of the term please see: "Khimar," accessed May 27, 2024, https://quransmessage.com/articles/a%20deeper%20look%20at%20the%20word%20khimar%20FM3.htm.

69 See for detail: Muhammad b. Saad, Al-Tabaqaat al-Kubra, vol. 10 (Cairo: Maktaba al-Khaanji, 2001), 57; Musnad of Ahmed, No: 25241.

70 See: Ibn-e-Ishāq; Yahya b. Sharf Nawawi, Kitab Tahdhib al-asmaa wallughaat, vol. 2, (Lebanon: Dar al-kutub al-`ilmiyya, n.d), 351; Ibn-e-Hisham, Al-seerah al-nabawiyya, vol. 1, (Damascus: Dār al-Khayr, 1999), 604.

71 See: Ibn Hisham, Al-seerah al-nabawiyya, [Chap. 'Mention of those of the Companions who became Muslim by the invitation of Abu Bakr, may Allah be pleased with him]', Publ. Dar al-Khayr, Damascus (1999), vol. 1, pg. 604.

72 See entries on Jaariya in Lisan al-Arab of Ibn Manzoor and al-Qamus al-Muhit of al-Fayruzabadi.

73 That Aisha was 10 years younger than Asma and Asma was born 27 years before Hijra is testified by: Yahya b. Sharf Nawawi, Kitab Tahdhib al-asmaawal-lughaat, vol. 2, (Lebanon: Dar al-kutub al-`ilmiyya, n.d), 328-9.

74 Abu al-Fidaa, Ibn e Kathīr, al-Bidaaya wa al-Nihaayah, vol. 8, (Cario: Isaal-Baabi al-Halbi, 1986), 91, 131.

75 Kate Wong, "The Face of the Earliest Human Ancestor, Revealed," Scientific American, November 26, 2019, https://www.scientificamerican.com/article/the-face-of-the-earliest-human-ancestor-revealed/

76 For a detailed analysis of the theory that behavioral modernity arose suddenly in humans around 50,000 years ago see Klein, Richard G.. "Anatomy, My Discovery of God, Islam & Judgment Day 335 behavior, and modern human origins." Journal of World Prehistory 9 (1995): 167-198; Also see: "The Transition to Modern Behavior | Learn Science at Scitable," accessed May 27, 2024, https://www.nature.com/scitable/knowledge/library/the-transition-to-modern-behavior-86614339/.

77 "If She Stipulated That He Should Not Take Another Wife, Does He Have to Adhere to That? - Islam Question & Answer," accessed May 27, 2024, https://islamqa.info/en/answers/143120/if-she-stipulated-that-he-shouldnot-take-another-wife-does-he-have-to-adhere-to-that.

78 Javed Ahmad Ghamidi, "Rajam Ki Saza," in Burhan, (Lahore: Al-Mawrid, 2010), pp.

79 Ibn Qayyim, Zaad al Ma'aad, vol. 5 (Beirut: Dar Ibn Hazam, 2019), 379.

80 Mustafa Khattab's Commentary on 2:282 in his translation of Quran entitled "The Clear Quran".

81 Biography of Ibn e Hisham & also see Abu al-A'laa Maududi commentaryon Surah Ahzab (Q 33) in Tafheem ul-Quran.

82 See for details: Watt, W. Montgomery, Prophet and Statesman, (Calcutta:1961), 170-176; Daniel C. Peterson, Muhammad, prophet of God, (Wm. B. Eerdmans Publishing, 2007), 125-127.

83 Watt, Prophet and Statesman, 175.